A TREATISE ON LANGUAGE

Alexander Bryan Johnson

A TREATISE ON
LANGUAGE

Edited by David Rynin

1959

UNIVERSITY OF CALIFORNIA PRESS

Berkeley and Los Angeles

University of California Press
Berkeley and Los Angeles, California

Cambridge University Press
London, England

*A new Introduction replaces the Introduction
and Critical Essay of the hard-cover edition*

Printed in the United States of America

EDITOR'S PREFACE

THIS WORK comprises the full text of the most important early American work on semantics, Alexander Bryan Johnson's *A Treatise on Language*.[1] The *Treatise*, first published in 1836, is itself an expanded and revised edition of Johnson's earlier work, *The Philosophy of Human Knowledge*, published in 1828, based on lectures delivered in Utica in 1825. The present edition also contains passages from the first edition (I) that were omitted from the 1836 revision, as well as important variant readings. The material from (I) will be found within brackets in the main text or in footnotes which contain the variations. Thus one who goes through this edition reading only the unbracketed paragraphs will have before him the complete text of (II), while the addition of bracketed materials and the footnotes will give him the substance of (I) and (II) minus only repetitions.

In the present edition, except for the correction of a few printer's errors and minor bibliographical changes, the text of (II) appears without alteration. Wherever possible, Johnson's references have been traced and identified. Most of his quotations, while substantially correct, exhibit discrepancies from the original, as if he were quoting from memory, or were interested only in giving the general sense of the passage, not the exact wording. Guides to location of the passages to which Johnson refers will be found preceding the Index.

I should like to acknowledge my very great indebtedness to

---

[1] Johnson's works on language referred to in this volume will usually be designated by the symbols (I), (II), (III), as follows:

(I) *The Philosophy of Human Knowledge, or A Treatise on Language* (New York, 1828).

(II) *A Treatise on Language: or The Relation Which Words Bear to Things* (New York, 1836).

(III) *The Meaning of Words: Analyzed into Words and Unverbal Things* (New York, 1854).

Mr. Stillman Drake, who first brought Johnson's *Treatise* to my attention, and whose collection of works by and relating to Johnson, together with important bibliographical investigations, he has very kindly put at my disposal during the preparation of this volume.

University of California, Berkeley
January, 1947

DAVID RYNIN

CONTENTS

INTRODUCTION

THE AUTHOR of this work, Alexander Bryan Johnson, was born in Gosport, England, May 29, 1786. He spent his early youth in the seaport towns of Sheerness and Deal, and in London, where his father Bryan Johnson was engaged in business relating to the fleet. In 1797 Bryan Johnson emigrated to America and settled in what was then known as Old Fort Schuyler (later Utica), New York, where he opened and operated a general store. Four years later Alexander, with his mother, joined the elder Johnson and began to keep books and tend store for his father, ending at this time his formal education.

Although the business flourished, it was abandoned soon after Alexander came of age, when his father retired with "a handsome competency." The family fortune was then turned over to the management of the son. After some preliminary business ventures, including the opening of a glass factory, in which he was joined by the later eminent traveler, ethnologist, and authority on American Indians, Henry R. Schoolcraft (who many years later, in 1851, dedicated to Johnson with high praise his important *Residence of Thirty Years with the Indian Tribes of the American Frontier*), Johnson embarked on his long and successful career as a banker. In this field he was well known in his day and published significant works on economics and finance. Joseph Dorfman in his *The Economic Mind in American Civilization* (New York, 1946) devotes some attention to Johnson as an economist. An account of his life and work appears in the *Dictionary of American Biography*.

He was active in and wrote on political matters, both state

and national, but never ran for or occupied public office. He studied law and was admitted to the bar, but never practiced. Although outwardly devoted to business and public affairs, Johnson's main interest in life was intellectual. The bulk of this brief introduction will deal with his intellectual activities and achievements, which although still practically unknown deserve to rank him with the most original of philosophic thinkers. He died September 9, 1867, aged eighty-one years, having been thrice married and having fathered eleven children. His first wife was a granddaughter of President John Adams, and a niece of President John Quincy Adams, being the daughter of the latter's brother Charles.

Johnson's dominant interest was philosophy, in particular the theory of knowledge and the philosophy of language, or the problem of meaning. His highly original views on these topics were based upon studies eventually published under the title *The Physiology of the Senses: or How and What We See, Hear, Taste, Feel and Smell* (New York and Cincinnati, 1856). He published (in addition to the aforementioned *Physiology of the Senses*) three works on meaning: (I) *The Philosophy of Human Knowledge, or A Treatise on Language* (New York, 1828); (II) *A Treatise on Language: or The Relation Which Words Bear to Things* (New York, 1836); and (III) *The Meaning of Words: Analysed into Words and Unverbal Things, and Unverbal Things Classified into Intellections, Sensations and Emotions* (New York, 1854). On these his main claim to consideration and fame rests. He also published two other works of a philosophical character: *Religion in Relation to the Present Life* (New York, 1841) and *Deep Sea Soundings and Explorations of the Bottom: or The Ultimate Analysis of Human Knowledge* (Boston, 1861). The former was "designed to present a summary of morality in small compass," and concerns the laws governing our feelings and conduct; the latter, a somewhat metaphysical work of his old age, he described as "little more than a very brief epitome of several books heretofore published by me."

The present work is a conflation of (I) and (II); the latter itself being a revision of (I). Johnson thought that the title of (I) was misleading or inadequate, and replaced it by its subtitle, adding a new descriptive subtitle indicating more precisely the nature of the work. The third work (III) repeats much that appears in (II), but contains a significant change or emendation in doctrine which will be mentioned shortly.

In his lifetime Johnson's philosophical works attracted practically no attention, and were completely unknown until 1938 when Mr. Stillman Drake by chance found a copy of (II), which luckily he recognized for what it is, a philosophical classic. He set up and printed by hand an edition of forty-two copies for his friends in 1939–1940, which marks the date of the birth of Johnson's reputation as an important and in many respects great philosopher. M. M. Bagg in his *The Pioneers of Utica* (Utica, 1877), in a brief sketch of Johnson's life, reports that: "His philosophical writings were welcomed . . . by an ardent though limited circle of admirers, and if they did not gain a more extended following the reason is chiefly to be found in the abstruseness of the subject and the little interest it has for the general mind, as well as to the compact form in which he delivered his teachings, and their lack of harmony with prevailing opinions." (P. 329.)

Johnson's work on language—(I), (II), and (III) may be thought of as variations of a single work—is indeed highly compact in style, almost aphoristic. It consists mainly of brief paragraphs expressing the most profound insights in capsule form, usually by way of striking examples. The original was prepared as a series of public lectures, some but not all of which were delivered in the Utica Lyceum to his fellow townsmen in 1825. These lectures Johnson describes as "little more than heads of discourses."

In all likelihood the principal reason for the failure of Johnson's teachings to reach an audience capable of appreciating and transmitting his insights is to be found in their radical implications for the prevailing philosophical and religious views of his day. Although capable of doing justice to the widest variety of views, Johnson's doctrines give the appearance of being nihilistic and sceptical in the highest degree. Furthermore he was quite out of touch with the main stream of thought of his day, having practically no connections with universities and learned men, immersed as he was in an atmosphere of business and politics.

The only contemporary references to his philosophical works which have been found are the following: Edward Johnson in his *Nuces Philosophae* (London, 1842) gives a few quotations from (II). Horace Bushnell in his *God in Christ* (Hartford, 1849) refers briefly to it also; while earlier the feminist freethinker Frances Wright, in her weekly *The Free Enquirer* (New York, March 18, 1829), in a prophetic mention of (I) wrote:

The Philosophy of Human Knowledge

A work of the highest merit, under the above title, issued from the press of this city during the past year; and, while calculated to advance the human intellect by a full century, in the path of true knowledge and sound thinking, we believe its appearance remains as yet unnoticed, and all but unknown. This inattention, its enlightened author will know how to interpret.

The diamond of true water is distinguished only by the lapidary; and unfortunately, in the present state of human knowledge, the brighter jewels of intellectual truth, are appreciated only by the philosopher. It is only the reasoner who can appreciate reason, the profound thinker who can appreciate thought, and the scholar who can appreciate the originalities of genius amid the stores of learning. Such characters may, therefore, be few, but they will not be lukewarm admirers.

We shall take an early opportunity of noticing this inestimable volume in more detail.

The opportunity apparently never offered itself, for no further notice has been found.

In a pamphlet issued in 1832 bearing the title *A Discourse on Language,* Johnson said of (I): "The book received no praise, nor censure, nor perusal. I seek not to animate the dead." However, a lengthy and on the whole very favorable review did appear in 1829 in Volume II of *The Western Monthly Review* (Cincinnati) written by its editor, Timothy Flint. Flint described Johnson as "an original thinker," and refers to the book as "this singular, learned and acute work."

Johnson's third work, *The Meaning of Words,* which he later said should have had the title *The Meaning of Language,* fared no better, for it excited no attention. In general Johnson was unsuccessful in interesting the learned world in his work. For example, he sent a copy of (I) to Professor Benjamin Silliman, the Yale scientist, who thanked him for the volume with explanations that "because of the number and pressure of my avocations, it may be some time before I can read your work." There was apparently no further communication from the professor. He sent a copy of (III) to the eminent Victor Cousin, and received an acknowledgment, but nothing more. Upon sending a copy of the same work to August Comte, who might have been expected to find it of some interest, Johnson received the following letter:

> Paris, Sunday
> October 15, 1854

Sir,

I pray you to accept my entire thanks for the small volume which I received yesterday, with your honored letter of the thirteenth of September. But although the question which you have broached may be one of the most fundamental which we can agitate, I cannot promise

you to read such an essay. For my part, I read nothing except the
great poets ancient and modern. The cerebrial hygiene is exceedingly
salutary to me, particularly in order to maintain the originality of
my peculiar meditations. Nevertheless, without reading your book, I
will confide its scrupulous examination to one of my best disciples.
The question which occupies you has not been directly treated in my
positive philosophy, but I have fully demonstrated my positive theory
of Human Language in the fourth chapter of the second volume of
the great work, or system of positive polity of which I have just
published the fourth and last volume, and according to the general
plan of my labours, I can never return to the subject. Salutations and
fraternity.

August Comte

Johnson's own attitude toward the reception of his works
may be indicated by a passage in his autobiography (from
which the above letter is also taken) in which speaking of (III)
he says:

The only use I made of the book, was to distribute some copies to
my friends; but I never made any effort to give any book of mine
a notoriety with the public, and to this probably may be owing the
little notoriety any of them ever acquired. I thought if they merited
public notice, they would eventually obtain it, and I left them to float
or sink by their own buoyancy....

He ends his autobiography with some reflections on his
philosophic work:

... And now in taking a review of my various writings that have
engrossed a large portion of my active and long life, I feel that I have
laboured in vain so far as my teachings have been accepted by the
world or influenced the thoughts of reflective men. Teachings which
like mine, require an eradication of existing notions, labour under
disadvantages that may well be deemed insurmountable, while teachings which harmonize with prevailing opinions are readily accepted.
My studies have been intellectually beneficial to myself and to that
extent they solace me for the time I have devoted to them. In artistic
construction I believe they are unsurpassed for brevity of expression
and perspicuity of meaning....

In the preface to (II) Johnson tells us that "all that the book contains is the elucidation of but one precept: namely, to interpret language by nature. We reverse the rule and interpret nature by language." (*Treatise*, pp. 27–28.) In his first lecture of the same work (p. 40) he states: "My lectures will endeavour to subordinate language to nature,—to make nature the expositor of words, instead of making words the expositors of nature. If I succeed, the success will ultimately accomplish a great revolution in every branch of learning." And in his *Conclusion* (pp. 299–300) he sums up by asserting that "to illustrate the foregoing positions is the design of all that I have stated. Theoretically, the positions may be admitted by every person, and may be deemed already known; but practically they are violated by all men, and understood by none."

From a failure to abide by this precept flow, in Johnson's opinion, the vast majority of intellectual errors and confusions of philosophy and science: "Our misapprehension of the nature of language has occasioned a greater waste of time, and effort, and genius, than all the other mistakes and delusions with which humanity has been afflicted. It has retarded immeasurably our physical knowledge of every kind, and vitiated what it could not retard. The misapprehension exists still in unmitigated virulence; and though metaphysicks, a rank branch of the errour, is fallen into disrepute, it is abandoned like a mine which will not repay the expense of working, rather than like a process of mining which we have discovered to be constitutionally incapable of producing gold." (*Treatise*, p. 300.)

Johnson was thus perhaps the first thinker who consciously and consistently based his whole approach to the problems of philosophy on a critique of language. He was in fact an isolated, self-taught philosophic genius who anticipated by a hundred years most of the insights and perhaps some of the errors associated with the contemporary school of logical positivism.

(Further bio-bibliographical information regarding John-son and more extended comment on his work are contained in the Introduction and Critical Essay of the 1947 edition of this work.)

In order to assist those readers who may not be fully pre-pared to judge what is sound and what is unsound in Johnson's highly original but often perplexing classic of semantics, I shall in the remaining pages of this new introduction attempt to place the work in the context of contemporary semantical theory.

The term "semantics" as used to characterize Johnson's study is to be understood as the discipline concerned with the study of meaning, with investigating what Johnson in his sub-title to (II) refers to as "the relation which words bear to things." This is to be contrasted with another, broader usage, according to which semantics goes beyond language to attempt the formulation of a general theory of signs, a discipline some-times called "semiotic." This latter includes in its scope in-vestigations not merely of linguistic signs but of natural signs, such as symptoms, e.g., blushing as a sign of embarrassment, and symbols, such as the cross (Christianity) or the flag, repre-senting one's country. Johnson's concern is only with words, whether standing by themselves or combined into sentences, i.e., with verbal or linguistic signs.

His description of the subject his work deals with as the relation which words bear to things is however in need of clari-fication. For Johnson distinguishes between two main cate-gories of things, namely *verbal* and *unverbal*—words being verbal things, all others however diverse being unverbal. The study of the relation which words bear to things is thus in fact more adequately characterized as the study of the relations of verbal to verbal and to unverbal things.

Now it is customary in contemporary discussions to distin-

guish at least three main investigations of this general type:
(1) the study of the relation words bear to things; (2) the
study of the relations words bear to other words; and (3) the
study of the relations that words bear to their users—these
three often being referred to as "semantics," "syntactics," and
"pragmatics" respectively. What in this scheme is called "semantics" coincides therefore with but a part of Johnson's discipline, falling within that branch of his study which concerns
itself with the relation holding between verbal and unverbal
things. Syntactics and pragmatics, which in the above classification are to be distinguished from semantics, thus fall within
the subject matter with which Johnson is concerned. If we are
to be accurate, Johnson's study coincides approximately with
the general theory of verbal signs, going beyond semantics in
the narrow current sense, yet falling short of a complete
semiotic.

Yet another ambiguity resides in Johnson's subtitle, for although it suggests that there is but one relation that words
bear to things, there are in fact many. And the triple classification—semantics, syntactics, pragmatics—reflects this. The
type of relation that connects, say, an exclamation of surprise
or anger with some inner state (feeling or emotion) of its
utterer is hardly the same as the type of relation that connects
one statement with another that logically follows from it. And
neither of these is identical with the relation that holds between
a class name and individual members of the class named by it.
The exclamatory sentence is often said to *express* the feeling;
the statement from which another is logically derivable is said
to *entail* the latter; the class name is said to *denote* the individuals.

It would be of course petty and unintelligent to make anything of the form in which Johnson characterizes his study in
the subtitle to his work if he were not in fact inclined to be
misled by it himself. But there are grounds for believing that

Johnson did fall victim to this language, or perhaps better, that it did in fact express a prevailing and overriding preoccupation of his, which had some unfortunate consequences for his views on language. For Johnson exhibits a very strong tendency to assimilate all such and many other relations to but a single one, which we may call "naming" or "denoting," and which is represented by the relation holding between a name and that which it names.

Johnson in dealing with the relation which words bear to things makes use of a number of terms, viz., "to refer," "to signify," "to name," "to mean." And in referring to the things to which words refer, signify, etc., talks of the meaning of these words, of their signification, of what they refer to, and the like. These terms are generally used by him indifferently: one easily replacing the other. What a word means or signifies or refers to, i.e., its meaning or signification or referent, turns out for Johnson to be invariably some existing thing, or as he often says "phenomenon"—i.e., a verbal or unverbal reality. Where there is no thing to which the word refers, that is, no referent, to use the preferred current term, the word will be without meaning or signification, an "empty salvo."

It is important to realize, however, that for Johnson it is rarely if ever that a word lacks some meaning or referent. The fundamental problem of semantics is for him not so much to determine whether a term has meaning as to determine what that meaning is. In this he exhibits a very great degree of tolerance, unlike some of those concerned with semantics in our own day, who often seem mainly concerned with trying to show that much of what goes on in discourse is without meaning.

This intolerance derives in large part from some arbitrary limitation on the kinds of things that may, in the opinion of a given theorist, be the objects of reference—many seeming to hold, for example, that unless a word refers to some object accessible to one of the external senses it refers to nothing and is therefore without meaning. This narrow viewpoint is wholly foreign to Johnson. His classification of things into verbal and unverbal is simply intended to serve as a convenient classification, which itself throws no light whatever on the nature of what is so classified.

Johnson's precept that we should interpret language by nature, not nature by language, prevents him from falling into the common error of supposing that names or words are in some way capable of revealing the nature of things. The fact is that only through our senses or feelings or intellect do we come into contact with reality, which presents itself to us in such ways as it does, to be apprehended not through theorizing but directly in awareness. These deliverances of the outer senses, and of the feelings or emotions, as well as those objects of thought not of this nature, i.e., what Johnson called "intellections," and especially certain recognizable groupings of them, constitute what Johnson means by "things" or "phenomena."

It is obvious that if language is to serve as a means of communication its constituent words must be relatively few in number, but the number of things, in Johnson's sense especially, is for all practical purposes endless. Hence a given word must serve in many capacities, be used to refer to many things, be, thus, ambiguous. This ambiguity is inevitable, and even essential for language to serve its function of communication. But it is not without harmful consequences in misunderstandings. It is in our attempt to overcome the evils of ambiguity that the main sources of linguistic confusion arise. For our tendency is to fix upon a single sense of a given term and to assume that whoever speaks differently speaks erroneously, or meaninglessly.

But it is not only in interpersonal communication that difficulties arise. We tend in our own thinking and speaking to

overlook the variety of referents that a word has and to identify its meaning with but one thing or type of thing. The nature,
cause, and consequences of this blunder are copiously exhibited in the present work; in what Johnson says on this and
related points lies his great originality and merit. I shall therefore not advert here to such matters, but turn now to an indica-
tion of what seems to be Johnson's main shortcoming, from
the point of view of an adequate system of semantics, even
conceived broadly as his is.

But before taking up these criticisms I must warn the reader
that as he studies the present volume he will find in it, except
in a footnote reference to (III), no mention of intellections,
which in Johnson's later thinking play so important a role.
In the first two of his works on language, (I) and (II), Johnson was dominated by the notion that words that could not
be shown to refer to other words, or to sensible things, or to
inner feelings or emotions were without signification, "empty
salvos." And consequently since he found that many words
do in fact occur in discourse that cannot with plausibility be
referred to deliverances of our feelings, or outer senses, Johnson was of the opinion that they are without significance. Much
of what he says on this topic of meaninglessness is of great
interest and importance, even if his later position leads him
to find in intellections many meanings that could not be found
in words, feelings, or objects of sensations.

But it is not in an inadequate list of types of objects of awareness, such as he thought he became aware of as he continued
his studies and reflections on language, that Johnson's main
shortcoming is to be found. It is rather in his preoccupation
with what we may call "the referential function" of language;
and with a somewhat too narrow conception of it. Earlier I
mentioned the current distinction between semantics, syntactics, and pragmatics, and attempted to show how typical semantical, syntactical, and pragmatical relations differ, how for

example the relation that a word bears to something of which it is a name differs from the relation that one statement bears to some other from which it logically follows or is derivable, and how both of these types of relation differ from the kind of relation that the utterance of an exclamation or interjection bears to the feeling of which it is an expression. Johnson is inadequately aware of the force of these distinctions, and tends to use terms such as "refers to," "signifies," "means" indifferently in all three cases.

Thus in dealing with synonyms, words or sentences having the same meaning, Johnson tends to speak of one meaning another, when in fact they are synonyms not by virtue of referring to or naming each other, but by virtue of naming or referring to (if this is their function) some common thing, in Johnson's sense of "thing." Similarly, he tends to confuse expression and naming when dealing with words or sentences that relate to feelings. Thus while the word "toothache" refers to a certain kind of feeling of pain, Johnson's inclination is to treat exclamations and interjections much as if they too refer to or name the feelings of which they are expressions. But "Ouch!" does not refer to or name pain, as does the word "pain"; rather it expresses it—as "toothache" does not express the pain but names it. This tendency is not apparent in his earlier works, in which he deals very little with exclamations, but becomes evident in (III) where, for example, he tells us "A man's imprecations of curses on his eyes, body, and soul are words; but they are also signs of an unverbal internal feeling *in* the organism of the imprecator . . . the internal organic feeling which prompts an imprecation is the unverbal meaning of the imprecation. . . ." ([III], p. 202.)

Now it is indeed correct that the imprecation is a sign of the feeling that produces it, but only in the sense of being a *symptom* of it, not in the sense of referring to or signifying it, as the name of the feeling refers to the feeling.

Johnson's expansion of his earlier views on language is interesting seen in the light of this distinction. Whereas his early reflections on language and meaning led him to the view that if language did not refer to other words, or to deliverances of sensation, or feelings, it was empty or void of meaning, he came later to hold that most such words have meaning peculiar to them. Thus, although nothing in the realm of feelings or sensations is referred to by such words as "cause," "substance," "identity," "thought," it does not follow that they are, as he earlier thought, devoid of any unverbal meaning. For they refer to the objects peculiar to thought or intellect, i.e., to intellections, which he identified with subjective tendencies in our intellectual organism.

When, for example, we speak of our personal identity, there is nothing (let us suppose) that we sense or feel that is referred to by this expression "identity," but there *is* in us an irresistible tendency to unify our diverse sensations and feelings in such a manner as leads us to think or conceive of an identity behind all its manifestations. This identity is not felt or sensed, but is conceived. That it *is* conceived is shown by the regular way in which questions and statements regarding identity crop up in everyone's discourse. Similarly, with respect to "cause" and other such terms: Not finding anything in the world of sensation or feeling that is referred to by them (assuming they are not meant to refer to words, or feelings, or sequences of events), Johnson finds their referents in the organic tendency that leads us to conceive or talk about causes, identity, and the like. Just "as therefore, the internal organic feeling which prompts an imprecation is the unverbal meaning of the imprecation; so the organism of the intellect that conceives any given words is the unverbal meaning of the verbal conception." ([III], p. 202.)

But there is a confusion here similar to that disclosed a moment ago. The putative organic tendencies that lead us to use words like "cause," "identity," in seeking to comprehend the world are certainly not what these terms refer to, but are at best what their use in some sense expresses. Hence these words do not signify such organic tendencies, nor are these organic tendencies their meanings, in the sense in which Johnson normally uses "meaning" or "signification." What causes us to use a certain word or make a certain utterance is rarely if ever what the word or utterance refers to.

Therefore Johnson's belief that in the doctrine of intellections he found an escape from sceptical conclusions of his early work on language is largely a mistake. It is a mistake because when one talks about causes or personal identity one is not talking about or referring to one's tendency to use these words. Meaning may be saved for them, but not the kind of meaning with which Johnson was typically concerned, that is, with meaning as referent.

It is an error to suppose that all words, as well as sentences, function referentially, are used to name things. This may be demonstrated without recourse to interjections, exclamations, or imprecations, which obviously have a quite different role in language. So-called logical constants, or connectives, words such as "and," "or," and the like, used to form compound sentences out of simple sentences obviously do not refer to anything. There are no *ands* or *ors* which these terms might be thought to name, as say there are *hands* and *oars* of which the names are "hands" and "oars." In "The dog and the cat were there," the words "dog" and "cat" at least may be thought of as referring to certain animals, but the word "and" serves a quite different function.

But that a word *refers* to nothing, signifies no thing, does not have as a consequence that it has no meaning. Or at least if this does follow it is clear that some kind of blunder has been committed in identifying meaning or signification with referent. We have good reasons for wishing to maintain that many words have meaning, or at least are significant, even though they have no referents. It is a mistake to think that the sole function of language is referential.

But even with respect to terms that do in fact function in some way referentially, a finer distinction is required than that supplied by Johnson. His view is that meanings are things or phenomena. And he supposes that we can mean only what we know and that we can know only what we sense, or feel (emotions), or intuit intellectually, i.e., think of or conceive. Things known in these three different ways are essentially different and incomparable, but in each case what we know if anything is something given: a complex of sights, sounds, tastes; an emotion or passion; a concept or thought or intellection. Where we have not sensed, or felt, or conceived, we have not known, and what has not been known cannot be meant, or signified.

This view elaborated at length in the present volume is clearly untenable, but Johnson finds himself committed to it because of an unduly narrow conception of knowledge, or at any rate of meaning. There being no (flesh and blood) unicorns, Johnson would be required to hold, and does hold, that a word like "unicorn" must either refer to some other words that constitute its definition or synonym, or to an image, or picture, or to a thought of a unicorn, since that which does not exist cannot be referred to: that term "a" refers to or signifies thing b entails, for Johnson, that b in some appropriate sense exists. If it does not, it cannot be meant.

This puzzle which Johnson was never able to overcome is due to a failure to distinguish meaning from referent. It is clear that "unicorn" has meaning, in the sense that we know how to use the term, that we could, say, recognize a unicorn if by chance one happened to be found in some out of the way corner of Africa, or Asia. We know how to tell whether an animal is a unicorn, just as well, at least in principle, as we know how to tell whether an animal is a Jersey cow. This we know or can know even though we may assume there are no unicorns and never will be. We know what the word means, even if there is no such thing. Hence to identify its meaning with its referent, if any, is to make meaning dependent upon accidents of nature or biology. It is clearly putting the cart before the horse to hold that unless we have seen a unicorn we cannot understand the word (in its sensible signification); on the contrary, only because the word already has signification for us could we ever know that we had or had not seen one.

It is clearly necessary in some sense to divorce meanings or significations from things, at least in the respects just indicated, for the identification of meaning with things has such absurd consequences as that meanings can be born, grow, decline, and die; eat hay and give birth to quintuplets. The separation is commonly made by distinguishing between: (1) sense or connotation and (2) referent or denotation. The denotation or referent of a term is comprised of such things as are named or referred to by it—it being understood that for a term to name something that something must exist. What *is not*, cannot be named, as "to name" is here understood. But a term may have meaning even if there exists nothing which it names or refers to, as "unicorn" has meaning although there are no such animals. We say the term has sense or connotation, despite having no referent or denotation. The sense or connotation is understood as the set of properties such that those and only those things (if any) that exhibit them will be denoted or referred to by the term. The referents of a term are those things that exhibit the properties that constitute the sense of the term.

In the sense of "meaning" according to which the meaning of a term is identified with its sense or connotation, not with its denotation or referents, words like "unicorn" will have meaning, despite the fact that they have no referents. And in this manner we are able to overcome the difficulty that gave Johnson so much trouble.

Of course this distinction between meaning as sense and meaning as referent will not suffice to provide all intelligibly used words with meanings, for, as was pointed out, such words as "and" do not merely *happen* to have no referents, but they lack sense or connotation as well, in terms of the formulation given. For unlike "unicorn," "and," in its occurrence as a connective, is not a word that happens not to have any referents, but conceivably might. There *are no* properties such that if something exhibited them it would be an and. Hence an adequate account of the meaning of words will have to go beyond the formulations presented above which enable us to deal with Johnson's typical difficulty.

One way of dealing with such terms, although not a very satisfactory one, would be to treat them as expressing certain feelings. In fact some suggestions along this line have been made by Bertrand Russell, in his *An Inquiry into Meaning and Truth* (New York, 1940, p. 102), who tells us that "or" corresponds psychologically to hesitation, i.e., in our language *expresses* such a feeling. This may well be true sometimes, but it will hardly give us a meaning for "or" in either the referential or the connotative sense. And if we go so far as to treat as meaningful all terms that express psychological states, we would be hard put to deny meaning to gibberish and nonsense, for we must suppose that they express certain feelings that give rise to their utterance.

The usual way of dealing with terms that occur in discourse but have neither connotative nor denotative meaning is to qualify them as meaningful if and only if their presence or absence in larger units of language, say in sentences, affects the meaning of these larger units in certain ways. Thus if in place of "or" as it occurs in a compound statement we put "and," the truth value and hence the meaning of the resultant

statement will often change. If I alter "John loves Mary or
I am mistaken," to "John loves Mary and I am mistaken," a
statement that may have been true will probably become false.
We associate the meaning or meaningfulness of these connectives with their contribution to the meaning of the compounds
of which they are constituents, but not in the sense that they
express feelings or have referents or sense. Connectives are
not meaningless because they lack referents or sense, or possibly express no feelings; they do not function in the same way
as do interjections, or nouns and adjectives, and the question
of their meaning or significance in the sense of *what* they mean
is misguided. Such so-called "syncategorematic" words that
gain their meaning only in larger contexts, not by way of reference to things, are not discussed by Johnson, but how he
would treat them is clear in terms of his treatment of words
that do not refer to sensible objects.

Although Johnson's discussions deal mostly with words, he
does not neglect the all important topic of the meaning of
sentences. And in fact his treatment of this topic is similar
to his treatment of words taken in isolation. Just as his tendency is to seek the meaning of words in the things they refer
to or denote, so when dealing with statements, declarative sentences, he seeks for facts or states of affairs referred to or
denoted by them. A statement may refer to some fact given in
sense experience, or to some circumstance of feeling, or to
other words. If it refers to none of these, then, according to his
earlier doctrine, it is void of meaning; but according to the
later doctrine, it may still refer to some organic tendency to
formulate hypotheses, to which there need be nothing corresponding in the outer world. Theoretical explanations of hap-
penings in nature are all of this character, giving answers
congenial to the intellect but having nothing sensible corresponding to them. Thus we invoke the theory that air has weight
to explain the phenomena of the barometer and the pump, al-

though the weight is not the felt weight that we bear with difficulty when carrying some heavy body.

Johnson's fundamental position on the meaning of statements is revealed in the following passage, the essential portion of which I italicize for emphasis:

> To say the earth is a sphere, that it revolves round the sun, and round its own axis, and that we possess antipodes, are truths so long as we consider the expressions significant of certain phenomena to which the propositions refer. If you inquire of an astronomer whether the earth is a sphere, he will desire you to notice what he terms the earth's shadow in an eclipse of the moon, the gradual disappearance of a ship as it recedes from the shore, etc. *After hearing all that he can adduce in proof of the earth's sphericity, consider the proposition significant of these proofs. If you deem it significant beyond them, you are deceived by the forms of language.* (*Treatise*, p. 128.)

His position is similar to what goes nowadays by the name of the "verifiability principle," in one of its versions: Ascertain what evidence the speaker can adduce in support of his proposition, and this will constitute its meaning. But if he can adduce none, it will have none; and if he adduces at different times different facts, his proposition will have different meanings correspondingly. If he adduces sensible matter of fact, it will have sensible meaning; if he adduces other sentences, it will have verbal meaning; and if he adduces necessities of thought, it will have intellectual meaning. And it may have any of these while lacking others.

For example, visible space is divisible up to a point, but no farther, whereas conceptual or mathematical space is infinitely divisible, the verbal process of dividing in thought being extendible without end. Hence, that space is infinitely divisible is an ambiguous assertion; in one sense it is true, namely when we refer to conceptual space, but in another it is false, namely when we refer to the space given to vision or to the sense of feel, which themselves differ from each other.

Similarly, the old question whether the greenness of the leaf is in the leaf, that is, whether so-called "secondary qualities" are in objects, is to be answered in the affirmative if "in" in the question relates to what we see, but in the negative if the evidence adduced be what we feel, "The color is in the leaf" having different meanings depending on the sense of "in," which is revealed by the kind of evidence adduced in support of the statement or its negation.

From this identification of the meaning of a statement with the evidence that the speaker adduces in support of it, Johnson is enabled to derive the most interesting and profound philosophical and scientific insights, many of which are astonishingly modern and frequently anticipate by many years what has been thought their first formulations. He derives from it the fundamental insight of the duality of psychological language, with all the consequences for settling the dispute between behavioristic and mentalistic psychology; he resolves the ancient paradoxes of Zeno; formulates the basic principles of operationalism; anticipates the views of Mach on the economical character of scientific theories; and disposes of most of the hoary puzzles of metaphysics and the problem of knowledge of the external world. But as these and other triumphs will be revealed to the reader as he goes through the text, it may be worth indicating here some of the errors Johnson got himself into by a too narrow interpretation of his principle.

In his formulation of the principle for ascertaining the meaning of propositions, Johnson says that we should ascertain all the speaker can adduce in support of his statement, and identify its meaning with those facts. He understands by "can adduce," the actual presentation of or verbal referring to the facts themselves. But one cannot adduce nonexistent facts, one cannot refer to what is not. In this he follows his earlier position on the meaning of words. The consequences are remarkable: If a statement means or signifies only what it refers to, and if it refers only to existing facts, it follows that no meaningful statement can be about the future, or can be false. For a statement purporting to speak of the future will be attempting to do what is impossible, namely to refer to what is not yet or, worse, never will be. Since in calling a statement "false" we simply mean that what it asserts is not the case, by Johnson's principle it will be without significance. But insignificant statements cannot in the proper sense be said to be true or false, since meaning is presupposed by both truth and falsity. Hence every meaningful statement in Johnson's sense will be true—the very facts referred to by virtue of its having meaning being identical with those from which its truth follows. And Johnson almost admits this paradox, holding that "Nearly every proposition is true when interpreted as the speaker interprets it." (*Treatise*, p. 133.) He should in fact drop the qualification, which probably reflects some dim awareness of the paradoxical nature of his position.

The difficulty in his view is here again his failure to distinguish between meaning as sense and meaning as referent. Just as a word may have meaning even if it have no referent, so a statement may have meaning even if it is not true, that is, even if what it asserts is not in existence, is not a fact. This forces us to distinguish between the sense of a statement and what it denotes, or refers to, if anything. We identify the referent of a statement (if it have any) with that fact that made it true, but we identify the sense of a statement as that condition which *if* it existed *would* make the statement true, and which if it did not would make the statement false. That is, we identify the meaning of a statement with the necessary and sufficient condition for its truth. Such a condition may be *specified* or *described* for a given statement even if it does not actually exist. For example, I know perfectly well what it means to say: "I shall have seven grandchildren," although I have no idea whether it will be true or false—for I know what would make it true and what false.

If Johnson had reached the point of distinguishing between sense and denotation, he would have been able to avoid the paradox that according to his view every meaningful statement must be true. Whereas the so-called "verifiability criterion" of statement-meaning may be thought of as holding that a statement means the state of affairs which if it existed *would* make it true, and which if it did not exist *would* make it false, Johnson's related view amounts to holding that the meaning of a statement is the fact that *has made* it true.

Even in its inadequate formulation, Johnson's principle of statement-meaning is as powerful a principle as any ever formulated in the history of philosophy up to and beyond his day. And there is nothing in his way of thinking that would have prevented him from altering his position in the required direction, provided he could have overcome the basic source of his trouble, namely the view that knowledge is direct awareness. As was indicated, his reasoning came to the following: we can mean only what we know, i.e., sense, feel, conceive. But to know what something is, is not, in most senses of "to know," the same as to sense or experience it. When we know what oxygen is, this is not the same as to breathe or otherwise come into intimate contact with it; when we know what electricity is, this is not the same as to experience an electric shock or see a spark. These experiences give us the object to be known, but do not give us the knowledge of it in the important sense of knowledge. Of course, there is a sense of "to know" which can be assimilated to "to sense" or "to experience," namely the sense in which to know is to be acquainted with something. But this sense is by no means the only or most important one.

To know or understand what electricity is, is to have at one's command the laws that enable one to predict and thus produce and control electrical phenomena—to make and operate a dynamo or a motor or a radio. The mere experience of electrical phenomena is not knowledge of electricity. If it were, the

dullest man in the street would be almost as learned as a professor of electrical engineering or of physics. Similarly, to
know the meaning of a word is not the same as to be acquainted
with what if anything it denotes; nor is knowledge of the meaning of a statement identical with having direct awareness of
the state of affairs if any that makes it true, that is denoted
by it. We know about electricity when we can predict what
would happen *if* certain kinds of apparatus were arranged
and operated in certain ways. We know about oxygen when
we can predict how it would react with various substances
under various conditions. And none of this involves sensing
directly any of these things.

Likewise, to know the meaning of a word is not to sense or
otherwise intuit the object if any named by it, but to be able,
in the case of certain kinds of words, to recognize something
if it properly goes by that name, that is, to know what a thing
would be like if it were to be a referent of, or denoted by, that
word. And to know the meaning of a statement is not to be
directly aware in some perceptual situation of the state of
affairs that makes it true, but to be able to specify or recognize
such a state of affairs if it happens to exist and one is suitably
located and properly equipped. With this emendation of his
doctrine we can free Johnson's teaching of most of its errors,
yet retain all its advantages and powers.

That he was acutely aware of the likelihood that his formulations, especially those based on the inadequate science of
his day, might betray him is shown by a touching passage in
his preface (in part quoted earlier) where he writes:

... All that the book contains is the elucidation of but one precept:
namely, to interpret language by nature. We reverse the rule and
interpret nature by language. The precept itself which I have sought
to illustrate, I profoundly respect; but whether I have demonstrated
its importance, the publick must determine. Amid active and extensive
employments, and with no external stimulus to literary pursuits, I

shall be satisfied if the succeeding discourses shall commend the doctrine to the efforts of men whose understandings are more comprehensive than mine, and whose labours the world is accustomed to respect. As, however, the following sheets are the painful elaboration of many years, when my language or positions shall, in a casual perusal, seem absurd, (and such cases may be frequent), I request the reader to seek some more creditable interpretation. The best which he can conceive should be assumed to be my intention: as on an escutcheon, when a figure resembles both an eagle and a buzzard, heraldry decides that the bird which is most creditable to the bearer, shall be deemed the one intended by the blazon. (*Treatise*, p. 28.)

Now it would be a bold man who thought he possessed a more comprehensive understanding than Johnson's; and although it is not impossible for a small mind to increase by a grain of knowledge the monumental achievement of a genius, it would, in view of Johnson's appeal, be ungenerous of us not to end by admitting that perhaps these criticisms are based on misapprehensions of what Johnson intended, that our impression that the noble bird before us ever so faintly resembles a buzzard may be due to a blurring of the vision that comes from gazing at too much brilliance. But buzzard or eagle, that few have flown so high or seen so keenly as A. B. Johnson, the following pages will make amply clear.

AUTHOR'S PREFACE
TO THE 1836 EDITION

IN 1828 the following work was first published. It was entitled
"The Philosophy of Human Knowledge, or A Treatise on
Language"; and was the first part of a series of experimental
investigations which were to include language, physical actions,
thoughts, and feelings. The publication of 1828 was limited
to the investigation of language; and as the present publication
possesses the same limitation, and the other topicks, though in
progress, may never be completed, the first half of the original
title is omitted, and the present publication is designated A
Treatise on Language.

Except many gratifying letters received by me from strangers
in various states of our Union, and one extensive review,[1] the
preceding edition of this work excited no attention. The edition
has, however, been long since absorbed spontaneously by the
publick, and I have received repeated applications for further
copies.

The form of lectures, to which the preceding work was subjected, has been retained as a means of lessening the natural
wearisomeness of instruction. In other respects, the work has
been newly arranged and simplified. The present edition contains also much that is not in the former; yet the lectures are
still little more than heads of discourses. They are sufficient
to indicate my views of language; while persons who shall ac-
cord with me in these views, will readily discover new illustrations of the rules which I have given, and new rules for verbal
positions to which I have not adverted. Indeed, all that the book

[1] In the *Western Monthly Review*, Cincinnati (March, 1829, pp. 575–587; April,
1829, pp. 623–629), by the editor, Timothy Flint.—D.R.

contains is the elucidation of but one precept: namely, to interpret language by nature. We reverse the rule and interpret nature by language. The precept itself which I have sought to illustrate, I profoundly respect; but whether I have demonstrated its importance, the publick must determine. Amid active and extensive employments, and with no external stimulus to literary pursuits, I shall be satisfied if the succeeding discourses shall commend the doctrine to the efforts of men whose understandings are more comprehensive than mine, and whose labours the world is accustomed to respect. As, however, the following sheets are the painful elaboration of many years, when my language or positions shall, in a casual perusal, seem absurd, (and such cases may be frequent,) I request the reader to seek some more creditable interpretation. The best which he can conceive should be assumed to be my intention: as on an escutcheon, when a figure resembles both an eagle and a buzzard, heraldry decides that the bird which is most creditable to the bearer, shall be deemed to be the one intended by the blazon.

THE AUTHOR

A TREATISE ON LANGUAGE

Lecture I

INTRODUCTORY

[IT IS my misfortune to possess a strong inclination for abstruse studies. Its indulgence has diminished my convivial enjoyments, and employed the ardour which, at my age, is usually expended in political discussions;—vociferous in the defence of rights not invaded, and vindictive in the redress of wrongs not inflicted. It has driven me from the whispers of the counting-house, and the war of judicatories, to an unambitious avocation; which, whilst it affords the conveniences that our plainness renders essential, enables me to gratify my unenviable propensity.

[Among the results is a Treatise on the Philosophy of Human Knowledge. From the obscurity in which my life has passed, I have reason to suspect an absence, rather than the possession, of instructive talents: hence the Treatise has long lain unregarded, and, till within a few days, undivulged. An accidental intimation of its existence, has produced from the Lyceum a request with which I shall endeavour to comply, by moulding the Treatise into short and occasional lectures.]

§ 1.—*To know the extent of our powers will save us from impracticable pursuits.*

Man exists in a world of his own creation. He cannot step, but on ground transformed by culture; nor look, but on objects produced by art. The animals which constitute his food are unknown to nature, while trees, fruits, and herbs, are the trophies of his labour. In himself nearly every natural impulse is suppressed as vicious, and every mortification solicited as a virtue. His language, actions, sentiments, and desires, are nearly all factitious. Stupendous in achievement, he is boundless in attempt. Having subdued the earth's surface, he would explore its centre; having vanquished diseases, he would subdue death. Unsatisfied with recording the past, he would anticipate the future. Uncontented with subjugating the ocean, he would traverse the air. Success but sharpens his avidity, and facility but augments his impatience. To know the extent of our powers is therefore important, that in our restlessness for further acquisitions we may neither dissipate strength in designs for which our faculties are unsuited, nor attempt practicabilities by incompetent methods.

§ 2.—*We are in little danger from the pursuit of physical impracticabilities.*

What we can accomplish in physicks, may be safely left to the development of experiment; for though alchymy and perpetual motion have occasioned some waste of time, tangible bodies oppose so sturdily our errours when we attempt physical incongruities, that we lose little by such attempts. Even royalty, which seldom hears unsophisticated truths, is treated by physical bodies as unceremoniously as the commonalty.

§ 3.—*We are in danger of wasting time in verbal investigations.*

Speculative researches are accommodating to human weakness. From geology, which teaches us what exists in the centre of the earth, to astronomy, which reveals what is transpiring in the empyrean;—and from physicks, which discourse about the body, to metaphysicks, which treat of the mind; the mass of verbal doctrine assumes any shape which ingenuity strives to create:—like the pebbles of Rockaway, that change their position as every wave, rising on the ruins of its predecessor, rushes, (lord of the moment,) proudly over the beach.

§ 4.—*To ascertain the capacity that language possesses for discoursing of external existences which our senses cannot discover, will enable us, more understandingly than at present, to estimate theories.*

To fix the fluctuating mass of theories, no man has suggested any other expedient than the construction of some new theory, to whose authority, (like to Johnson's orthography,) all persons shall submit. The remedy is constantly augmenting the disease. I shall not imitate so unsuccessful a procedure; but as theories are the means by which we attempt to discourse of external existences that our senses cannot discover; and as the desire for such discourse originates a large portion of our theories; I will teach you the capacity of language for such an employment, and thereby enable you to judge more understandingly than you can at present, the utility of most theories, and the signification of all.

§ 5.—*No knowledge is more important than a correct appreciation of language.*

But not in theories only is a correct understanding desirable of the capacity of language. Words constitute a great part of all our thoughts. An infusion of words is the means of nearly all instruction, and an ability to repeat words is the substance of much of our learning. When a man is distressed, we administer to him words for his consolation; and when he rejoices, we proffer words to heighten his felicity. Even when medicine admits itself vanquished,—when wealth can no longer purchase a gratification, nor power excite ambition,—words not only maintain their influence, but their potency is augmented by the surrounding desolation.

§ 6.—*Verbal discourse contains defects which have escaped detection.*

Language possessing this important relation to man, the duty is imperative of becoming acquainted with its defects; especially if it contain any which have hitherto escaped detection:— and such it actually contains.

§ 7.—*Significant verbal inquisition is not unlimited.*

Language possesses also an illimitable power of interrogation. Nothing is too sacred to escape its inquiries,—nothing

too remote,—nothing too minute. We employ it, if not without
suspicion that it contains any latent incapacity for unlimited
inquisition, with certainly a very indefinite apprehension of its
limitations:—hence the importance of defining the limits, (if it
possess any,) within which interrogatories are significant. I am
prepared to show both that it possesses limited powers in these
particulars, and to define the limits.

§ 8.—*Language may be formed into propositions whose results, though incontrovertible by logick, are irreconcileable
with our senses.*

Language is also mouldable into propositions that can neither be controverted by any known rules of logick, nor cred-
ited without violence to the evidence of our senses:—hence the
importance of ascertaining whether language, when thus employed, possesses not a covert signification that will save us
from the alternative of either disbelieving our senses, or disbelieving the best demonstrated conclusions. I will satisfy you
that it possesses such a signification, and I will teach you the
signification of language that is thus sophistically employed.
The propositions to which I allude may be known from the following examples:—

1. Mathematicks assures us that the water which placidly
flows in our canal, is no where level;—that the walls which constitute the sides of this chamber, are not parallel;—that a line
no longer than an inch, is diminishable interminably.

2. Astronomy declares that we are whirled momentarily a
thousand miles in one direction, and fifteen miles in another;
and in this giddy rotation, our heads travel faster and further
than our bodies:—that a portion of mankind walk with their
feet diametrically opposite to ours;—that the world is a ball,
and assumes at a given distance the appearance of a star;—that
comets are hotter than red hot iron, and the sun a body of fire
thirteen hundred thousand times larger than the earth;—that
tides are caused by the attraction of the moon, and weight produced by the attraction of the earth.

3. Opticks assert that while I look around, and perceive distant hills, spacious streets, lofty buildings, and prosperous activity, I truly see neither spaciousness nor distance, but a miniature, not an inch in diameter, that is painted on the retina of my eyes.

4. Physiology affirms that a ray of light, though it seems colourless, is iridescent; while roses are a mere blank apparatus, to display the tints which exist latently in light. Botany has, however, compensated the queen of flowers for this disparagement. Botany insists that plants eat, drink, sleep, and breathe;—that they are male and female;—that their fragrance is amorous sighs, and their motions nervous irritability.

5. Chymistry is peculiarly the science of enchantment. It asserts that water is principally composed of the most inflammable substance in nature;—that our flesh is but a combination of disgustful gases, and diamonds but a preparation of charcoal.

§ 9.—*The verbal defects which these discourses will discuss, are inseparable from language, and differ from any defects that you may anticipate.*

You must not expect that I can, at present, make you understand the defects of the foregoing propositions. All that I shall say hereafter, I deem necessary to convey that information. Indeed, I can afford no better guide to lead you ultimately to a correct understanding of the defects of language, than to say, at a hazard, that I allude to no defects that you ever heard of or conceived. I also allude to none that can be obviated. The most that I hope to perform is to make them known; as we erect a beacon, to denote the presence of a shoal which we cannot remove.

§ 10.—But though you know not the defects to which I refer, still, when you read the conclusions of astronomy that I have above adduced, the conclusions of opticks, of physiology, and chymistry, may you not infer, that if such doctrines are incontestible by logick, the doctrines are more repugnant to reason, than the belief that some latent sophistry exists in the language by which the doctrines are expressed, or in the processes by which the doctrines are sustained?

§ 11.—When you hear further, not as an item of revelation to which the judgment is bound to submit, but as a reality, elaborated proudly by the judgment itself, that all things were created out of nothing;—that every existence had a beginning, except the first, which had no beginning;—that every existence sprang from some cause, except the first, which is uncaused;—may we not catch some glimmering of a suspicion, that our words have lost their intelligence in these heights of speculation?—as we read in a book of ingenious absurdities, that a man in a balloon ascended so high, that his hat, which he accidentally removed from his head, flew upwards, having lost its original gravity, and become attracted by the moon's.

[You perceive, then, that the Philosophy of Human Knowledge deserves attention. There has always existed an indefinite impression that such a science is attainable. It has been to metaphysics, what alchymy has to chymistry; or what perpetual motion has been to mechanics;—sufficiently plausible to stimulate our efforts, and sufficiently subtle to elude them.

[In such a science, I must, however, confess myself a believer; though the progress which has been made in it is inconsiderable. The labours of antiquity have descended to us embarrassed with mutilation and obsoleteness. Yet we may discover that ancient metaphysics consisted principally in the formation of general propositions, which, though dictated by the senses, were supposed authoritative beyond their purview. Thus, it was maintained, that "nothing can be erected out of nothing"; hence that the power of deity, in the construction of the world, extended only to arrange materials, which were co-eternal with himself. Clouds and darkness soon enveloped such speculations, and reason looked aghast at the monsters of its own invention.

[With modern writers also, the science is in its infancy. Etymology has pursued it through all the torturous wanderings of words, up to their pristine signification. Discovering hence, that *spirit* signified originally *breath,* she concludes that the word has still no other import. Instead, therefore, of expounding a word by narrating the phenomena to which it is now affixed, she seeks its meaning by groping for the phenomena to which it was originally applied:—overlooking the most important characteristic of language, that every word possesses as many meanings, as it possesses applications to different phenomena.

[Induction is another method by which our science has been attempted. We upbraid the ancients with reasoning from general propositions to particular facts. This process induction reverses. She discovers that my hand cannot draw on a glove without touching the glove; that you cannot light a candle, unless an igniting body be conveyed to the candle: hence induction forms a general proposition, "that nothing can act where it is not." The proposition would be abundantly harmless, were it deemed significant of those facts only from which it is elaborated; but induction estimates facts as the mere ladder by which she is enabled to climb beyond the senses; then, like the ambition described by Shakspeare,

> She unto the ladder turns her back,
> Looks in the clouds, scorning the base degrees
> By which she did ascend.

[Lord Monboddo maintained, that, (as nothing can act where it is not,) when we see distant objects, our soul passes from us to the object. The conclusion was too gross to be permanent, therefore we now suppose, that sight is produced by rays, which rebound from visible objects, to the optic nerve;—that sound is conveyed by appulses of air, which strike the tympanum; and that smells are diffused by small corpuscles, which are wafted to the olfactory nerve.

[There is still another way in which philosophy has expended itself, when employed metaphysically. We show to a child an

iron red with heat, and we assure him that pain will follow
its contaction. The monition vanishes with the iron, never to
recur, but on a recurrence of the danger. Painfully industrious
we peruse biography, theology, legal intricacies, and medical
properties. To nature we unheedingly commit the whole un-
sorted, unarranged. Yet a hero's name no sooner strikes the
portals of hearing, than memory, like an officious chronicler,
announces his fortunes, qualities and actions. A legal injury
summons all the methods of redress:—anticipation awards a
verdict, and imagination exults in the triumph.

[These are briefly the services of thought. Its ministrations
are incessant, its uses infinite; and they are divisible, by the
copiousness of language, into recollection, retrospection, anticipation, ratiocination, imagination, deliberation, and various
other operations. But, instead of recording the phenomena, and
leaving them to be marshalled under the names which use shall
determine, philosophers have considered the marshalling to
be their province: hence, what is denominated the Philosophy
of Mind, consists of but little more than a contentious verbal
criticism.

[Such then is the present state of the philosophy which I propose to investigate. Judgment is wearied in examining chimeras,
that possess no interest but their deformity; and exploring labyrinths, which have no merit but intricacy. The science has long
lost the favour of practical men, and is almost abandoned, with
alchymy and catholicons, to the dreams of enthusiasm. These
are formidable impediments, and they are peculiar to this
science. But there are many others, which are incident to the
promulgation of every new doctrine; and, that you may behold
the extent of my temerity, I will adduce a few of them.

[Words may be compared to music. When a Briton listens
to a certain tune of Handel, the notes articulate distinctly, "God
save great George the King"; but, when an American hears it,
the notes articulate, "God save great Washington." Hence the

difficulty in understanding a strange doctrine. The words will constantly excite old opinions, though the speaker intends new.

[When Columbus informed the Spaniards that he had discovered a new world, inhabited by men, the Spaniards attached to the word man its ordinary signification; nor were they undeceived, till Columbus exhibited the natives. I saw once, in a Roman Catholic cathedral, a wax candle burning before the altar: you will suppose that the word candle intimates sufficiently my meaning, but it will be wholly unrevealed;—what I saw, possessed the circumference of my arm, and the height of this table.

[Of the mistakes to which we are thus liable, I can adduce nothing more explanatory than the philosophy of Epicurus. He maintained, that happiness consists in pleasure. Shortly every libertine sought protection under this philosophy; and now its name is synonimous with luxurious sensuality. But fortunately for the reputation of the philosopher, we eventually discover that the pleasure to which Epicurus alluded was virtue.

[Modern researches escape not obscurations equally gross. We read of volcanoes that are discovered in the moon; of immense mountains nine miles perpendicular—in the moon; of a country six thousand miles in circumference, devoid of atmosphere and water,—in the moon; of awful chasms as broad as oceans and as deep,—also in the moon. We read, likewise, of small planets that were created by the explosion of a great planet; and that the roofs of houses would appear, (if we could divest ourselves of prejudice,) lower than the foundations. These expressions are amply significant, when correctly understood; but whoever shall affix to the words their ordinary import, will err as widely as the remote disciples of Epicurus.

[Such examples should instruct us that the puerilities of ancient metaphysics had probably a sensible signification to their authors; and should restrain our perverse assumption, that every writer is to be literally interpreted, though we thereby make him utter the greatest absurdities. Ancient speculations of the above description are frequently made significant by modern discoveries. After we acquire thus a meaning to the heretofore unintelligible sentences, we announce that the ancient author intended the modern signification, though probably nothing was further from his apprehension. This principle induces us to attribute to Pythagoras the astronomical system of Copernicus; and enables us to discover in Homer a profundity of knowledge that he never conceived; and to find in the general suggestions of Bacon every art and science that has succeeded him.

[The next obstacle which every new doctrine encounters, is prejudice. When Copernicus asserted the sun's quiescence, the theory was deemed subversive of scripture, which declares that Joshua protracted day by arresting the sun. Better interpreters have succeeded in establishing, that the prolongation of day constituted the only material fact; and if Deity should even now promulge the process, it would surpass our comprehension.

[This historical instance is trite, but very illustrative of the identification of erroneous conclusions with indisputable truths. Whatever contradicts the former, we deem incompatible with the latter. Such prejudices oppose a sturdy barrier against any new doctrine connected with the philosophy of human knowledge; for on no subject are artificial conclusions so widely diffused, and implicitly believed. Every man possesses some metaphysical system which he has imbibed, he knows not how; and credits, he knows not why. Its incomprehensibility renders him sensitive to its preservation. It is an unfortunate child, whose very idiocy endears it to his feelings.

[Besides, every science is so encumbered with propositions which are hostile to the information of our senses, that repugnance to them has ceased from obstructing credibility; hence the most subtle deductions, and extended analogies, are implicitly adopted by the illiterate as phenomena, which, though above their perception, are pervious to the learned. You cannot find a person who does not as readily believe that the earth moves, as that his cart moves. The word motion, he supposes to possess the same signification in both cases; while truly, when applied to the earth, it means certain phenomena only, which are explicable in no way so well as by assuming a motion of the earth. The earth's motion means all the proofs which can be adduced in support of the theory. Whoever believes that the motion purports more, is deceived by language.

[Amid this dreary host of ambiguities, prepossessions, and prejudices, exist a few enlivening auxiliaries. When Cicero visited the groves of Academus, Socrates had long been sacrificed to envy, and his great disciple had realized, in eternity, some of their sublime conjectures. Yet Cicero's imagination re-peopled the Academy. It saw Plato surrounded by the youth of Athens, and heard his eloquence captivate again the understanding. Why then may not a name produce enthusiasm now, and our Lyceum gleam with a faint glory from a recollection of the immortal Aristotle, the founder of the first Lyceum, and the Philosopher to whom the honour is due of discovering the only principle on which reasoning must for ever depend: a discovery which time cannot simplify nor enlarge; which eulogy has been unable to obscure by comment, or prejudice to subvert by proscription; and which teaches that argumentation may mould knowledge into new forms of speech, but cannot extend it beyond our premises?

§ 12.—*These discourses concern not the relative meaning which words bear to each other, but the relation which words bear to created existences.*

I have gained my present object, if I have excited your attention to the succeeding discourses, and removed some prepossessions that would have prevented you from discovering in language the defects to which I refer; for when I speak of defects in language, most persons suppose that I allude to the admitted ambiguity of speech. My remarks will not concern the relative meaning which words bear to each other, but the relation that words bear to the phenomena of the universe.

§ 13.—*We translate sensible existences into words, instead of interpreting words by the information of our senses.*

When an Englishman is learning to read French, he learns to translate French words into English words. A French word he estimates as a mere representative of some English word. We translate creation much in the same way. Every natural existence we deem a mere representative of some word. Language usurps thus, to an astonishing extent, the dignity which truly belongs to creation. I know we usually say that words are signs of things. Practically, we make things the signs of words.

§ 14.—*We must make our senses the expositors of words, instead of making words the expositors of what our senses reveal.*

Our misuse of language may be illustrated by another simile:—we estimate creation by means of words, much in the same way as we estimate the gravity of bodies by means of weights. My lectures will endeavour to subordinate language to nature,—to make nature the expositor of words, instead of making words the expositors of nature. If I succeed, the success will ultimately accomplish a great revolution in every branch of learning.

§ 15.—*To understand these discourses, a slight perusal of detached parts, or of the whole, will be insufficient.*

That language will eventually receive the construction for which I shall contend, I feel no doubt, though I may not possess the talent to introduce the reformation. Before we commence our discussions, I must warn you, that the perverted estimation of language is so habitual, that you will be constantly liable to misapprehend my remarks. Should a person, unacquainted with geometry, read Euclid's Elements, he may meet with no word for which he possesses not a definite signification; yet, when he shall have read to the end of the volume, he will know but little of geometry. To understand geometry, it must be studied slowly and painfully. No effort of mine can indoctrinate you with the knowledge of language on any easier conditions.

§ 16.—I will labour intently to state my views as intelligibly as possible, and as concisely; and as I am aware that in oral instruction to voluntary auditors, the speaker must conciliate his hearers, or be taught by the solitude which will soon environ him, that his labours are vain, I will endeavour to believe that Philosophy is not necessarily so frowning and sluggish a divinity as her ministers usually represent.[1] Her limbs are masculine I admit, and her discourse is grave; but her language may be tasteful, and her decorations gay. I pause at these promises. All the stimulation which you can yield will probably be necessary to my perseverance. If I stagnate in the midst of your kindest efforts, the result should disappoint my hopes, rather than your expectations.

§ 17.—When fame has produced for an individual an elevation to which all eyes are continually directed;—when his opinions are impatiently expected, and rapidly disseminated;—when they are applauded in anticipation, and their adoption secured

---

[1] In Johnson (I) the passage reads:

In oral instruction to voluntary auditors, the speaker must conciliate his hearers, or he is taught by the solitude which soon environs him that his labours are vain. Hence the Grecian philosophers were the most eloquent men of their age; while probably, from a resort either to typography, or lectures to involuntary hearers, philosophy exhibits now no traces of fascination. Usually it combines slovenly composition with sterility of ornament; and custom has even moulded these deformities into a canon of criticism. Professor Blair recommends the style of Locke's Essay as a model: a work which, though it carries the philosophy of knowledge as far as it has yet been extended, presents no page that will not bear an expunction of a quarter of its words with benefit to perspicuity.

by prepossessions;—the labour of composition assimilates to the progress through Spain of the Duke of Angoulême,*—a progress in which every city was approached but to be entered with a bloodless triumph; and every enemy pursued, but to be received by a resistless surrender—a progress whose labour is only the fatigue of pleasure, and whose dangers are merely the inebriation of success.

§ 18.—Startled at the difference between such a writer and me, I have more than once cast aside my pen as an insidious enemy, that lures me from the substantial pursuits of life. Even the consolation of yielding an amusement to you cannot well be expected; and while I have been distracted in seeking a worthy motive for exertion, I have not been exempt from apprehensions that I may, unconsciously, be influenced by the demon who delights to revel in our infirmities: the demon who makes the taciturn exult at his own dulness, and the loquacious enamoured of his own frivolity; who makes ill-timed gravity increase its frown, and incessant levity augment its laughter.

§ 19.—The demon at whose pernicious suggestions even moral deformities are heightened. Surgeons, thus induced, will boast of an insensibility that they cannot feel; and libertines, of profligacy that they never practised. The avaricious will falsely magnify his selfishness, and the prodigal his expenses. The liar will laugh at an exaggerated recital of his infamy, and the extortioner at an aggravated list of his oppressions. Nor escape personal deformities, the malice of this evil counsellor. Dwarfs, at his suggestion, endeavour to appear smaller than nature intended, and giants larger. The stammerer he urges to incessant conversation, and the freckled to an unnecessary nudity.

§ 20.—While I was reflecting on the eccentricities which proceed from his persuasion, imagination presented him unexpectedly before me. His language was harmonious,—his actions were profoundly respectful. Delight hung upon his lips,

---

* This discourse was pronounced in the winter of 1825.

and conviction attended his communication. An unusual complacency expanded my breast. I extended my arms in the attitude of oratory, and prepared to welcome him with all the figures of rhetorick; when suddenly, approaching the fiend, his eyes were averted, and his face was distorted in ridicule. He dissolved into air, and, as he vanished, I discovered his name, Vanity, stamped upon his back.

PART FIRST

OF LANGUAGE WITH REFERENCE TO EXISTENCES
WHICH ARE EXTERNAL OF MAN

Lecture II

§ 1.—CREATION is boundless, whether we estimate its objects numerically, or its extent superficially. We cannot, by penetrating the earth, discover a vacuity;—we cannot exalt our vision beyond created objects;—we cannot fathom the fulness of the ocean.

§ 2.—To bring this immensity of existences within our definite comprehension, naturalists divide the whole into a vegetable kingdom, a mineral kingdom, and an animal kingdom: with various subdivisions of classes, orders, species, &c.

§ 3.—Chymists subject creation to a still more concise classification. All objects are convertible, chymically, into about forty different substances; and chymists classify objects with reference to the substances into which they are thus convertible:—hence, with chymists, the universe is reduced into about forty different substances.

§ 4.—*To understand the relation which words bear to created existences, we must contemplate creation apart from words.*

Creation is susceptible of a classification more definite, and even less multifarious, than that of chymistry. This classification will constitute the present discourse. You must understand it, because I cannot teach you the relation that words bear to created existences, till you can contemplate the existences apart from words.

§ 5.—*The external universe may be divided into sights, sounds, tastes, feels, and smells.*

The classification which I propose, refers to our senses. We derive from them our knowledge of the external universe; hence, by marshalling under each of our five senses, all the information that the sense reveals to us, our knowledge of the external universe becomes divided into five classes. Each·class can be confounded with no other. A triangle is not more distinguishable from a circle, than the information of one sense is distinguishable from the information of every other. To make each class as distinct in name, as in nature, every information that is revealed to me by hearing, I shall call a sound;—every information that is revealed to me by seeing, a sight;—every information that is revealed to me by feeling, a feel;—every information that is revealed to me by smelling, a smell;—and every information that is revealed to me by tasting, a taste.

§ 6.—*Sights, feels, &c., are presented to us by nature in certain groups.*

When considered with reference to our senses, and divested of names, the external universe is a mass of sights, sounds, tastes, feels, and smells. Nature presents these to us in certain groups. A sight and a feel that are invariably associated, we call fire. Another group, consisting of a certain sight, feel, taste, and smell, (associated in a manner peculiar to nature,) we call an orange. Another group, consisting of a certain sight, feel, and taste, we call bread. Another group, consisting wholly of sights, we call a rainbow.

§ 7.—*Sights and feels are the most frequently associated.*

The associations which are most frequent in nature, are sights associated with feels. Of these associations, one sight and feel we call silver; another, gold; another, mahogany; another, marble; and another, wool.

§ 8.—*Sights, feels, tastes, and smells, are frequently associated.*

The associations which are next in frequency, are composed of a sight, feel, taste, and smell. The word lemon names an association of this description, and the words brandy, apple, grass, sulphur, oil, tar, tobacco, cheese, beef, cinnamon, &c.

§ 9.—Sights, feels, and tastes, are found in frequent association. To some of the associations we apply the words salt, sugar, water, honey, milk, wheat, chalk, &c.

§ 10.—*Sights, sounds, tastes, feels, and smells, nature some-times presents singly to us.*

In some cases, sights, sounds, tastes, feels, and smells, are presented to us disjunctively. One sight, which is thus presented to us, we call moon. Another sight we call light; and another, aurora borealis, meteor, ignis fatuus, &c. A certain unassociated feel, we call air. Another feel, we call wind; and another, cold. A certain unassociated sound, we call echo. Thunder can hardly be designated as an unassociated sound, for it is usually associated with a sight which we call lightning. Tastes and smells are never presented to us, unless in association with some other existence. I recollect only one exception, and we designate it, when it occurs, by saying, we have an unpleasant taste in our mouths.

§ 11.—*We must discriminate between the extent and variety of creation, and the paucity of language.*

The number of unassociated sights is very small, if we estimate them by the number of words which name such sights. They are, however, far more numerous than this mode of estimating them will imply. The word star, for instance, names an unassociated sight, (a sight not associated with any feel, &c.;) but the word which thus seems to name but one sight, names a great number of sights, that differ in magnitude, brilliancy, colour, shape, &c. I state this, to enable you to perceive, that verbal designations are an inadequate means of estimating the variety and number of natural existences.

§ 12.—The sights which are presented to us in association with feels, &c., are also far more numerous and various than language implies. Colours alone are almost infinite in variety, while our names for them are comparatively a few words. But a large portion of sights we never attempt to designate by specifick appelations. When I look at a chair, I discern a different sight from what I see when I look at fire; still, for the sight alone of neither the chair nor the fire, language possesses no

name. The words chair and fire apply severally to an associated
sight and feel. When we speak of the sight alone, we employ a
periphrasis, and say the appearance of the fire, the appearance
of the chair, &c.

§ 13.—*Tastes, smells, sounds, and feels, are seldom designated specifically by names.*

Men have been more sparing of names to tastes, smells,
sounds, and feels, than even to sights. Fragrant, fetid, and a
few other words, are all that we have deigned to appropriate to
the information of the sense of smelling. Hot, cold, pain, &c.,
are all which we have appropriated to specifick feels, though
nature presents them to us in boundless variety. When I touch
iron, I realize a different feel from what I experience when I
touch wood, silk, wool, linen, &c.; but to none of these feels is
a name appropriated. The word iron names an associated sight
and feel. The same may be said of the words wood, silk, wool,
linen, &c.

§ 14.—*We create names when we deem them useful.*

But not only numerous sights, sounds, tastes, feels, and
smells, possess separately no name; many associations of them
possess no name. We name such associations only as utility
requires us to designate. A certain associated sight and feel we
designate by the word square, and others we name round, flat,
&c.; but a hundred shapes which may be assumed by a piece
of glass, on its accidental fracture, we have not designated by
any name.

§ 15.—*The associations of nature are sometimes separable.*

If a piece of gold is held in front of a mirror, the mirror will
exhibit the sight, gold, separated from the feel. In many other
instances, art can separate the sights and feels which nature
associates. If you thrust a stick into water, and leave a part
unimmersed, the stick will exhibit the sight, crooked, without
the feel, crooked. If you look at a candle, and press with your
finger against the external angle of one of your eyes, you will

experience the sight, two candles, unaccompanied by the feel, two. If you look at the sun, and then close your eyes; or, without looking at the sun, if you press for a moment rather painfully against either of your eyes; you will see various colours, unaccompanied by any of the feels with which colours are generally associated. If you whirl your body, and produce dizziness, every object on which you look will exhibit the sight, rotation, unaccompanied by the feel.

§ 16.—*Feels can also be separated from the sights with which they are naturally associated.*

If you cross the third and fourth fingers of your right hand, and rest the tips of the crossed fingers on a bullet, you will experience the feel, two bullets, unaccompanied by the sight, two. I have seen a wheel whirl so rapidly and evenly, as to present the feel, motion, without the sight. Blindness and darkness effectually separate all feels from their associated sights. To the blind, iron is a feel only, fire a feel only, sunshine a feel only.

§ 17.—*Painting, slight of hand, natural magick, &c., consist in the separation, either artificially or spontaneously, of the sensible existences which nature usually associates.*

The art of painting consists principally in producing sights separated from their usually attendant feels:—the sight, prominence, without the feel,—the sight, distance, without the feel,—the sight, shape, without the feel. Perfumery consists in separating the smell, rose, jessamine, &c., from the sights and feels with which the smells are naturally associated. Ventriloquism and mimickry consist in separating sounds from the sights and feels with which the sounds are naturally associated. Slight of hand and natural magick are either the apparent or actual separation of phenomena which nature generally associates:—usually some sight separated from its associated feel. If a wine glass be half filled with cotton wool, and immersed, (in an inverted position,) in a bowl of water, the cotton will exhibit the sight, wet, as you slowly emerge the wine glass. To the feel, the cotton will be dry. Sights are far more frequently and easily separated from their associated feels, than feels are from their associated sights.

§ 18.—*When we see a sight, experience alone induces us to expect that it is associated with a feel.*

An ignis fatuus is the sight, fire, without the feel. Our surprise at the phenomenon, and the alarm of the ignorant, is not occasioned by the sight, but at the absence of any associated feel. We forget that experience is all the warrant which we possess, in any case, for expecting a feel, where we discover a sight. We erroneously deem the sight a proof that a feel exists, and hence we suspect no possibility of mistake when we predicate tangibility of the sun, moon, and stars. We suppose that we can see their tangibility; a supposition which involves the absurdity that we can feel with our sight. When we look at space, and know that our hand will encounter no resistance in passing through it; and when we look at glass, and know that our hand will encounter resistance in passing through it; the knowledge in both cases is experimental, and no part of the sight of either the glass or space. That a fog is not tangible, and that a stone wall is; that the moon cannot be reached by our hand, and that the table can be; are all revelations of feeling, and not revelations of vision.

§ 19.—*When we perceive a feel, experience alone induces us to expect that it is associated with a sight.*

Should we feel a violent external pressure, and discover no accompanying sight, we should be alarmed at the invisible annoyance;—still, experience alone induces us to expect a visible accompaniment, when we experience a feel: and hence, an external pressure produced by a gust of wind, disconcerts no person by its invisibility. External feels, unassociated with a sight, are very few. The wind is such an existence; and temperature, both hot and cold, is another. A person unaccustomed to the experiment, to whom you should exhibit a bladder inflated with air, would expect its contents to be visible, as strongly as he would were the bladder filled with stone:—he would in both cases believe that the feel of the bladder testified to a visible contents:—a belief that involves the absurdity, that we can feel visibility. In the dark, when we place our hand on a window, and know that what we feel is visible; and when, at the same time, we feel a current of wind rushing through a broken window, and know that what we feel is invisible; the knowledge in both cases is experimental, and no part of the feel of either the window or the wind:—the knowledge is a revelation of vision, and not of feeling.

§ 20.—*Language refers to the groups which nature presents to us, and not to the individual phenomena of any group.*

I shall not pursue these remarks, as they belong more properly to the future physical investigations referred to in my preface. I introduced them here with no object but to enable you, amid the groups of sensible existences which compose the external universe, to discriminate the separate existences of each group. The discrimination is peculiarly important, language referring to the groups, and seldom regarding the individual phenomena which compose any group. All the incidents which I have stated are mere illustrations of the proposed discrimination, and probably I need not burthen you with further examples.

§ 21.—*Words are confounded with things.*

The benefits which you are to derive from the discrimination will be gradually disclosed in our progress; but the first benefit is to enable you to contemplate created existences apart from their names. The names are at present so identified and confounded with the external existences, that we cannot discover the subordination which language bears to the realities of nature, but are continually, (as I shall show hereafter,) imputing to nature limitations, classifications, ambiguities, imperfections, and properties, of various kinds, which truly belong to language alone. A child comprehends with difficulty, that in France, the people eat apples, and still know not the meaning of the word apple. We smile at the child, but we all conform more nearly to the child than we imagine, in our identification of language with the existences to which we apply it.

§ 22.—*We should endeavour to regard words as merely the names of things.*

Should a person point to an object, and ask me what it is, I might answer, it is a sight and a feel. My children are so accustomed to such answers from me, that they never address me as above. They ask me to tell them the name of the object. This question keeps the name distinct from the object, and gives language its proper subordination to created existences.

§ 23.—Besides, by answering that the object is a sight and a feel, I direct your attention, not to the name, but to the group of existences, to which the name refers. Examine it, and discover the sight. Handle the object, and discover the feel. Elicit all the sights and feels which it presents. Try if it possesses a taste and smell. This category conduces to physical knowledge, and at least separates distinctly physical existences from language.

§ 24.—For the same purposes, when a child reverses the inquiry, and asks me what is a rose; I reply, it is a word with which we name an associated sight, feel, and smell. For the sensible existence itself, I refer him to his senses, as alone able to communicate the information:—words being unable to perform the functions of our senses. Words can refer us to sensible information which we have experienced; but they cannot reveal to us what we have not experienced.

§ 25.—If you have succeeded in catching my analysis, you no longer see in the heavens, light, clouds, sun, galaxy, moon, stars, meteors, space, vacuity, distance, shape, &c.; but you see various sights, to which the above words are names. You no longer feel, in a knife, iron, hardness, weight, matter, substance, impenetrability, external, cold, edge, sharpness, &c.; but you experience various feels, to which Englishmen apply the above words, and Frenchmen apply other words, and uneducated mutes no words.

§ 26.—To investigate the sights, sounds, feels, tastes, and smells, which separately, and in various associations, constitute the external universe, is not my present object; nor shall I discuss whether sights, sounds, tastes, feels, and smells, are words which appropriately designate external existences. I adopt the phraseology, as a means of investigating the nature of language; and if I shall establish the utility of the adoption, I trust you will tolerate the expressions, how much so ever they may offend against euphony and custom.

Lecture III

LANGUAGE IMPLIES A ONENESS TO WHICH NATURE CONFORMS NOT IN ALL CASES

§ 1.—*The existence which we name a shadow, possesses more natural oneness, than the existence which we name gold.*

HAVING, in my last discourse, divided the sensible universe into sights, sounds, tastes, feels, and smells; the analysis shows that language implies a oneness to which nature conforms not in all cases:—for instance, the word shadow implies a unit. If we refer to nature for the meaning of the word shadow, we discover a sight. Here language implies a unit, and nature presents one. But the word gold implies a unit also; and if we refer to nature for the meaning of the word gold, we discover a sight and a feel:—two distinct existences.

§ 2.—*The oneness of natural existences must not be interpreted by their names, but by our senses.*

Each of our senses is known to be so peculiar, that its loss is irremediable by the others. That no sense but seeing can inform me of sights,—that no sense but hearing can inform me

of sounds,—that no sense but feeling can inform me of feels,
&c.—are obvious truths. Still, the obviousness exists only while
we use the words sights, sounds, feels, &c.; for if I assert that
no sense but seeing can reveal to you gold, I shall be told that
feeling can reveal it as well as seeing. The oneness of the information exists, however, in language only. A man void of sight,
and another void of feeling, (if we may imagine such a man,)
could possess a definite meaning for the word gold, without
possessing in common any sensible knowledge of gold. To the
blind man, the word would name a feel only; and to the other,
a sight only. The knowledge which they might seem to possess
in common, would be verbal and not physical.

§ 3.—*We must subordinate language to what we discover in
nature.*

You may ask whether I mean to assert that gold is not a unit?
It is a unit, but its oneness must be interpreted by what our
senses reveal. In all the uses of language, to thus subordinate
it to nature, is the object of all my lectures. Language has
usurped over nature a superiority which is so inveterate and
unsuspected, that we constantly appeal to words for the interpretation of natural existences, instead of appealing to natural
existences for the interpretation of words.

§ 4.—*Verbally, the oneness of every existence is equally
simple, but the natural oneness varies in different existences.*

The English language contains but a few thousand words,
while the objects to which we apply the words are innumerable.
To effect these infinite appliances, every word receives many
meanings: snow is white, paper is white, silver is white, the air
is white, glass is white, you are white, and the floor is white;
hence, after you are satisfied of the propriety of calling an object
white, I shall know but little of its appearance, without I take
an actual view of the object. The word white names, you perceive, certain general characteristicks, and disregards less
obvious individualities. The generality of language is an irre-

mediable defect in its structure; for were we to invent a separate name for every sight which we now denominate white, language would be too voluminous for utility, and perhaps for our memory. The same remarks apply to every word. To know, therefore, the sensible meaning of the word unit in any given case, our senses must examine the case, and we shall find that the oneness of a shadow differs from the oneness of gold; the oneness of gold differs from the oneness of water; and the oneness of water differs from the oneness of an orange. Imagine, for instance, four men so misformed, that each possesses only one sense. Let the senses which they possess be seeing, tasting, feeling, and smelling. To one of the men, the word orange will name a sight; to another, a taste; to another, a smell; and to the other, a feel: four dissimilar existences. An orange is, however, one existence, as appropriately as a shadow; but we must interpret the oneness by what we discover in the orange, and not interpret what we discover in the orange by the word one. Such a misinterpretation is common, and it has exceedingly perplexed speculative inquiries.

§ 5.—*In all our speculations, we estimate created existences by the oneness of their name.*

Bishop Berkeley perceived that the word roundness signifies a sight and a feel. He knew not that the duality of nature controls the oneness of the name. He supposed that the oneness of the name proves the duality of nature to be fallacious; and that either the sight is the true roundness, or the feel. He decided in favour of the feel, and hence he proclaimed roundness to be invisible:—invisible, because he restricted the name to the feel!

§ 6.—*Because nature exhibits not the oneness which we find in language, we impute the discrepancy to a fallacy of nature, instead of knowing that it is simply a provision of language.*

When we look at roundness, we know the feel with which nature has associated the sight. This knowledge is derived from experience, for seeing cannot inform us of a feel; but we need not mysterize a truth which is founded on the organization of our senses, and is applicable to all their information. Saint-Pierre states that a philosopher who lost his sight by gazing too intently at the sun, imagined that the darkness which ensued, proceeded from a sudden extinction of the sun. This ingenious sarcasm is frequently applicable to human conclusions, and thus Berkeley never imagined that invisibility was predicable of roundness by means of our restricting the name to the feel; but he accused vision with the production of a fallacy.

§ 7.—*Instead of employing our experience to teach us that the oneness of language is fallacious, we employ it to show that the duality of nature is fallacious.*

Rees's Cyclopedia, (title, Philosophy,) records a sudden acquisition of sight by a person who had been always blind. "When he had learned to distinguish bodies by their appearance, he was surprised that the apparent prominences of a picture were level to the touch." The experience of this person is adduced by the Cyclopedia to show that the senses are fallacious, hence the person is made to ask which sense deceived him. Neither sense, however, deceived him. The sight prominence, and the feel prominence, are so generally associated, that we expect the feel when we see the sight; but they are distinct phenomena, and may be separated, as the picture evinces. If we assume that the sight and the feel are invariably associated, the mistake is in our inexperience, and not in our senses, nor in nature. A deaf mute, when he should first observe, in either a picture or a mirror, the sight prominence separated from the feel, would be as much disappointed as we; but he would immediately learn the duality of nature, and be satisfied. But we contrast the duality of nature with the oneness of the word prominence; and instead of employing the discrepancy to show that the oneness of language is fallacious, we employ it to show that the duality of nature is fallacious. The delusion is extraordinary by which we thus exalt language above nature:—

making language the expositor of nature, instead of making nature the expositor of language.

§ 8.—*We make language the expositor of nature, instead of making nature the expositor of language.*

In the Gentleman's Magazine of July, 1796, published in London, another blind person testifies that figure is not visible.[1] "When he first acquired vision, he knew not one shape from another." We are prepared to hear him announce, that he knows not the name of colours; but a different ignorance seems implied by an inability to determine by sight a globe from a plain. Our surprise proceeds less from any practical ignorance of the duality of nature, than from unsuspicion of the fallacious oneness of language; an unsuspicion which induces us to believe that when a blind man knows globes and plains by the feel, he knows the same units that he subsequently may be made to see. But I introduced the above quotation to show that the blind man's experience is not employed to expose the fallacious oneness of the word shape, but to convict either nature or our senses of a fallacy in not exhibiting the same oneness that the word shape implies. We assume that language is the expositor of nature; and as language implies that shape is a unit, we restrict the word to the feel, and announce (not as a conventional provision of language, but as a detected fallacy of nature,) that

---

[1] In Johnson (I) the passage reads:

In the Gentleman's Magazine of July, 1796, published in London, another blind person testifies that figure is not visible. "When he first acquired sight, he knew not one shape from another." Related thus, the fact excites astonishment; yet it signifies only that he knew not the names of the sights which he was then first beholding. In one of the dramas of Shakspeare, a fanatic is arrested for asserting that he has just been miraculously cured of blindness. The king, after showing him a scarlet cloak, and desiring him to name the colour, orders him to announce the name of an officer who is near him. The restored blind man cannot. Then, says the king, you are an impostor, or the name of scarlet would be also unknown to you.

figure is invisible:—invisible, because we restrict the name to the feel.

[Professor Reid, in his Inquiry on the Mind, states, "that a young man, who was couched by Cheselden, thought at first that every thing he saw touched his eyes."

[This is supposed to manifest the invisibility of distance. But what did the young man mean? Seeing can inform me when my hand touches the table, and feeling also can inform me. The word names then a sight and a feel. The young man was opening his eyes for the first time, hence he could no more know by name the sight touch, than he could the sight scarlet. He meant by the word touch, what during his blindness he had meant—a feel. He knew no way to discover exterior existences, but by feeling, smelling, tasting, or hearing; consequently, he supposed that his eyes operated by one of these methods. His expression was merely an hypothesis to account for the intelligence of his new organs. If a person should suddenly acquire feeling, he would probably say that every thing which he touched was seen by his fingers. Something similar did occur: a man who had been deaf from his birth, acquired hearing by a surgical operation. His first expressions intimated that his ears saw the sound which they announced.]

§ 9.—*We invent theories to reconcile the duality of nature to the oneness of language.*

"When I look at a book," says Professor Reid,[1] "it seems to

---

[1] Johnson's treatment of this topic in (III) is of interest as introducing a system of word indexing. He says (III, pp. 89–92):

I want to suggest a mode to speculatists by which the generic diversity of the unverbal components of any such nominal unit may become sensibly apparent. The alphabet is a nominal unit, and possesses as much intellectually conceived oneness as the letter A; but even the letter A possesses less sensible oneness than nominal oneness, for it names four different sounds. Orthoepists designate which of the four sounds the letter A denotes in any given use of it, by plying over the A some

possess thickness, as well as length and breadth; but we are certain that the visible appearance possesses no thickness, for it can be represented exactly on a piece of flat canvass." The painting exhibits the sight thickness without the feel. If we had

---

character which conventionally reveals the intended sound. Philosophers might adopt a like contrivance when using any nominal unit that aggregates objects generically different. I, might denote intellection; S, sight; F, feel; T, taste; L, smell; D, sounds; G, internal feeling. For instance *thickness* is a nominal unit, but sensibly I can feel thickness and I can see thickness; consequently, the intellectually conceived nominal unit thickness names a sensible duality. We, however, possess an entire control over the definition of the word thickness, and can define it to signify the *feel* thickness, excluding the sight thickness. This definition is as good as any other when we understand the intended limitation; but we may convert such a limitation into a puzzle when the limitation is not avowed. Professor Reid thus puzzled himself, as follows: He says, "When I look at a book, it seems to possess thickness as well as length and breadth; but we are certain the visible appearance possesses no *thickness*, for it can be represented exactly on a piece of flat canvass." Now, if he had placed the letter F over the word thickness, so as to denote he was limiting the word to the feel thickness, he would have seen the quibble which arises from saying we can represent thickness on a piece of flat canvass. We cannot represent the *feel* thickness on a flat canvass; we can represent the *sight* thickness only, which is just what we see when we look at the canvass. . . .

Hume announces a like unconscious quibble, when he says, "The table (S) which we see, seems to diminish (S) as we recede from it, but the real table (F) suffers no diminution (F)." The whole zest of the proposition consists in the sensible duality of each of the nominal units table and diminution. That the *sight* diminution and the *feel* undiminution can exist thus together, is a physical fact of much interest; but we make a mystery of it only when we play bo-peep with words, by neglecting to discriminate the intellectually conceived oneness of diminution, and its physical duality.

(The passage from Hume here quoted differs slightly from the same passage quoted in (II), Lect. XIII, § 3, and from the original: Hume (1), Sec. XII, pt. I, p. 161, Open Court edition. The original does not of course exhibit the indexing, which is Johnson's innovation.)

always supposed thickness a unit, this experiment ought to have undeceived us. But we are not accustomed to subordinate language to the revelation of our senses; hence we invent theories to reconcile the revelation of our senses with the implications of language. The theory in the above case consists in restricting the word thickness to the feel, and pronouncing the sight a delusion. That seeing cannot acquaint us with the feel thickness, is an interesting item of experimental knowledge. We need not give it an artificial piquancy by limiting the signification of the word thickness to the feel, and asserting that thickness is invisible. The feel thickness and the sight are equally realities of the external universe;—equally entitled to honour;—equally inconvertible. We may, if we choose, restrict the word to the sight, and assert that the feel is a fallacy; but nature is no party to our philology. She exhibits her phenomena just as our senses discover, unaffected by our theories, and unchanged by our phraseology.

§ 10.—*To assert that distance is invisible, is only an enigmatical mode of relating the simple fact, that seeing cannot reveal to us a feel.*

When I look at a picture, one part appears remote, and another near. To the feeling the parts are equi-distant. From the frequency with which the sight distance and the feel distance are associated, we suppose them identical; but pictures would always have taught us the contrary, if we had not deemed the authority of language, which calls the sight and feel a unit, superior to the authority of experience, which teaches us that they are not a unit. A restored blind man, who should see distance for the first time, would no more expect that it was associated with the feel distance, than he could tell, by looking at a red hot iron, the feel with which that appearance is associated. We may, if we please, restrict the word distance to the feel, and assert that distance is invisible; but this is only an enigmatical mode of relating the simple and undisputed fact, that seeing cannot reveal to us a feel.

§ 11.—*Whether seeing can or not inform us of an external universe, depends on the meaning which we attach to the word external. The question relates to language, and not to nature.*

That seeing, tasting, smelling, and hearing, can yield us no intimation of an external universe, is another puzzling tenet of speculative philosophy, founded on the errour of estimating sensible existences by the oneness of their name, instead of estimating the name by the duality of nature. The word external names usually a sight and a feel. If I look at this table, I discover the sight external; if I touch the table, I realize the feel external. When we speak of external, we should therefore explain to which we allude,—the sight or the feel. This ambiguity was discovered by Locke, but he knew no alternative but to select whether the feel is the real external, or the sight. He selected the feel, and succeeding philosophers have obeyed his decision. Seeing, therefore, cannot reveal to us an external universe, because we restrict the signification of the word external to the feel.

[The puzzle is susceptible of another elucidation. What is the external universe? A mass of existences. The table before me is one. But do I allude to the sight table or the feel? Table, though a unity in language, is two existences. The feel table is familiar to the blind, but the sight table is so dissimilar, that were a blind man to suddenly obtain vision, he would be unable to select thereby a table from the carpet on which it stands.

[Like remarks are applicable to nearly every part of the external universe. There is a sight candle and a feel candle; a sight chair and a feel chair. If now we restrict the word candle to the feel, we may contend that seeing cannot inform us of the existence of candles. This restriction philosophers accordingly impose on all words which name external existences: hence the paradox that seeing cannot discover them.

["The table which we see," says Hume, "seems to diminish as we recede from it; but the real table suffers no diminution."

Here the real table is evidently intended to designate the feel; while the table which diminishes, and is deemed deceptious, is the sight.

[In the paradox under discussion, I have spoken of that part only which asserts that seeing cannot teach us the existence of an external universe. This part is the most paradoxical, because external is usually the name of a sight as well as of a feel; still we experience some perplexity when we are told that hearing, tasting, and smelling cannot inform us of an external universe. An instance of this will appear in the following quotations. "If any man will stand blindfolded in the middle of a room, and allow his most intimate friend to walk repeatedly round him without speaking, and afterwards to stand still and address him, he will not know, in several trials, the position of the speaker."

[When we resolve the above information into sensible phenomena, it amounts to an intimation that hearing cannot inform us of a sight and a feel. The word position is a name of these, and the author intended so to employ it. Still position is not obviously a sight and a feel only; and hence is not known to be undiscoverable by hearing. If, however, we wish to teach a child the signification of position, we shall be unable except by the agency of either seeing or feeling. We may know from experience the position of a sound, but all that hearing discloses is the sound. If a man should deafen his ears with cotton, and be surrounded by persons who move their lips, he will not know, by looking at them, whether they articulate or feign. This would not constitute an interesting experiment; still it differs not from the former, except that articulation is known to name a sound, and therefore to be undiscoverable by seeing; while position is not obviously a sight and a feel only, and hence is not evidently undiscoverable by hearing.

[The writer continues: "We might have had sensations of taste, without the application of sapid substances to the palate; for nothing is more common than to experience a taste, without an ability to ascribe it to an external cause."

[He intends to prove that tasting cannot inform us of an external universe. If the word external means any thing which is not a taste, the position is evident. It exemplifies, however, the sophistry to which we are liable, when we designate sensible information by other names than sights, sounds, tastes, feels, and smells. To announce that tasting cannot teach us a sight and a feel, would be insufferably simple; yet it is precisely what appears momentous, when we say that tasting cannot inform us of an external universe.

[That external does not designate a taste, may be evinced by the inability of taste to teach a child the signification of external. He will, however, easily comprehend its meaning, if you operate on the senses to whose phenomena the word refers. Delineate a circle, and write therein the figure 2, and place without the figure 3, he can immediately learn that the position of 2 is internal, and the position of 3 external: or place his hand in a tankard, and thereby teach him the feel internal, and the feel external. External is, therefore, a sight and a feel; hence tasting cannot discover it.

[I think Professor Reid says, "if we enter a room and observe a collection of roses, we readily attribute the fragrance that we inhale to the roses; but," continues he, "if instead of roses we should perceive a range of closed jars, we should be unable to determine from which jar the odour issues."

[He wishes to prove that smelling cannot inform us of an external universe; and that experience only enables us to know that odours proceed from external objects. His doctrine is correct, but it assumes an unnecessary mystery. Smelling cannot take cognizance of a sight or a feel; and when external is thus resolved, all mystery vanishes.

[By restricting the word external to the phenomena of feeling, philosophers prove not only that seeing, tasting, smelling, and hearing, cannot inform us of an external world; but that nothing which is intactible constitutes any part of external objects. Sweetness, say they, is no part of sugar; whiteness no part of snow; and fragrance no part of a lily. They persevere in a similar exclusion from all objects; and this constitutes the second branch of the paradox.

[We must not suppose that Locke or Descartes, with whom these assertions originated, intended to propagate a deception. They perceived that the word sugar implies but one existence while it exhibits three existences, a sight, a taste, and a feel. Instead, however, of attributing the disagreement between the unity of the word sugar, and the plurality of the phenomena, to a latent sophistry in language, they accused the senses of a delusion.

[We will examine the positions separately. What is sugar? Usually the name of a sight, a feel, and taste. If we restrict the word to the feel, we may safely pronounce that sweetness is no part of sugar. Touch it, I may say, and be convinced. Whatever is truly in the sugar, you can feel. There is hardness, figure, texture, and mobility; but nothing like sweetness.

[When we know that philosophers restrict thus the significa-tion of sugar to the phenomena of feeling, their conclusion becomes grossly evident. No man imagines he can feel sweet-ness; yet this is all that their position purports.

[Let us consider, says Locke, the red and white in porphyry; "hinder light from approaching, and the colours of porphyry vanish. But," continues he, "can any person think that any alteration is thus made in porphyry; and that redness and white-ness are really in it, in the light, and not in the dark? It has indeed such particles as are apt, by the rays of light rebounding from some part of that hard stone, to produce in us the idea of whiteness; and from other parts the idea of redness: but neither redness nor whiteness is in it at any time."

[What is porphyry? In the language of Locke, it is a hard stone. Here is an elucidation of the mystery: Locke restricts the name to the hard stone, to the feel: hence the presence and absence of light produce no alteration in the porphyry, and whiteness and redness are not in it: that is, they are no part of the feel. Even so insignificantly can speak a wise man, when he does not discriminate between the information of different senses.

[To strike on a drum, and assert that the sound constitutes no part of the drum, will be admitted by most persons; for the word drum, names usually only a sight and a feel: but if I inquire whether sound constitutes any part of thunder, the question embarrasses. With most men, thunder is the name of a sound, to subtract which makes the word insignificant. Some, however, vanquish this difficulty even. The word thunder they resolve into other words, then they can deny that the sound constitutes any part of thunder—that is, the sound forms no part of their definition.

[After philosophers determine that the phenomena of feeling alone constitute every external object, and that colour is no part thereof, they inquire where colour exists? Before we reply, it is well to know whether the answer must be verbal. If you ask me the appearance of my hand, you will concede that a display of the hand is the best information. If you demand whether my hand is hard, the submission of it to your touch is the most conclusive solution. But when you ask where colour is, you deem it a poor reply to be shown the colour, and told that it is where you see. You touch the place, and say colour is not here. Nothing is here, but figure, extension, and texture.

[This dissatisfaction is highly significant; and as it elucidates the paradox that colour constitutes no part of an external object, we will slightly discuss it. The appearance of my hand is a sight: hence you deem the question that relates to its appearance well answered by seeing the hand. The hardness of my hand is a feel: hence to touch it is the best elucidation of its consistence; but when you ask where colour is, the word where is a sight and a feel; therefore to see the colour is an unsatisfactory answer.

You allude to the feel where. But the feel is not applicable to colour; and when I direct your hand to it, you justly exclaim that the colour is not there. I can feel, say you, solidity, extension, and texture, but nothing that resembles colour.

[To dispel the ambiguity of the question which inquires after the location of colours, we must, therefore, understand that the word place, with all its concomitants, here, there, where, &c. is the name of two phenomena—a sight and a feel. If we converse metaphysically of location without attending to this distinction, we shall involve ourselves in a comedy of errors; nor are the Dromio of Ephesus and the Dromio of Syracuse more diverse existences than the feel place and the sight place.

[As philosophers restrict external objects to the phenomena of feeling, and thus prove that flavour, odour, sound, nor colour, constitute any part of external objects; so they limit the signification of sugar, and every other external object, to a few only of the phenomena of feeling, and exclude hardness, temperature, roughness, and other feels. This constitutes the last branch of the paradox.

[Every external object produces not one feel only, but several. When I touch a piece of wax I can experience smoothness, weight, tenacity, external, mobility, temperature, substance, figure, extension, and many other feels, to which also we have given distinct appellations. If we restrict the word wax to a part only of these feels—to figure, extension, and substance—we can confidently assert that the other feels constitute no part of wax. They are, I can say, sensations which the wax excites, but they are not in the wax: that is, they are not included in the phenomena to which I restrict the signification of wax.

[While philosophers are discussing the number of phenomena which the name wax shall embrace, they imagine that the discussion penetrates deeply into the arcana of nature; though truly it relates to language alone. Phenomena exist precisely as we discover them, and all the control which we possess is to comprehend them under such names as we deem expedient. When estimated thus, it may be useful to debate whether hardness constitutes any part of iron, or tenacity any part of wax; but to suppose the inquiry is an investigation of nature, is as erroneous as to suppose that we are deciding the character and fortunes of our children when we are deliberating whether to call them Cleopatra or Lucretia, Arnold or Washington.

["When I am opposite to fire," says Locke, "I feel heat; when I approach I feel greater heat; when I advance nearer I feel pain. Why then," continues Locke, "do we not think that pain is in fire as well as heat?"

[He wishes to prove that neither is in the fire, and nothing can be more easily accomplished. Fire, when restricted to the phenomena of feeling, is usually a name of the feel heat, the feel burn, the feels solidity, external, and some others: hence heat is in the fire—that is, we include it among the phenomena to which the name fire is applied. But if we restrict the word to the feels solidity, substance, external, and figure, we can maintain that heat is not in the fire.

[Professor Reid states a similar proposition: "If you recline against a stone, you will feel hardness; if you press against it, you will feel pain: why then," he asks, "do you not affirm that pain is in the stone as well as hardness?"

[He adduces the argument to prove that hardness is not in the stone: and doubtless with him it is not. He says that nothing is truly in the stone but figure, substance, and texture. This elucidates sufficiently why hardness is not therein. Substance also might be excluded, if he would banish it from his definition.

[An inattention to the principle of language that I have endeavoured to designate, has produced more errors than many volumes can comprehend; yet I will intrude upon you an enumeration of only one additional class. This relates to the generally received impression that the senses are fallacious. If we thrust a stick into water, and leave a part of its length unimmersed, the stick will appear crooked, which we are told is a fallacy of the senses; for the stick is straight. Crooked is supposed to name but one existence, though it names two—a sight and a feel. The sight crooked and the feel possess no identity except the name, by which we confound them. True, they are generally associated, but if we hence infer that they are identical, or even that they never exist disjunctively, we must blame our inexperience. The senses would always have taught us the separability of the sight crooked from the feel, if we had thrust a stick into water. They are no more chargeable for our erroneous conclusions in this particular, than they would be if we had never seen any black body but what would discolour our hands, and should thence believe (as I have known some children) that the discolouration is a necessary consequence of blackness.

[If you half fill with cotton wool a wine glass, and immerse it (in a reversed position) in a bowl of water, the cotton will, on slowly emerging the glass, appear wet, while to the feel it will be dry. We may exhibit this experiment as another fallacy of our senses; but such a use of the experiment will be rather another instance of the latent sophistry of language. Wet is a sight and a feel, two phenomena, though they possess but one name. The sight wet and the feel are frequently associated, but that they are not inseparable, the experiment in question will demonstrate.

[Again: by a slight pressure on one of my eyes, I can see two candles, where feeling certifies there is but one. This also is deemed a deception, for we assume that the sight candle and the feel are identical, though experience would always have taught us that the two phenomena are separable by a slight pressure on one of our eyes. If I write at a table on which there are two candles, my pen produces two shadows. If a third candle be lighted, the pen will produce three shadows. Why do we not esteem the multiplication of the shadows a deception, as well as the multiplication of the candles? Because the word shadow names a sight only, while candle designates a sight and a feel, which hence we assume to be identical; and when the sight is multiplied without the feel, we suppose that seeing deceives us.

[Seeing is most obnoxious to the charge of deception, but feeling is not wholly exempt. If you place across each other the third and fourth fingers of any one's right hand, and rest the tips of those fingers on a bullet, the person will suppose that he is touching two bullets. Here also the senses are innocent. Two, when applied to bullets, designates a sight and a feel. The feel is so seldom discoverable without the sight, that we suppose them identical. But feeling can never inform us of the sight two. The sight and the feel are different existences, which the experiment shows may be disconnected.

[Finally, we may come to this conclusion, that what any sense informs me of, no one or more of my other senses can reveal to me. This position seems to violate the experience of every moment; still all violations may be reconciled by an investigation of language. When I look across this table, seeing informs me that there exists no impediment to the extension of my arm. This information feeling also can give me: hence both seeing and feeling seem to yield the same information; but when we resolve the information into the phenomena which give it significancy, we shall find that seeing informs us of a sight, and feeling of a feel:—two existences which cannot be identical. Experience alone enables us to determine, by vision, that my arm will meet with no obstruction.

[Again, a physician may say that seeing informs him of the approaching dissolution of his patient, and that the sick man's pulse yields to feeling the same information. But feeling announces nothing, except certain phenomena which experience evinces precede death; and seeing announces another class of phenomena which also precede death. The information of the two senses agree in nothing but in being joint precursors of the same catastrophe.

[If the physician say that death is discoverable by seeing and feeling, the identity is even in this case verbal. Perhaps every sense can reveal some phenomenon to which the word death may be appropriately affixed, so that no man, how defective soever his formation, may be wholly ignorant of life's extinction; still the information of the different senses is identical in nothing but in the name death that is common to the whole.]

§ 12.—*Estimating nature by the oneness of language is a fallacy which enters deeply into every system of philosophy.*

I hope you are now convinced that language implies a oneness to which nature conforms not. The discrepancy has greatly perplexed philosophy, and produced some of its most enigmatical speculations. A few of these I have discussed, not to subvert them, but to elucidate the errour on which they are founded. I might pursue the discussion illimitably, for the errour enters deeply into every system of philosophy; but I shall have gained my object if I have stated examples enough to teach you the latent sophistry of language to which I have alluded.

Lecture IV

THE ONENESS IMPLIED BY LANGUAGE AFFECTS NOT ONLY METAPHYSICAL DISQUISITIONS, BUT PHYSICAL SPECULATIONS

§ 1.—*When a word names the phenomena of two or more senses, the oneness of the name is peculiarly embarrassing.*

IN MY last discourse, I showed that sensible existences are presented to us variously grouped, and that we estimate the oneness of each group by the oneness of its name, and not by the revelation of our senses. The errour is peculiarly embarrassing when the group consists of existences (like figure, magnitude, distance, &c.) that are revealed to us by two or more senses; because the imputed oneness of the group seems to manifest that two or more senses reveal to us the same information; a position which contradicts the known limitation of our senses.

§ 2.—The errour affects principally metaphysical disquisitions, and the examples which I adduced were extracted from the abstruse speculations of Locke, Hume, Descartes, Berkeley, Reid, and kindred writers. But in many other cases, and of a nature quite different, language implies a oneness, and we credit the implication, to the vitiation of our most familiar speculations and pursuits. To an exposition of the evil in this new guise, the present discourse will be directed.

§ 3.—*We seek in nature for a unit which exists in language only.*

I am speaking, I am standing, several persons are present. Each of these assertions is a truth; but if we seek among these truths for truth itself, believing it to be a unit, we are seeking in nature for what is merely a contrivance of language. "What is truth?" said Pilate. He supposed it a unit, and hence the difficulty of the question. All things that we call truths, possess certain general characteristicks; just as snow, salt, silver, and glass, possess certain characteristicks, which entitle them all to the designation of white: but if we wish to ascertain the meaning of the word white in any given case, we must examine the object to which it is applied; and if we wish to know the meaning of the word truth in any given case, we must examine the circumstances to which the word is applied. The oneness of a thousand whites is verbal; and the oneness of a thousand truths is verbal. The unit is a creation of language; hence the fallacy, ambiguity, and difficulty, when we seek in nature for a corresponding unit.

§ 4.—*Groups of natural existences and relations may be deemed units, but we must estimate their oneness by our sensible experience, and not by the implication of language; nature being no party to our language.*

Temperature is hot, cold, tepid, freezing, melting, burning, &c. Temperature seems a unit, but these examples exhibit it multiform. Shall we interpret the oneness of temperature by the multiformity of nature, or shall we estimate hot, cold, tepid, freezing, &c., by the oneness of the word temperature? We choose the latter course, and fallaciously perplex ourselves to discover in hot, cold, tepid, &c., the unit which exists in language only. Hot, cold, tepid, &c., may be deemed a unit; but we must estimate their oneness by what we discover in nature, and not by the implication of language. The oneness of the name is a contrivance of language. The oneness of the phenomena is the similarity which induces us to class them under one name.

§ 5.—*The oneness of nature is different in different cases, but the oneness which language implies is always complete.*

The health of a country is as much a unit in language as the health of Thomas. In nature, the oneness of the two cases is dissimilar. Even Thomas's general health during a year, is less a unit in nature, than his health at the present moment. The oneness which language implies is always entire; while nature presents but different approximations to a simple oneness. The saltness of the ocean is a unit in language, and the saltness of any given drop of the ocean is another unit; but the oneness is more unique in the drop than in the ocean. The oneness of an army is as much a unit in language as the oneness of Napoleon who commands it; while in nature their oneness is very dissimilar.

§ 6.—In these cases, experience neutralizes the implied oneness; but the delusion is subtle, where we cannot obviously compare the multiformity of nature with the oneness of language;—for instance, wisdom is as much a unit in language as the moon. The countless actions, &c., which are denominated wisdom, possess a homogeneity which makes one name applicable to them all; but to impute to these countless actions the oneness of the name, is to commit the errour that I am anxious to display:—it is to interpret nature by language, when we ought to interpret language by nature.

§ 7.—*The particulars which we can discover in nature, are all which truly pertain to nature.*

The main delusion of alchymy consisted in assuming that the colour, weight, fixedness, malleability, &c., of gold, are append-ages of a mysterious unit. To discover this unit, constituted alchymy. The alchymist never supposed that the above qualities and others are the unit of which he was in search. He disre-garded these, and sought for some unit that would agree in oneness with the oneness of the word gold. He sought in nature for what exists in language only. We laugh at the exploded labours of alchymy, but we laugh more from having abandoned the search in despair, than from having discovered the fallacy on which the search is founded. Kindred researches are still common. Magnetism is sought as a unit, and gravity, electricity, repulsion, aurora borealis, vitality, impregnation, animality, power, causation, &c.

§ 8.—In nature, we find magnet A, that will suspend a weight of twenty pounds, and magnet B, that will suspend but an ounce. We find the polarity of a magnetick needle, with its variations, its wanderings, and its dip, &c.; and while we apply correctly the word magnetism to these and as many other phenomena as we deem sufficiently homogeneous to be included under a com-mon name, we gain nothing but delusion in attributing to them a oneness like that which is implied by the name. Their true oneness is the homogeneity that we discover in them, and which induces us to call them all magnetism. The verbal oneness is a property of our own creation.

§ 9.—*Medical science is probably embarrassed by our imput-ing to diseases and their incidents, the oneness which pertains to their names only.*

The medical question of contagion is embarrassed by not dis-criminating the oneness of language from the plurality of na-ture. The contagiousness of cholera generally is less a unit than the contagiousness of a single case. Even the contagiousness of a single case, during its whole continuance, is less a unit than its contagiousness on any given moment:—hence, to investigate the contagiousness of cholera, and to proceed by supposing that the contagiousness possesses the oneness which the word contagion imports, is like seeking for magnetism as a unit among the numerous magnetic phenomena. It is seeking in nature for a unit that exists in language only.

§ 10.—But cholera itself is not a unit. Whether medical science suffers not by the implied oneness of each disease, merits the consideration of physicians. Many medical theories seem to owe their origin to this errour. But not only is cholera in general not a unit, the particular cholera of Thomas is not a unit. It consists of many feels, sights, and other phenomena. I admit the propriety of combining them under one name; but if we would escape delusion, we must construe their oneness by nature, and not by the oneness of their name.

§ 11.—*Our moral speculations also are embarrassed by imputing to nature the oneness which exists in language only.*

Is a man a unit, as strictly as language implies? Should I attempt to discover wherein his oneness consists, (and volumes have been written on the subject,) I might seem to discuss humanity very profoundly, but I should discuss it very ignorantly. I should seek in nature for what is merely a contrivance of language:—for instance, amputate one of Peter's arms, will the remainder of Peter be a man? How much excision of his body must occur, before the remainder will cease to be a man? Such questions are not deemed trifling. We interpret nature by the oneness of the word man, instead of interpreting the oneness of the word man by the exhibitions of nature. The errour seems to me so gross, that I should doubt its existence, were not the evidence too explicit to be mistaken.

§ 12.—In what consists the consciousness of a man? in what consists his identity? have been debated, and they are still debated, with the most surprising ignorance of the delusion which gives to the questions their perplexity. Consciousness is supposed to possess as much natural oneness as it possesses verbal oneness; while, in truth, the consciousness of a man is the many phenomena to which the word refers,—precisely as the wealth of a man is the various items of his property to which the word wealth refers.

["I now proceed," says Professor Brown, "to a most important inquiry—the identity of the mind; whether the mind is truly one and permanent, amid all the variety of its fugitive affections?"

[But wherein is this inquiry important? To collect facts may be important; but whether they shall be named mental identity is unimportant. The name cannot raise or depress them, but sinks in its signification to the phenomena to which you affix it. I shall be what I am, call me by what name you please; and so will the phenomena of the mind. Hence it is wisely observed by Lord Shaftesbury, in view of the conflicting opinions which relate to the identity of the mind, that there is (to use his own language) "no impediment or suspension of action on account of these refined speculations. Agreement and debate go on still. Conduct is settled. Rules and measures are given out and received. Nor do we scruple to act as resolutely, on the mere supposition that we are; as if we had proved it to the full satisfaction of our metaphysical antagonist."]

§ 13.—What governs the will?—how acts volition on our limbs?—how is the soul united to the body?—and how mind acts on matter, and matter on mind?—are questions which derive their perplexity from severally implying the existence of some unit. The search after the unit is the delusion.

§ 14.—Gravity, which effects so much in astronomical theories,—which has displaced Atlas, and equals him in oneness,—is still, so far as relates to its oneness, but a delusion of language. The word gravity names many interesting and important phenomena; but if, in addition to these, we look for gravity itself, we act as ignorantly as the child at the opera, who, after listening with impatience to the musick, singing, and dancing, said, "I am tired of these; I want the opera."

§ 15.—The delusion by which we look for the unit gravity among the various phenomena of which gravity is the name, and for the unit man among the various parts of our formation, is analogous to the ancient puzzle denominated sorites:—A heap of wheat is exhibited to a person, and you proceed with him among the individual grains, to look for the heap itself. You take up a grain, and ask him if that is the heap. You proceed thus with every grain, till the whole will be exhausted without finding the heap.

§ 16.—*Some units are a sensible aggregation, and some a verbal aggregation.*

The word heap signifies a sight and a feel, and hence possesses an existence and a oneness without reference to the separate grains of which the heap is composed;—while the unit gravity possesses in nature no existence independently of its constituent parts. Gravity, as a unit, is a verbal aggregation; while the heap, as a unit, is a sensible aggregation. This distinction is highly deserving of consideration. Language disregards the distinction; the verbal oneness being equally complete in both cases.

§ 17.—*We invent theories to supply the unit which we suppose must exist, but which we fail from finding in nature.*

To the mistake by which we transfer to nature the oneness that exists in language, we owe a large portion of our theories. The theories supply the unit that we vainly seek in nature, but which we erroneously suppose must exist:—for instance, the unit magnetism is alleged to be some subtile and invisible emanation or fluid;—the unit temperature is another radiating and insensible fluid;—gravity another. The unit vitality is an irritability of fibre, and the unit sound is a vibration of the atmosphere. The unit is sometimes deemed an undiscoverable essence; sometimes an agitation of the brain; sometimes an insensible repulsion of insensible parts; sometimes an internal combustion; and sometimes an external explosion.

§ 18.—So far as theories are useful, they are of course desirable. I wish to merely show that we attribute to nature the oneness which exists in language; and that we usually invent a theory to supply the exigency created by our mistaken apprehensions of nature. The practice will continue till we shall learn to interpret and qualify words by the revelation of our senses; instead of interpreting and qualifying the revelation of our senses by the implied oneness of words.

Lecture V

LANGUAGE IMPLIES IDENTITIES TO WHICH NATURE CONFORMS NOT

§ 1.—HAVING, in my last two lectures, shown that we impute to nature a oneness which belongs to language only, I shall now show that we impute to nature an identity which belongs to language only.

§ 2.—*Language is a collection of general terms, but creation is a congregation of individual existences.*

Nine hundred and ninety-seven millions of beings exist, to whom we apply the word man. Amid the varieties of their complexion, stature, hair, features, age, sex, structure, habits, and knowledge, enough similarities are discoverable to make the word man appropriate to all. No two are, perhaps, identical in their general appearance, nor in the appearance of any particular part. They differ, also, individually from each other, in many qualities besides the appearance.

The word man, therefore, refers to a mass of dissimilar individuals. Every word is equally general in its signification. By means of their generality, a few thousand words comprehend all created existences. Nature is a congregation of individual existences, and language a collection of general terms.

§ 3.—*We interpret the identity of existences by the identity of their name.*

When we wish to disparage Napoleon, we say, he was but a man; and when we wish to exalt a simpleton, we say, he is a man as well as Napoleon. The alleged identity is correct, if we interpret it by the similarities that we discover in the compared individuals; but the identity is alleged to imply a similarity beyond what we discover in the two individuals, and even to control the differences that they exhibit. This is an insidious errour, and it constitutes the subject of the present discourse.

We disregard the individuality of nature, and substitute for it a generality which belongs to language.

§ 4.—*The identity which language implies has embarrassed medicine.*

Medical science long suffered by the delusion which we are investigating. It still suffers measurably. Diseases possess sufficient resemblances to be classed under general names; hence we possess the words peripneumony, pleurisy, rheumatism, &c. I censure not physicians for constructing the names, nor for deciding that Thomas and Henry are severally afflicted with pleurisy; but their diseases are not as identical in nature as in language.

§ 5.—*Individuality is characteristick of nature.*

The identity which language implies is responded to by nature very nearly, or we could possess no medical science; but the most skilful physician is often defeated by the individualities of nature. Physicians have long detected these individualities, and deemed them anomalies of nature. The anomaly is, however, in language, which unites under one name, as identities, what is only partially identical. Individuality is no anomaly of nature. It is nature's regular production, and boundless richness.

§ 6.—No two parcels of calomel possess the perfect identity which the sameness of their name implies. No two men possess the perfect identity which the sameness of their manhood implies; nor possesses any one man, at all times, and under all circumstances, the complete identity with which language invests his individuality.

§ 7.—*The identity which language implies is always complete, but nature approximates in various degrees only to a perfect identity.*

Language implies always a perfect identity; nature exhibits, in some cases, a greater approximation to identity than in other cases. For instance:—in two flakes of snow, the snow presents an identity which is almost complete; but in a whale and an anchovy, the fish of both animals presents a very incomplete identity. The fish of the whale and anchovy is, however, as identical verbally, as the snow of the two flakes.

§ 8.—Again, a polypus and an elephant are animals, and the animality of both is identical in language; in nature, the identity is less than even the identity of the fish.

§ 9.—Iron is matter—a sunbeam is matter. Their materiality is identical in language, while in nature we discover in it less identity than we discover in even the animality of the polypus and elephant.

§ 10.—*We should not confound the verbal identity with the realities of nature.*

I complain not of language for its implied identities. We can construct a language on no other principle. A whale and an anchovy present sufficient similarities to render the word fish appropriate to both: still we need not confound the verbal identity with the realities of nature. In nature, the identity is just as we discover it to be. It must not be measured by names, but ascertained by observation. We reverse this rule: we interpret the natural identity by the verbal.

§ 11.—*Failing to discover in nature the identity which language implies, but believing that it must exist somewhere in nature, we mistake it for a mysterious property of creation.*

No man observes so superficially as not to discover in natural productions an endless diversity. Children say, that no two blades of grass are alike. Still, the difference in the blades we estimate as not affecting their identity as grass. But what is the identity of grass, beyond the sensible resemblance, &c., of the different blades? Nothing but the name grass. We deem the identity a hidden property of nature, while it is only a property of language.

§ 12.—*We transfer to nature a generalization which belongs to language.*

Botanists say, that oats, barley, and wheat, are also grass; and when we become botanists, we see that the name is appropriate. We are, however, deceived, if we suppose that in these different existences some property exists, which is as identical as the identity of the word grass. We are transferring to nature a generalization of language.

§ 13.—*The diversity which we discover among natural objects, &c., that possess the same name, should teach us to correct the identity implied by their name; but we employ the verbal identity to excite wonder at the natural diversity.*

The question is deemed profound which asks how the soul is united to the body;—how the movements of a man's limbs are united to his volition;—how heat and light are united in flame;—how coldness and hardness are united in ice. The union, in these cases, is deemed identical with the union of the arm to the shoulder; and hence the wonder and the fallacy. Should a man ask how the arm is united to the shoulder, we could show him the ligatures, &c., and he would be satisfied. He would be equally satisfied with what he discovers of light and heat in flame, did he not believe that the word union, as applied to the light and heat, meant the same as the word union when applied to my arm and shoulder. The diversity which he finds in nature between the two unions, fails to teach him that the verbal identity is fallacious. He employs the verbal identity to show that the natural diversity is mysterious.

[Locke admires that the coldness and hardness of ice, though inseparable, produce in us separate ideas. If, however, we inquire into the alleged inseparability, we shall find that it is predicated of the coldness and hardness of ice, because they do not exhibit the phenomena to which the word separable is applied in some other cases.

[I can tear a piece of paper, and tell you to see that the fragments are separate. The word now is the name of a sight. I can direct you to feel that the fragments are separate. The word is then the name of a feel. Did Locke mean that coldness and hardness are so united in ice that the sight separation cannot be produced in them? Coldness and hardness are not visible. But can we not produce the feel separation in the coldness and hardness of ice? What feel? That which is experienced from the fragments of the paper when held asunder? This feel can no better apply to the coldness and hardness of ice, than the sight can: hence, when Locke asserts that the coldness and hardness of ice are not separable, he limits the signification of separable, and means only that coldness and hardness will not produce the sight and feel which are produced by the fragments of paper—a meaning which no man intends to contravene, when he asserts that the coldness and hardness of ice are separable.

[As Locke shows that the coldness and hardness of ice are not separable; so another philosopher has shown that they are not united. To understand this, we must recollect that the word united is ordinarily applied to the sight and feel exhibited by the links of a chain. As neither this sight nor feel are discoverable in the coldness and hardness of ice, we consider the application to them of the word united as a curious irregularity of nature, instead of a simple contrivance by which men prevent an inconvenient multiplicity of words.

[If a congress of metaphysicians should assemble to designate the phenomena to which the word united truly belongs, there would probably be much disagreement; and whilst every member might assert the claim of some adverse phenomenon, all would admit that the name can belong properly to only one. They would affirm that its signification is independent of men, and exists in some subtle definition to whose test every advocate would subject his favourite phenomenon;—not to decide whether it shall be named united, but whether it be the existence, that the word inherently typifies.

[Admit they shall adjudge that the sight and feel exhibited by the links of a chain constitute the phenomena to which alone the name united belongs: the assembly would immediately declare that coldness and hardness are not united in ice; that sweetness is not united with sugar, nor whiteness with snow, nor fragrance with a rose, nor an effect with its cause—enunciations which mean simply that sweetness and sugar, whiteness and snow, &c. do not exhibit the sight and feel that are produced by the links of a chain: a meaning which, if expressed plainly, is as puerile as any declaration that can be framed. The whole is founded on an ignorance of the fundamental truth, that words have no inherent signification, but as many meanings as they possess applications to different phenomena. The phenomenon to which a word refers, constitutes in every case, the signification of the word.

[We may now understand the metaphysical puzzle of Hume, that there is no visible union between any cause and its effect. The union to which he referred is the sight and feel exhibited by the links of a chain. But such a union can never be intended by any person who asserts that a cause and its effect are united. Cause and effect exist successively; and how instantaneous soever may be the succession, the cause must precede its effect. One only can be present—the other must be either future or past. To talk, therefore, of seeing a cause and its effect united, as we see the union of two links, is to talk of seeing at the same

time a present phenomenon and a past, or a present phenomenon and a future. It is to speak absurdly.*]

§ 14.—Light passes through solid crystal. This many persons
deem a standing miracle. What we see excites no surprise. The
passage through the solid crystal is the marvel. We know the
difficulty which would attend the passage of our hand through
the crystal, and we deem the passage of the light identical with
the passage of the hand. Nothing is more fallacious than thus to
construe the word passage in these different uses of it. The two
operations possess the requisite analogy to make the word passage applicable to both, but its meaning in each application is
what our senses reveal, and not what the identity of the word
implies. The passage of the light through crystal is a sight only;
the passage of my hand is a sight and a feel.

§ 15.—A spark causes gunpowder to explode. This is curious.
But speculation wonders not at the explosion, but that we cannot discover the connexion which exists between the touch of
the spark and the explosion. Mankind would not have attached
the word connexion to the spark and explosion, if the word was
not appropriate; but if we infer that the connexion is identical
with the connexion exhibited by two links of a chain, and seek
in nature for such a link, we are deluded. Nature is boundlessly
diverse; and all that we can accomplish is, to group the diversities under such general terms as alone can compose a finite
language.

§ 16.—*Language, in its ability to designate individual existences, is like colours in their ability to depict the variety of
nature.*

---

* That a chain will move on drawing towards us one of its links, is a result
which we learn from experience, and which we could not discover, *a priori*, any
more than that the uttering of a sound will be succeeded by an echo.

Again: that a chain resists separation, constitutes none of the information
which we obtain by looking at the union of its links. The resistance is an effect of
the union, and disclosed to us by experience only.

Hence, if we could, as Hume desired, see every cause and its effect entwined
like the links of a chain, our knowledge would be exactly what it is now. The link
would prove nothing. None of its effects can be seen or felt, *a priori*, any more
than we can see or feel, *a priori*, the effects of arsenic.

When a painter undertakes to represent nature, he finds an infinity of natural tints, while he possesses only a finite number of artificial colours with which to effect the representation. So, when he undertakes to discourse of nature, he finds an infinity of phenomena, while he possesses only a finite number of words with which to form his discourse.

§ 17.—The colour which on one occasion the painter employs to portray the moon, he, on another occasion, employs to represent water;—so the word which on one occasion a speaker employs to designate the relation that exists between two links of a chain, he employs on another occasion to designate the relation that exists between a spark and an explosion.

§ 18.—The painter and the speaker act from a kindred principle; the painter discovers in the moon and the water an analogy which makes one colour appropriate to both; and the speaker discovers in the links, and the spark, and explosion, an analogy which makes the word connexion appropriate to both.

§ 19.—*Verbal disquisitions will be erroneous till we cease from imputing to nature the identities which belong to language.*

But in one point the painter differs from the speaker. The painter knows that the identity of colour (between the water and the moon), exists only in the imperfection of his materials; while the speaker knows not that the identity of "connexion" (between the links of a chain, and the spark and explosion), exists only in the imperfection of language. Yet this truth must be learnt before we can extricate ourselves from the errours in which nearly all verbal disquisitions are involved.

§ 20.—*The meaning of the word identity varies with the object to which it is applied.*

The word identity itself is merely a general term, expressive of a multitude of varying existences and relations. A man who is blind from his birth, knows roundness by the feel. Should he attain sight and see a ball, he will not recognise it as the round object of his former amusement. When, however, he shall have learnt roundness by the sight, he may inquire how the visible ball and the tangible are identical. Their identity is different from the identity of his person now, and his person a few moments previously. The identity of John when an infant, and the same John when a decrepid old man, differs from both the other identities. The identity which exists between an acorn and the oak from which it originated, differs from all the other identities. To seek in each of these cases for something that is common to them all, and as similar in all as the similarity of the word identity which we apply to them all, is to seek in nature for what is only a contrivance of language.

§ 21.—*We subordinate nature to language, instead of subordinating language to nature.*

To ask how the visible ball and the tangible are identical, displays the perverse manner in which we interpret language. Instead of asking language how the two phenomena are identical, we should ask our senses what the verbal identity signifies. We apply the word identical to many dissimilar phenomena; and instead of imputing the verbal identity to a necessary stratagem of language, we impute the natural diversity to a mystery of nature. The visible ball and the tangible exhibit not what some other identities exhibit; hence we are perplexed. Nothing but a long habit of subordinating nature to language can account for our not discovering, in the diverse applications of the word identical, that the alleged identity is a mere license of language, and the discoverable diversity but the ordinary individuality of nature.

§ 22.—*No two existences are as identical in nature as in name.*

After an assayer pronounces two bars to be gold, I shall not know correctly what even their identity signifies, till he shows me the phenomena to which his decision refers. Their identity possesses not the unqualified sameness which exists in the name gold.

§ 23.—*The identity which language implies is the expedient by which a finite language comprehends an infinitely diverse creation.*

Men agree on the standard which decides whether two bars are gold, but a like agreement exists not in every alleged identity. One man will deem no two things identical, unless they exhibit the phenomena which constitute his personal identity. He knows not that the natural identity of any two objects is only what the objects display; and that the complete identity which is implied by the sameness of their name is merely a human contrivance, by which an infinitely diverse creation is comprehended by a finite vocabulary: comprehended as well as we can, in groups of much similarity, under the word gold; in groups of less similarity under the word metal; and in groups of but little similarity, under the word mineral.

§ 24.—*Imputing to nature the identity which exists in language, causes much fallacious speculation.*

Heat, whether solar or culinary, chemical or animal, is deemed as identical in nature as in language. So far the fallacy is free from much absurdity. But the prepossession which induces us to deem all heats identical, induces us to deem their causes equally identical; hence, solar heat is considered either chemical or igneous. An alternative is pleasant, but philosophers are almost unanimous that the sun is fire. Even the years are numbered which must elapse before its combustible parts will be exhausted. Whether this continues the scientific romance of the day, I know not, and care not. The theory may be changed, but the errour which originated it remains. Pursuing the verbal identity of solar and terrestrial fire, astronomers find that some planets, by approaching the sun, become periodically hotter than iron in fusion; and comets accumulate heat enough to retain, after a century's absence, a sufficiency for comfort.

§ 25.—These are the calculations of men with whom I presume not to contend, except where they delusively impute to nature the identity which exists only in language—a delusion which has been indulged by astronomers, till they have fabricated wilder romances than ever fiction created intentionally.

§ 26.—Again, stone is matter; air, light, water, man, earth, and sun, are severally matter. That matter is as identical in nature as in name, is believed with all the simplicity of an undisturbed prepossession in favour of the errour. Creation displays in vain its diversities. The variety only augments our admiration at the implied identity.

§ 27.—So far, however, the absurdity is moderate compared with the chimeras which we produce, when, in pursuance of the implied identity of matter, we invest a sunbeam with hardness, bulk, particles, resistance, and every other essential property of stone. We are then taught to admire that light, so constituted, can fall with a velocity almost inconceivable, and from a height almost inexpressible, and not merely leave our houses unbattered, but leave us unconscious of the blows which are inflicted on even our eyes.

§ 28.—Light moves from the sun to the earth, and a coach moves from Utica to Albany. The word motion is proper in both phrases; but when we deem the motions as identical in nature as in language, we are transferring to nature what is simply a property of language. The mistake is unimportant, till, by virtue of the supposed identity, we attribute to the motion of light the concomitants of the coach's motion. Proceeding thus, we calculate that during one vibration of a clock's pendulum, light moves, as consecutively as the coach, one hundred and sixty thousand miles.

§ 29.—I lately saw a little book (The Child's Book on the Soul) which teaches children occult doctrines. The child's curiosity is excited by the information that he and stones possess many properties in common:—colour, form, substance, hardness, bulk, resistance, mobility, &c.

§ 30.—That the child and the stone are identical in some particulars, is the marvel and the fallacy. So far as the identity is verbal, the child knows the identity. So far as you impute to nature the identity which exists in the words, you are deluding him. In the same way, youth are taught that male and female, when applied to plants, are identical in meaning with male and female when applied to animals; and thus we obtain from youth an interest for botany at the cost of their understanding.

§ 31.—We teach a child that certain stars are suns. We court his belief that the identity is as complete naturally as verbally. Beyond all ordinary visibility and all telescopic, other suns, we say, exist; still wishing him to believe that the identity of language and of nature are one. This verbal delusion, to which teachers and scholars are usually alike victims, exalts, we say, creation. Miserable compliment! Creation needs not romance for its exaltation, nor the perversion of reason for its glory.

§ 32.—We tell a pupil that the earth travels with various velocities, and various motions, wishing him to believe that the motions and velocities are identical in nature with the motions and velocities of a steamboat. This errour is so monstrous and so general, that it presents a wonderful example of the delusion by which we transfer to nature the identity of language. The motions and velocities of the earth are a good theory; but that they are more than our senses reveal, and especially that they should be deemed identical with the motions and velocities of a steamboat, are neither necessary to the theory, nor useful. That men have invented laws and calculations, whose results coincide with the sensible phenomena of the heavenly bodies, is creditable to human knowledge, and useful to human pursuits; but we need not vitiate our knowledge, and sully its glory, by interpreting astronomical theories by the identities of language, instead of the revelation of our senses.

§ 33.—*Estimating nature by the identities of language misleads us in natural history, geography, &c.*

Natural history suffers by the implied identity of its objects.

Eagles are discussed as identical, men as identical, whales as identical, lions as identical. So far as we can speak of properties that are discoverable in every lion, a general account is not delusive; but we are prone to attribute to every lion the property of each, misled by an identity among them which exists no where completely but in their name. To discourse of groups of animals as identities is probably the only method by which we can possess any natural history; but we need not aggravate the evil by deeming their verbal identity a property of nature.

§ 34.—To read Captain Parry's narrative of his Arctic expedition, seems to make my knowledge identical with his; but he acquired new sights, and new phenomena of every sense; while his narrative gives me new combinations of words only—or any way, a knowledge different from his, how identical soever may be the words with which we speak of it.

§ 35.—*Two men, who assent to the same general proposition, may possess very diverse meanings.*

In the use of general propositions, much misunderstanding occurs from the identity of language and the diversity of nature. If I assert that George is good, you may assent. Under this verbal identity, I may refer to actions of George that are unknown to you; and you may refer to actions unknown to me. Nay, the actions to which I refer might cause you to reprobate George.

§ 36.—*Our expressions are often identical, when our meanings are diverse.*

You and I may be well acquainted with Thomas; still, when we see his portrait, you may deem the likeness excellent, while I may call it execrable. While we speak of the appearance of Thomas, our knowledge seems identical; but our different estimations of the portrait prove that our knowledge is diverse. When we view Thomas, we take not necessarily the same view. I may habitually contemplate his profile, and you his bust; I may notice his chin, and you his forehead.

§ 37.—*Estimating thoughts by the identity which their name implies, has prevented us from noting the natural diversity which thoughts exhibit.*

I will burden you with only one further illustration of the difference between the identity which language implies, and the diversity which nature possesses. The illustration possesses, however, an importance which makes it merit your attention.

§ 38.—*Thoughts are divisible into six different classes.*

We can think of the appearance of the moon, and we can think of the word moon. In both cases we are said to think of the moon; but, in nature, the two thoughts differ from each other, as much as a sight differs from a word. Instead of possessing the identity which the name implies, thoughts are divisible into six different classes. A disregard of this diversity produces much of the mystery with which thinking is usually invested in our discussions of it.

§ 39.—*One class of thoughts are words.*

Professor Stewart says, "some men, even in their private speculations, not only use words as an instrument of thought, but form the words into sentences."

§ 40.—What is thus alleged, is true of all men; but the remark attaches to only one class of thoughts. Think the word million. The thought is a word. When we pronounce million audibly, it is a word; when we pronounce it inaudibly, it is a thought.

§ 41.—*In the production of verbal thoughts, an agency of the organs of speech is discoverable.*

If you repeat in thought the alphabet, you may employ your organs of speech so forcibly, that the thoughts will require but a little more energy to become audible words. Endeavour to avoid an agency of the tongue, lips, and breath, you will detect a slight agency, and of the tongue especially. The more freely we permit the tongue's movements, the more distinctly we can think the alphabet. If you stand before a mirror and protrude your tongue, you will see it either dilate or thicken, as each letter is pronounced in thought. The experiment must be made with letters whose articulation is lingual.

§ 42.—*Verbal thoughts are limited, like audible words, to a consecutive formation.*

We cannot think the word George, while we are speaking the word Thomas; nor can we pronounce Thomas, while we are thinking George. Speech is limited to an utterance of successive syllables. Verbal thoughts require a similar succession of syllables. The phrase "our father," we can no more condense into one thought, than we can pronounce the words in one articulation.

From long attention to these coincidences, my verbal thoughts are as evidently the production of my organs of speech, and located in my mouth, as words are.

§ 43.—*The identity which exists between verbal thoughts and mere words, is closer than the generality of identities.*

We do not think of words as our theories lead us to say, but we think words themselves. A Frenchman thinks French words, and an Englishman, English. An uneducated man thinks ungrammatical sentences, and a rude man, vulgar sentences. Professor Blair was more literally correct than he supposed, when he said, "that a person who is learning to arrange his words correctly, is learning to think correctly."

§ 44.—*One class of thoughts is characteristically sights.*

But verbal thoughts are only one class of the six classes into which thoughts are divisible. We can think the word moon, as I have stated, which will be a verbal thought; and we can think the appearance of the moon, which is a visual thought. Visual thoughts possess the evanescence of vision. They flash and vanish. They possess also the comprehensiveness of vision. We comprehend in one gaze the whole starry firmament, and our thought of the firmament is as capacious as the gaze, and apparently as remote from our contact.

§ 45.—*The remaining four classes of thoughts are character-istically sounds, tastes, feels, and smells.*

The remaining four classes of thoughts are characteristically sounds, tastes, feels, and smells. Each class conforms to the peculiarities of the sense with whose phenomena it is connatural. The last pressure of an absent friend, when it recurs to me in thought, rests seemingly upon my hand with the contaction which pertains to the sense of feeling.

§ 46.—*The thoughts which I class as smells, possess the limitation that pertains to the perception of odours.*

The thoughts which I class as smells, possess the limitation that pertains to the perception of odours. We can no more combine in one thought the distinct fragrance of a rose, and the fetor of assafœtida, than we can realize them separately in one inspiration.

§ 47.—*Tastes possess in thought the singleness which attends the reception of tastes.*

Tastes also possess in thought the singleness which attends the reception of tastes. Vinegar and water yield not their tastes separately when placed together on our tongue, but combine to form a single taste. Thought also cannot present us the two tastes simultaneously.

§ 48.—*The recollection of sounds differs from the recollection of articulations.*

To think of sounds conforms so nearly to actual hearing, that I have heard a musician require silence from his auditors when he was recollecting a tune.

Many voices, uttered confusedly together, are recollected in one clamour, as we heard them. In this, the recollection of sounds differs characteristically from the recollection of words. Words can be thought of in only the syllabick succession of oral utterance.*

---

* We can think of words as sounds, but they are usually thought of as words, by a very palpable agency of our organs of speech.

§ 49.—*We construe nature by the forms of language, instead of construing language by the revelations of nature.*

If you cannot catch my meaning by a few hints, you will not by a tedious detail. To me, the fact is evident, that the identity which is implied by the word thought, is not responded to by nature with any like identity, but by six classes of dissimilar phenomena. That this obvious truth has escaped detection by all the acute men who have investigated thought, is imputable to the inveterate prepossession which makes us construe nature by the forms of language instead of construing language by the revelations of nature.

§ 50.—*Dumb mutes possess neither verbal thoughts nor auricular thoughts.*

A knowledge of the preceding classification is exceedingly useful: for instance, what thoughts have the dumb? Their defect of utterance prevents the formation of verbal thoughts, and the defect of hearing prevents auricular thoughts.* The dumb, therefore, are deficient of all thoughts that consist of words, and of all thoughts that consist of sounds. They possess but four classes of thought, while we possess six.

§ 51.—*To acquire a written language will not give the dumb verbal thoughts.*

When the dumb acquire a written language, their misfortune is remedied less effectively than is usually supposed; for a written word, when thought of by the dumb, constitutes but a visual thought, possessing all the evanescence of vision. When we think oral words, the thoughts possess the stability of speech.

§ 52.—*Infants possess no verbal thoughts.*

While language is unknown, infants can possess no verbal thoughts. Sights, sounds, feels, tastes, and smells, they can think, to the extent of their experience. Children obtain not early a facility of thinking inaudibly. They usually think aloud

---

* Words are sounds to the hearer, but to the speaker they are certain movements of his organs of speech; hence verbal thoughts are more characteristically feels than sounds.

the few words which they first acquire; and hence the constant repetition of words by infants.

§ 53.—*A paralysis of the tongue impedes verbal thinking.*

Whether madness uniformly attacks all classes of the maniack's thoughts, may be worth the examination of physicians. A paralysis of the organs of speech affects verbal thinking nearly as much as it affects speaking; while the other classes of thought are unimpaired. The paralytick recognises, by sight, his friends, but he cannot recollect their names. He also recalls, in visual thought, his absent friends, with a like inability of recollecting their names.

§ 54.—*Practically, we are well aware of the difference which exists in the nature of our thoughts.*

I heard a gentleman refuse to look on his deceased friend, because he wished to think of his friend in no other way than as he appeared when alive. The remark surprised no one. It is founded on our experience of the limitation of visual thoughts. With verbal thoughts he can think of the deceased in any state of decay that language can express, whether he view him or not. To create a new verbal thought, and to construct a new sentence, are similar operations, except that the new sentence is articulated, and the new thought is inarticulate.

§ 55.—These observations on thought are simply to show that the identity which language implies is not responded to by nature with an equal identity. We measure the natural identity by the verbal, instead of interpreting the verbal by the natural. I am anxious to free you from this errour; and if I have succeeded, the tediousness of an abstruse discourse may well be endured.

Lecture VI

WORDS CAN BE DIVESTED OF SIGNIFICATION, AND STILL FORMED INTO PROPOSITIONS WHICH WILL NOT BE OBVIOUSLY UNMEANING

IN THE natural world, the objects which are most abundant are those that are most necessary to the preservation of life. Air and water, for instance, are so common, as to be pecuniarily valueless.

In the moral world, also, the qualities which are most prevalent, are those that are most essential to the preservation of society. Forbearance from homicide is so common a virtue, that it possesses not even a name.

By a like principle, objects, of both the natural and moral world, exist in rareness, just in proportion as they are unessential to the common ends of life. The exalted integrity, for instance, that spurns the slightest indirection,—and the scrupulous truth, that bends to no expediency,—compare in rareness with the diamond that sparkles on the breast of wealth only, and with the plate which loads the sideboards of the conspicuous few.

In the intellectual world, a kindred dispensation is discoverable. The knowledge which is sufficient to procure the necessaries of life, is discoverable in the most uneducated individual; while a knowledge either of the latent subtility of language, or of the muscular motions necessary to produce the portraits of Stuart, is as rare as it is unessential to the preservation of society.

Although, then, we may, without the information that I deliver, remain qualified for the stations in which Providence has placed us, yet all who would correctly understand speculative learning, can in no way so effectually secure the object as by acquiring a knowledge of the latent properties of language.

[In the last discourse which I had the honour to deliver, I showed that the same word names frequently phenomena of different senses; and that much speculative error is produced by estimating as identical, phenomena that have no identity but the name by which we designate them: for instance, we think roundness the name of but one existence, while in truth it names two—a sight and a feel.

[In the present discourse I shall attempt to show another essential property of language, namely: Every word is a sound, which had no signification before it was employed to name some phenomenon, and which even now has no signification apart from the phenomena to which it is applied.]

§ 1.—*Words can be divested of their sensible signification.*

William and Thomas, when spoken with reference to two men, are significant appellations; but if I apply the names to nullity, the words partake immediately of the nothingness to which I apply them.

This principle, how obvious soever it may seem, has escaped the vigilance of the most acute, and supplied speculation with its most perplexing doctrines.

§ 2.—The word weight names a feel. The feel is discoverable in a feather, in a piece of lead, and in nearly every object. The word possessed no significancy before its introduction into language, and it now possesses none apart from the feel that it designates.

§ 3.—Admit, then, that weight names a feel, and observe how speciously I can employ the word after I divest it of signification: thus, "many objects are too small to be seen with the unassisted eye; and some, the most powerful microscope can render but just visible; we may therefore well believe that numerous atoms are so small that no microscope can reveal them: still, each must possess colour, shape, and weight."

§ 4.—Now observe, if weight names a feel, how has the word any signification when we predicate it of an atom, in which confessedly the feel cannot be experienced? What feel is that which cannot be felt? We have subtracted from the word its significancy, and left a vacated sound. It becomes weight minus weight.

§ 5.—Again: take the word atom—what is it? The name of a sight and a feel. Its sensible meaning I can teach you only by showing you, or permitting you to feel, some object, of which thereafter atom will be a name. I can show that a microscope enables us to see objects where vision unassisted can discover nothing. These sights, also, I can inform you are atoms. But when I say atoms exist which cannot be seen or felt, I divest the word of signification. We may apply the word atom to a taste, sound, or smell, and speak of an atom of taste, or an atom of sound, or smell; but when we use the word where nothing is discoverable, it designates nothing, and is nothing but the sound of which it is constituted.

§ 6.—Again: colour is an attribute of the atoms that we have been considering. Colour names a sight; but in the above proposition, it is used for what is invisible: hence the word is divested of signification, and nothing remains but a vacated sound. A man that can neither be seen nor felt, is not a greater nullity than an invisible colour. The defect is similar in both cases:—the words are divested of signification.

§ 7.—*We are vigilant in detecting verbal contradictions, but we never detect the sensible contradiction which exists in affirming the presence of sensible existences, where none are discoverable by the senses.*

We may learn from even this slight investigation, that words can be deprived of intelligence, and still formed into propositions which will not be obviously futile. We are vigilant to detect any verbal contradiction in a proposition, but we never notice the latent contradiction which arises from predicating sensible phenomena where they are confessedly undiscoverable: thus, should you affirm that an object is heavy and not heavy, or visible and invisible, all persons would ridicule the affirmation: but no essential difference exists between such propositions and those which speak of a weight that cannot be felt, and of a colour that cannot be seen.

§ 8.—*Words, divested of signification, may still be employed in all the processes of logick.*

Zeno's paradox respecting motion is an example of the inanity to which we may arrive by the foregoing misuse of language, even when we pursue the most logical deductions. Thus, say that a tortoise is a mile before Achilles, and that Achilles runs a hundred times faster than the tortoise, yet he will never overtake it: because, says Zeno, when Achilles has run the mile, the tortoise will have moved forward the hundredth part of a mile; and while Achilles runs the said hundredth part of a mile, the tortoise has moved forward the ten thousandth part of a mile; so that it is not yet overtaken. In the same manner, whilst Achilles passes over the ten thousandth part of a mile, the tortoise moves on the millionth part of a mile, and is not yet overtaken; and so on, ad infinitum.

§ 9.—Though the proposition is palpably preposterous, the defect of its reasoning has never been explained; nor is it explicable on any other principle, than that its words become insignificant the moment they are used where nothing sensible is discoverable: for instance, "while Achilles passes over the hundredth part of a mile, the tortoise moves on the ten thousandth part of a mile." The ten thousandth part of a mile is between six and seven inches. It names a sight and a feel; hence the tortoise is not yet overtaken:—but the proposition proceeds,—"Whilst Achilles passes over this ten thousandth part of a mile, the tortoise moves on the millionth part of a mile." The millionth part of a mile leaves them asunder about the fifteenth part of an inch, which names a sight and a feel; hence the tortoise is not yet overtaken. But the next step is a quibble. It affirms, that whilst Achilles passes over this millionth part of a mile, the tortoise moves on the hundred millionth part of a mile. This is a name without any corresponding existence in nature, hence the sophistry and quibble. The last step is absurd, not from any defect of logick, but because the words are become divested of signification.*

§ 10.—The new Edinburgh Encyclopedia says, "it would not be easy to solve this quibble were we to measure motion by

---

* The words retain a verbal signification, which is discussed hereafter: see also Lectures XV, and XXII.

space merely, without taking in the idea of time." This explication is only the substitution of a new quibble. The tortoise will not be overtaken so long as it is a minute the start of Achilles; but when the time which separates them is the hundred millionth part of a minute, the words will have no archetype among sensible phenomena, and will be divested of signification.

§ 11.—Verbally, no limit exists to the divisibility of matter; for every thing possesses two halves, and when you have divided it, each half becomes immediately a whole endued with halves; and so in infinitum. The conclusion is irrefragable. It is also true practically, while the words possess any sensible signification; but after a certain number of divisions, the word half will refer to neither a sight nor a feel, and become as insignificant as the hundred millionth part of a mile which separates Achilles from the tortoise. The words in both cases become divested of meaning, hence the defect is alike in both propositions; but so little understood is the principle which creates the defect, that the infinite divisibility of matter is treasured among the truths of philosophy; while Zeno's kindred problem, (from interfering more grossly with our experience,) excites our ridicule.

§ 12.—I have heard intelligent persons deliberate gravely on the infinite divisibility of a drop of water; half of a drop is water, for the division alters not chemically the nature of water, but diminishes the quantity merely. But the half may be again divided, and the residue will be still water; and so in infinitum. The conclusion is regularly deduced from the premises, but during the process the word water loses its signification. Water is a sight, a feel, and a taste. A water in which these are not discoverable, is water minus water—a vacated sound.

§ 13.—*Words divested of signification may still be employed in the problems and demonstrations of mathematicks.*

We may imagine a circle that shall be larger than the orbit described by the earth in its annual revolutions. Still, no part of the circumference can be equal to a straight line; for no prop-osition in mathematicks is more satisfactory, than that a straight line can never constitute a circle; hence we arrive at the con-clusion, that a curve may expand in infinitum without becoming straight, though at every expansion it approximates towards straightness.

§ 14.—In view of this mathematical process, Hume says, "the demonstration seems as unexceptionable as that which proves the three angles of a triangle to be equal to two right angles; though the latter opinion is natural and easy, and the former big with contradiction and absurdity. Reason here seems thrown into a kind of amazement, which, without the suggestion of any skeptick, gives her a diffidence of herself, and of the ground on which she treads. She sees a full light, but it borders upon the most profound darkness. Between them she is so daz-zled and confounded, that she can scarcely pronounce with certainty concerning any object."

§ 15.—But the difficulty vanishes if we consider the words circle and curve as names of sights and feels. Mathematicians are correct so long as the words refer to sensible existences; but when they speak of a curve which can neither be seen nor felt, it is a curve minus curve, and the proposition is like the problem of Zeno.

§ 16.—*The fallacy enters largely into the speculations of every department of philosophy.*

Because a cubick inch of air weighs the third part of a grain, we calculate the number of cubick inches of air which rest on a man in a column of forty or fifty miles in altitude; and by call-ing every inch the third part of a grain, we conclude that every man supports fourteen tons weight of air. Is not this divesting the phrase fourteen tons of its signification? Weight, (and especially fourteen tons,) is the name of a feel; and to use the word where no feel is discoverable, is like talking of a tooth-ache which cannot be felt, or of an inaudible melody.

[But is it not demonstrable, that the weight of a column of atmosphere is equal to the weight of a column twenty-eight inches high of mercury? No, the experiment shows simply the facts which are exhibited. The weight of the atmosphere is merely the theory by which we account for the support of the mercury. So far as we use the weight theoretically to give a system to our discoveries, the use is desirable; but to deduce therefrom that a man sustains literally a pressure of fourteen tons, is to possess a very erroneous opinion of language. The fourteen tons refer to no existence but the few phenomena from which the conclusion is deduced; and so far only as the phrase is a name of these, it is significant.]

§ 17.—I met lately with the following speculation: "A small piece of sugar will sweeten a pint of water; consequently, every drop of the water will contain some sugar." So far, the speculation is sensible; the sugar which every drop of water is said to contain, refers to the sweetness that is discoverable in the water. But the theory proceeds:—"If we add a farther pint of water, we shall discover that the taste is gone; therefore, the last pint caused a farther division of the sugar, or some part of the water would continue sweet."

§ 18.—We find as yet no sophistry, but the next step is delusive. The writer continues:—"Have the particles of sugar been divided to the extent of their divisibility? If they have, the indivisibility must proceed from a want of power in water to effect a farther division, and not from a want of matter to be divided; because the last water could not have so divided the particles that each will not be larger than the half of it. But why shall we suppose that the power of water to divide ceases at the moment when our sense can no longer discover the effects of a division? We may as well suppose, that time ceases when we sleep. More philosophical is the supposition that the smaller the particles of sugar become by division, the more easily they will be affected by the water; and that the water continues to divide the particles so long as particles remain. But we have shown that particles will always remain; hence, no quantity of water can be added without causing a further division of the sugar. How infinitely divided must the sugar at length become, when a small piece is cast into a river! And if every soluble thing which is thrown into the ocean divides, so that every drop of the ocean contains some part of the dissolved substance, what a variety of particles must a drop of the ocean contain!"

§ 19.—In the above we find no weakness of argument. The defect lies in a misuse of language. The words particle and sugar are names of sensible existences; and to use the words where the existences are not discoverable, is to speak of invisible sights, or any other contradiction. Such a use of language is like the trick of a juggler, who, having adroitly conveyed a shilling from under a candlestick, talks of the money as still under the candlestick.

[I have now, I hope, established the assertion that words have no signification but as they refer to phenomena, and that an ignorance of this principle induces us to use words after their signification has been subtracted, and the words have thereby become insignificant. It is not my intention to apply this rule to any theory or science. My object in these Lectures is merely to establish principles—their application I shall leave to others. But as a farther illustration of the principle, I will adduce some examples of its abuse in the use of the word cause. I select this word because its abuse enters more deeply into metaphysical errors, and has in nearly all the sciences been more fruitful of delusion than the same error in the use of any other word.

[To teach a person the meaning of the word cause, I must operate on some of his senses. I can tell him to behold how I cause darkness. He looks and sees me extinguish the candles. The word will then have one signification; namely, the phenomena which he discovers. Again: I can tell him to halloo, and it will cause an echo. If he ask what I mean by causing an echo, I shall tell him to halloo, and he will discover my meaning. I can teach him by any other of his senses the meaning of cause.]

§ 20.—*Theoretical causes are frequently nothing but words divested of their sensible signification.*

If two billiard balls strike, they rebound. Till lately philosophers inculcated, that when the balls strike, a dent is produced in each ball; and the dent resuming instantly its rotundity, causes the balls to fly asunder.

§ 21.—A dent is a sight and a feel. But the dent which is here assumed, can be neither seen nor felt; hence the cause, in this case, is a word divested of its signification. A dent which our senses cannot perceive, differs but in sound from a house which our senses cannot perceive: both are names of sensible existences, and both are unmeaning terms when they are used where nothing sensible can be discovered.

§ 22.—*When we subtract from a word its sensible signification, the word returns, (so far as relates to the external universe,) to the pristine insignificance which the word possessed, before it was applied to the purposes of language.*

In relation to the motion of billiard balls, Professor Stewart says, "Some of the ablest philosophers in Europe are now satisfied that the effects which are commonly referred to impulse, arise from a power of repulsion, extending to a small and imperceptible distance round every element of matter."

§ 23.—A repulsion is, however, a sight or a feel, or both; but in the present case, we can neither see the repulsion, nor feel it; nor is it discoverable by any of our senses. It is a repulsion minus repulsion. It operates also at an imperceptible distance. This is the distance that for ever prevented Achilles from overtaking the tortoise. But distance is a sight and a feel; and when Professor Stewart subtracts these, the word returns to the pristine insignificance which it possessed before it was applied to the purposes of language.

§ 24.—*The law of nature, which makes the word scarlet in-significant to the blind, makes all words insignificant when they attempt to name external existences which our senses cannot discover.*

Let us consider, says Locke, how bodies produce ideas in us.[1] "Colour and smell are produced by insensible particles operating on our senses." The word particles names, however, existences which can generally be both seen and felt. It may be applied intelligibly to a sound, taste, or smell; but to employ the word as a name of some external existence, which none of our senses can discover, is a use that language cannot sustain and retain any significance.

§ 25.—If particles were known in the way only in which they are employed by Locke, you could never disclose their meaning to any person. You may as well attempt to instruct the blind in the import of scarlet, as teach another person the signification of particles when they refer to no sight, feel, taste, smell, or sound. The disability of the blind proceeds from a destitution of the sense which is conversant with scarlet; and a disability arising from a similar cause is experienced by us in the word particles when it signifies something that our senses cannot discover.

§ 26.—*We can no more subtract from an external existence its sensible qualities, and leave a subsisting reality, than we can subtract all sensible qualities from an orange, and leave a fruit.*

---

[1] In Johnson (I) the passage reads:

Let us consider, says Locke, how bodies produce ideas in us. "It is manifestly by impulse, the only way in which bodies can operate: hence, if external objects be not united to our mind, when they produce ideas therein, some motion from the external object must be continued by our nerves or animal spirits to the brain, there to produce in our minds the particular ideas which we have of the objects."

What is a motion? A sight or a feel. We may speak of an invisible and intactible piece of iron with as much propriety as of a motion that is undiscoverable by our senses. The defect is similar in both cases.

"Let us now suppose," continues Locke, "that a violet, by the impulse of such insensible particles, of peculiar figures and bulks, and by different degrees and modifications of their motions, causes the blue colour and sweet scent of that flower to be produced in our mind." The smell and colour of a violet are therefore imputed by Locke to an impulse which can neither be seen nor felt; and the objects impelled are undiscoverable particles that possess invisible and intactible figures and bulks, and move with various degrees of an insensible motion. We need not wonder that the study of metaphysicks is difficult, and that common sense has long ridiculed it. You can no more subtract from a particle its sensible qualities, and leave an entity, than you can subtract them from an orange and leave a fruit. [It must be a fundamental axiom of philosophy that the word cause, nor any other, can be used significantly, except as the name of some sight, feel, taste, smell, or sound; and we shall eradicate a mass of error with which every branch of knowledge is oppressed and disfigured. The phenomena which nature exhibits spontaneously, or which we can by any means cause her to exhibit, afford real knowledge, and the only subjects except revelation to which we can significantly apply language.]

§ 27.—*When the word cause is used significantly, it refers to a sensible existence.*

If I release my hold of a stone, it will fall to the earth. Natural Philosophy asks why the stone descends. Philosophers answer that the descent is caused by an attraction which exists in the earth.

§ 28.—We think we have gained much information. Needles rush to a magnet by virtue of its attraction, and we have only to suppose a similar power in the earth, and the descent of the stone is accounted for. An essential difference exists, however, in the two cases. The word attraction, when predicated of the magnet, refers to a sight and a feel. The attraction can be seen in the needle's uniform attendance on the movements of a magnet; or it can be felt in the effort that it is necessary to detach a needle from a magnet. But attraction, when predicated of the earth, is cognizable by none of our senses: hence the word is divested of its signification. It becomes attraction minus attraction.

[With the descent of a stone you will be unable to teach a person the meaning of the word cause. Caused by the earth? he will say, what do you mean? I see the stone fall, but I see nothing more. There is only one phenomenon. Not so, however, with the magnet. I can tell him to observe how the magnet causes the needle to move. He will see the motion, and that the approach of the magnet is a necessary prelude; farther, that the quiescence of the needle is uniformly disturbed by the advance of the magnet; that their conjunction is prevented with difficulty, and their separation produced by a sensible effort only. Here are phenomena to which the word cause refers; but when it is applied to the earth the word is divested of its signification.

[Again: the word attraction, when predicated of the magnet, refers to a sight and a feel. It can be seen in the needle's uniform attendance on the movements of a magnet; or it can be felt in the effort that is necessary to detach a needle from a magnet. But attraction, when predicated of the earth, refers to no phenomenon. It is cognizable by none of our senses; hence the word is divested of its signification. It becomes attraction minus attraction. The proposition, therefore, which we have been considering, errs in two particulars: it uses the word attraction, without intending that it shall name any sensible phenomenon; and it makes this insensible existence the cause of the descent of stones, hence using insensibly the word cause also.

[If I place in your hand a piece of lead, and inquire if you feel any weight, you will answer affirmatively. The weight I shall tell you is caused by the lead. The word cause is here significant. It refers to the invariable realization of the feel, in conjunction with the lead; and to its cessation on the removal of the lead. But Natural Philosophy inquires farther, and demands the cause of this feel. She answers, it is caused by the earth's drawing the lead downwards by the force of attraction.

[Here again the word cause refers to no phenomenon, and is therefore divested of signification. When a slender bar of steel struggles to touch a powerful magnet, the feel is caused by the magnet; for it ceases on the removal of the magnet, and thus gives to the word cause a sensible signification: but when we feel on our hand the pressure of a piece of lead, and say that the feel is caused by the earth, the assigned cause refers to nothing: there is only one phenomenon, and that is the pressure of the lead.]

§ 29.—*An ignorance of the limitation which nature has formed to the signification of language, is in no instance so productive of erroneous speculation, as in its application to the word cause.*

Doctor Darwin attributes all the phenomena of chymistry to a specifick attraction and a specifick repulsion, which belong to the sides and angles of the insensible particles of bodies. When the repulsions predominate, they cause the diffusion of light and odours, the explosion of some bodies, and the slow decomposition of others: but when the attractions predominate, they cause crystallization and solidity.

§ 30.—Attraction, repulsion, sides, and angles, are names of sensible phenomena; independently of which, the words are as insignificant as any that can be made by throwing promiscuously together the letters of the alphabet. We find, however, in Doctor Darwin's speculation, that words alone are made the cause of odours, sounds, fluidity, and explosion. The proposition is an instance as glaring as any that can be adduced of the absurdities into which even the wisest men fall when they investigate causation without knowing that the word cause (like every other word) is insignificant, when it relates to the external universe, and refers to no sensible existence.

§ 31.—If I look at this piece of silk, I discover the sight which we call red. The sight is caused by the silk. If you desire to know what I mean by asserting that the silk causes the sight, I can remove the silk, and show you that the sight will cease.

§ 32.—But opticians carry the inquiry further, and ask what causes the silk to produce the sight which we name red. They answer, that light is composed of red and other coloured rays. That the silk absorbs from light all its rays but the red, and that the red rays are reflected from the silk to our eyes.

§ 33.—The phrase red rays, when used significantly, refers to a sight. It may be discoverable in a prismatick spectrum; but here the rays can be neither seen nor felt; nor are they discoverable by any of our senses. They are rays minus rays—a word divested of its signification. Red rays which cannot be seen, are as gross an incongruity as a pain which cannot be felt. The errour in both cases is the same. Still, this phrase, divested thus of its signification, is made the cause of redness.

§ 34.—The inquiry is carried further, and we are asked how the reflection of red rays to our eyes enables us to see redness. The answer is, that the red rays converge on the retina of our eyes, and form there a very small picture of the piece of silk. This picture is what the mind perceives, though we ignorantly imagine it is the distant silk.

§ 35.—The word picture names a sight and a feel; but here it designates neither. You would in vain endeavour to teach a person the signification of the word, by referring him to what is exhibited on the retina of his eye. The word picture, when thus used, becomes nullified. It is nothing but the sound of which it is composed. In a dissected eye, a miniature of external objects may be discovered: hence the term is significant when thus applied; but to apply the word to a living eye, where no such phenomenon can be discovered, is to act less significantly than children; for when they say that a stick shall be a ship, or a lady, they give a wrong name only to their playthings; but when we apply the word picture where no existence is discoverable, we "give to airy nothing a local habitation and a name."

§ 36.—*Theories are useful, but we need not confound them with the sensible realities of creation.*

Let me not be understood as decrying the theories to which I advert, or the sciences that are erected on them; but we need not confound the theories of men with the realities of nature. We can award to Prometheus the credit of sculpturing a well proportioned statue, without straining our admiration to the belief that he endued it with animation.

[Recollect further, that what I have said of the word cause, is only illustrative of the general principle that words have no signification but as they refer to some phenomenon. The principle is applicable to every word. It is as broad as language, and has no exception, but when words refer to revelation. This principle will guide you safely through the most subtle labyrinths of metaphysics, and enable you to separate the tinsel of indolent conjecture from the gold of laborious observation.]

§ 37.—My remarks are only illustrations of the general principle, that words can be divested of signification, and still formed into propositions which will not be obviously futile. That words are insignificant when they are employed to signify external existences, but refer to nothing which the senses can discover, the present lecture assumes. Of this assumption I shall speak hereafter,* and I trust make its truth manifest, if so obvious a position be not self-evident.

§ 38.—*The principles of this lecture are correct, though some of my illustrations may be deemed incorrect.*

I would add in conclusion, that the principle of this lecture should be separated from the examples† with which I have

---

* See Lecture X.

† For an explanation of some of the examples, see Lecture VII, § 1.

sought to illustrate it. Some of the examples may be unskilfully adduced, and not obnoxious to the charges which I have brought against them; but the principle is true in every case in which it properly applies.

Lecture VII

THE MEANING OF A WORD VARIES WITH ITS APPLICATION

WHEN WE survey society, and discover the labourer bending beneath his toil; the merchant, sedentary at a scanty desk; and the scholar, wasting in the contemplation of a few propositions; we can scarcely believe that they are beings, to whom nothing is naturally more delightful than to roam without a limit, and to expatiate without a rule. Such, however, are some of the transformations of civilization. In condescension to human infirmity, every new enterprise may be preceded by a relaxation, and every new investigation by an excursion of fancy. But these indulgences must be brief. The sinews of the artisan must again be strung to toil, and the thoughts of the student contracted to a point.

Leaving, then, the above pleasant field of imaginative speculation, we also must return to the slow exploration of a single avenue of knowledge. My former lectures contained truths which are simple, yet highly important. They have singularly escaped the scrutiny of metaphysicians, while, practically, they have been admitted by all persons. We are prone to disregard what is obvious, and to believe, with an ancient philosopher, that truth lies at the bottom of a well. The contrary is uniformly a safer conclusion. I now beg your attention to another fundamental, yet simple principle of language. [Every word has as many meanings as there are different phenomena to which it refers.

[If we reflect, even cursorily, on language, we must be struck with the number of its applications. Creation is, literally, immense; still, the names of created objects form but one use to which language is appropriated. Every feeling, every desire, every action can be recorded by language. No event is so eccentric, no imagination so wild, no situation so peculiar, but language can publish it. To effect these innumerable appliances, we have but thirty-eight thousand words: hence the necessity that every word should possess a multitude of meanings.

[Nothing is more definite than colours; still, we take any one of them, we shall find how variously, even in this definite application, a word may be used. White is applied to snow, to this paper, to the glass which composes our windows, to our skin, to the floor of this room, to the walls, to water, and to silver. A perfect language should have a separate word for each of these appearances, and a separate word for every other phenomenon; but a language thus precise would be too copious for our memory: hence in every tongue the same word is applied to many phenomena.

[This versatility of language produces little embarrassment in the ordinary concerns of life, but in speculation it occasions controversy and confusion. When a metaphysician discovers that a word is appropriated to discordant existences, he supposes that the disagreement is an anomaly in nature, instead of a property of language.]

§ 1.—*Words may be compared to a mirror. It is naturally void, and varies its representations as you vary the object which is placed before it.*

In my last lecture I endeavoured to show that words which name sensible existences, are often divested of signification, and still formed into propositions which are not obviously futile. We seem not to know that when we employ the word water where no sensible existence is discoverable, the word partakes immediately of the nothingness to which we apply it. Words are in some respects like a mirror. When you remove all objects from before it, the mirror no longer reflects any image, but becomes void; and when you remove from a word all refer-

ence to sensible existences, the word no longer signifies any
sensible existence, but becomes void. We seldom, however,
use a word without referring to something for its signification.
This remark applies to even several of the instances adduced
in my last lecture; hence those instances will not strictly illustrate the errour which the lecture sought to illustrate:—for
example, the picture which is alleged to be on the retina of your
eye, I denounced as a word divested of signification. This is
not strictly true. The picture refers to certain experiments which
can be made with a dissected eye; and it refers also to various
other sensible illustrations which belong to the theory of which
the picture is a part.

§ 2.—*Words signify the objects to which they are applied.*

Words possess another analogy to mirrors. A mirror which,
at one moment, reflects the image of a man, may, at another
moment, reflect the image of a chair, a cat, or a canary bird.
The mirror conforms to the object which is placed before it,
and, in like manner, every word conforms in signification to
the object to which it is applied. The word William, when
applied to a child, signifies the child; and when applied to a
flower, signifies the flower. This estimation of words constitutes the topick of the present lecture.

§ 3.—*Every word is a general term, and applies to a multitude of diverse existences.*

After we find, by examination, that an object is a unit, red,
hard, solid; we must examine the object further, to learn the
meaning of the words unit, red, hard, and solid:—for the meaning of a word varies with every different application of it. My
hand is red, blood is red, hair is often red, the moon is sometimes red, fire is red, and Indians are red. These objects possess
a congruity of appearance that entitles them all to the appellation of red; but the precise meaning of the word in each application is the sight itself which the object exhibits. Whether an
object shall or not be called red is a question which relates to

the propriety of phraseology, and with which nature has no concern; but the meaning of the word red in each application, is a question which relates solely to nature, and with which language has no concern:—at least, language possesses over it no control.

§ 4.—*We attribute to nature the generality which belongs to language.*

Should we attend to the minute discriminations that can be discovered in the sights which we now denominate red, and instead of calling them all red, give a separate name to each sight; language would be too copious for memory, and no adequate benefit would result from our prolixity. We should still be forced to resort to nature when we wished to know the sensible meaning of each word. The necessity which prompts us to employ the word red as a general name to a mass of varying individual appearances, prompts us to employ nearly every other word in a manner equally general. The infinity of objects and relations about which language discourses, can in no other way be comprehended by the few thousand words that compose language. A curious inattention, however, to the nature of language, induces us to measure the sameness of different sights by the sameness of their name (red); instead of qualifying the sameness of the name by the diverse appearance of the different sights. A like errour exists in the use to which we apply every word.

§ 5.—*Instead of qualifying the meaning of a word by the existence to which we apply the word, we estimate the existence by the word.*

In a preceding discourse, we have discussed so much of our present lecture as relates to the sensible diversity which exists in objects that are nominally identical. Dismissing, therefore, that topick, I shall proceed to show that in the use of language generally, we invert the order of nature; and instead of qualifying the meaning of a word by the existence to which we apply the word, we estimate the existence by the word:*—for instance, after a moment's exposure, a drop of the otto of roses will fill with odour many rooms, while the drop will exhibit no diminution of size.[1] This phenomenon is too common to excite admiration, but much may be excited if you exhibit the experiment to teach a person the expansiveness of matter. He will now snuff the odour with astonishment. Bless me! how wonderfully a little matter may be expanded! A dozen rooms are full of it! The person is evidently interpreting the smell by the phrase "expansiveness of matter." He knows not that the phrase should be interpreted by the smell.

§ 6.—But if he is astonished at the preceding, what will he say of the particles of light? They fall, says natural philosophy,

---

* When men first attempted to spell, they resolved every word into such letters as would best express the sound of the word. The sound was the standard, and the letters approximated to it as well as they could. In our day, however, the process is reversed. The letters are the standard, (in our country at least,) of the sound of the word; and very awkwardly sounding words the superficially learned (who adopt this unnatural standard) occasionally make. Thus to subordinate oral words to the letters into which orthography resolves the words, is a species of retribution on words for the authority that words have usurped over natural existences.

[1] In Johnson (I) this passage reads:

After a moment's exposure, a drop of the otto of roses will fill with odour a large room; still, the size of the drop will betray no diminution: nay, the drop will remain undiminished, though fifty rooms should be surcharged with its odour. This is a common phenomenon, and its announcement excites no admiration; but if you adopt a different phraseology, much surprise will be produced. Tell a person that the particles of matter are so small that several rooms may be filled with a single drop of otto of roses, and the drop be apparently undiminished. As a proof of your position, expose a drop of otto of roses, and while he recognizes its fragrance in every part of the room, he will admire the wonderful smallness of its particles. Still it is not the phenomenon which surprises him. The phraseology seems to purport that the room is filled with particles, which would be tangible and visible were they less minute, or our senses more delicate. He does not know that the word particles, when applied to the odour, signifies the smell only. In short, he knows not that the meaning of a word is in every case governed by the phenomena to which it refers.

millions of miles, and with a velocity so wonderful, as to accomplish the descent in an instant; still they hurt not the eye though they alight immediately on that susceptible organ. A man, grown old under the rays of the sun, may be astonished at this recital. The astonishment is produced by the language, and not by light. He interprets the words fall and particles, not by what his senses discover in light; but he interprets what his senses discover in light, by the words particles and fall: hence, when he is informed further, that philosophers have in vain endeavoured, with the nicest balances, to discover weight in sunbeams, (even when the number of particles thrown into a scale has been multiplied by a powerful lens,) the experiment increases his wonder at the smallness of the particles; though it ought to teach him that the mystery is nothing but a latent sophistry of language. The word particle when applied to light, means the existence only to which it is applied. It names a sight. When applied to stone, it names a feel as well as a sight. To wonder that the eye cannot feel the particles of light, is to wonder that it cannot feel a sight. We may as well wonder that we cannot taste sounds, and hear smells.

§ 7.—*We must resort to our senses for the sensible meaning of a word, and not to a dictionary.*

We cast into a tub of water a small piece of indigo, and the water becomes tinged with blue; we cast into another tub of water a lump of sugar, and the water becomes sweet; we open our shutters, and light becomes perceptible throughout our room; we ignite a few sticks of wood, and the mercury will rise in a distant thermometer:—these results possess a certain congruity, hence we say, the indigo and sugar are *diffused* through the water;—the light and heat are *diffused* through the room. If, however, we wish to discover the sensible meaning of the word diffused, in these several uses, we must resort to our senses, and not to our dictionaries. The sensible meaning is so diverse in the above different applications of the word diffused,

that a blind man will possess no conception of the diffusion that
refers to the light and indigo; while a man who never possessed
tasting, will possess no conception of the diffusion which refers
to the sugar.

§ 8.—*We must discriminate between the question which relates to the appropriateness of a word, and its signification.*

Every word refers for signification as scrupulously to the
existence to which it is applied, as a pronoun refers for signification to the substantive whose place it supplies. I may say that
two sounds look alike. Whether the expression is appropriate
or not depends on custom; but whether the expression is significant or not, and what it signifies, depend on nature:—the
expression will signify any sensible revelation to which it refers; and if it refers to nothing, it will signify nothing.

§ 9.—*Interpreting nature by language enables us to communicate an artificial interest to scientifick experiments.*

When you exhibit the passage of light through a prism, you
may assert, that the light which enters on one side of the prism
is composed of the gorgeous colours that are emitted from the
other side. This language gives to the experiment an interest
which the exhibition alone will not excite. The spectator will
not interpret your language by what he is beholding; but he
will interpret what he is beholding by your language. You may,
however, say, that the prismatic experiment is not all that you
refer to when you say light is composed of the prismatic colours.
This impairs not my position. If you refer to other experiments,
they will constitute a part of the meaning of the phrase. The
phrase will mean every sensible revelation to which it refers, but
nothing more:—so long as you confine its signification to the
realities of the external universe.

§ 10.—*The language in which every experiment is announced
must be interpreted by the experiment. We must not interpret
the experiment by the language.*

The experimenter may tell you, that as you have seen a ray

of light untwisted by the prism, and split into its constituent threads; he will collect the filaments, and retwist them into their original form. With this preface, he will cause the coloured rays to pass through a lens which will converge them to a focus of light in its usual colour. The experiment is interesting. I wish not to depreciate it, but it constitutes all the sensible signification that the experimenter's language possesses. We must interpret the language by the experiment, and not interpret the experiment by the language. A dumb mute who may witness the exhibition will possess all the knowledge on the subject which we possess. If the language which we apply to the experiment tends in the least to increase, diminish, or alter the information that we receive from seeing the experiment, the dumb mute will estimate it more correctly than we.

§ 11.—In a small book on natural philosophy, after explaining the prismatick phenomena, the writer states, grass is green, because it absorbs all rays of light but the green; roses are red, because they absorb all but the red rays; snow is white, because it reflects the whole ray, &c. "You can never see objects," says the book, "without light. Light is composed of colours; therefore every object, though it is black in the dark, becomes coloured as soon as it is visible. It is visible by the coloured rays which it reflects: hence we can see it only when it is coloured."

§ 12.—This doctrine is delivered in a dialogue between an instructress and a female pupil. The pupil replies with emotion, "All you say seems true, and I know not what to object; yet it appears incredible: what! when in the dark, are we all as black as negroes? The thought makes me shudder!"

§ 13.—Who has not experienced that in the dark no discrimination exists between the colour of a negro and a European? The astonishment is produced by the supposition that the blackness, which is attributed to us in the dark, is not to be interpreted by the event to which it refers; but that the event is to be interpreted by the word blackness, according to its meaning when it refers to negroes.

§ 14.—When a chymist ignites a stream of hydrogen gas and oxygen, and permits the flame to pass through a glass tube, we find the inside of the tube become suffused with water. The interest of the experiment is usually heightened by the surprising announcement, that water is nothing but a union of the two gases. Instead of interpreting the announcement by the experiment, we interpret the experiment by the announcement, and hence the surprise.

§ 15.—*Interpreting nature by language enables us to very insidiously excite admiration.*

"That light, itself a body, should," says Professor Brown, "pass freely through solid crystal, is regarded by us as a physical wonder." Why? No man was ever surprised at finding light enter his room when he threw open his window shutters. Wonder is produced only when we interpret the occurrence by the language in which the occurrence is expressed:—when we suppose the passage of light through crystal to be the same as the passage of my hand through crystal. But when we know that the language is to be interpreted by the fact to which it refers,—(that it means only what crystal and light are continually exhibiting,)—our surprise vanishes with the delusion that created it.

§ 16.—Observe, also, in the above extract, how insidiously language enables us to infer that light ought to encounter opposition in its passage through crystal. If Mr. Brown had merely stated that light passes through crystal, no reason would have appeared why it should not pass through. But the addition of one word implies that the passage of light through the crystal is as wonderful, if not as miraculous, as the passage of Moses through the Red sea. I allude to the word body,—the wonder is that light, "itself a body," should pass through crystal. Body is generally the name of a feel: hence, when we say that light is a body, we know not that the signification of the word body is governed by the object to which it is applied. We suppose rather, that the character of light is determined by the word body. The wonder is produced, not by the sight which we experience, but by something else:—a something which is a delusion of language.

[Again: "If," says the same author, "there had been no such science as chymistry, who could have supposed that the innumerable animate bodies and inanimate, on the surface of our globe, and all which we have explored in the depths of the earth, are reducible, and in the imperfect state of the science, have been already reduced to a few simple elements?"

[This seems the climax of wonder, that every thing, even ourselves, "yea, the great globe itself, and all which it inhabit," are reducible to a few elements, which are possessed in common by "the giant and the poor beetle he treads upon"; by the sick man and the coals which warm his chamber; by the mason and the stones which he unfeelingly hews. Mr. Brown says correctly, if there had been no chymistry, these facts would not have been supposed. But why? Because the whole refers to the processes of chymistry; independently thereof, the language has no archetype in nature. The declaration evinces, however, the ignorance which exists of the nature of language, and the proneness of scientific men to exalt their pursuits by the excitation of wonder.

[Chymists do not say simply that they can produce hydrogen gas, and oxygen, from water, and vice versa; but that water is nothing but a combination of these gases. The assertion is true, so long as it means the phenomena to which it refers; but it produces wonder, because we suppose it has a meaning beyond the phenomena.

[A large portion of bodies will, on the application of fire, resolve into smoke and cinders. We may, if we wish to excite wonder, say that these bodies, how diversified soever in shape and consistence, how beautiful soever to the eye and delicate to the touch, are nothing but modifications and combinations of smoke and cinders. We may elucidate the assertion by a conflagration of several bodies, and our position will appear to be thereby proved; because it will constitute all that the assertion means. Chymical theories are much like the above. They are not exactly similar, for chymists proceed farther; and with the smoke and cinders produce additional transformations.]

§ 17.—*Interpreting nature by language enables us to both artificially exalt and degrade sensible information.*

An ignorance of the simple fact, that every word or phrase possesses as many sensible significations as it possesses a reference to different sensible phenomena, enables philosophers to encircle their experiments and speculations with an artificial importance, as I have just exemplified; and also with an artificial degradation, as will appear by the following examples:—Professor Brown says, "power is a word of much seeming mystery; yet all which is mysterious in it vanishes, when it is regarded as only a general term, expressive of invariable antecedence; or, in other words, of what cannot exist without being followed immediately by a definite event, which we denominate an effect. To express shortly," he continues, "the only intelligible meaning of the three most important words in physicks, power, cause, and effect, we may say that power is immediate invariable antecedence;—a cause is the immediate invariable antecedent in any sequence;—and an effect is the immediate invariable consequent."

§ 18.—We may now think, that power, cause, and effect, are vastly more simple than we had supposed:—a cause is nothing but "an immediate invariable antecedent." But what is the sensible signification of an immediate invariable antecedent? The sensible existence to which we apply the phrase. When we become acquainted with the sensible existence, we may call it either a cause, or an immediate invariable antecedent: our meaning will be the same in both cases. Mr. Brown's phrase can simplify causation only when we seek the meaning of the phrase from some other source than the revelation of our senses;—and hence seek a fallacious meaning.

§ 19.—But the most curious of simplifications relates to chymistry. Chymistry analyzes bodies, and out of water produces oxygen gas and hydrogen; out of glass, sand, alkali, &c. Now, says Mr. Brown,[1] "These processes of chymistry enable us only to discover what are always before our eyes, but our sight is not keen enough to see them." This greatly dissipates our admiration of chymistry. To produce oxygen from water, and sand from glass, is but little meritorious, if the operation enables us to see what only the weakness of our eyes prevented us from seeing. Unfortunately, however, the means which ordinarily assist vision, aid not chymists. With the most powerful microscope they are unable to discover, in water, the gases; or in glass, the sand.

§ 20.—*The sensible realities to which words refer, and which alone give words a sensible signification, are not affected by our phraseology.*

If we inquire soberly into the meaning of Mr. Brown, we

---

[1] Johnson (I) reads:

"Nothing," says Professor Brown, "appears more uniform than a piece of glass." Granted. Why should it not so appear? But he proceeds:—"Yet glass is a product of human art, and we know from its composition that it is a congeries of bodies which have no similarity."

We now discover matter for considerable surprise. A man who has all his life been employed in manufacturing glass, will be astonished, though he will laugh if you tell him, in plain language, that glass is composed of sand and alkali. This, however, is all that the assertion signifies.

"But," continues Mr. Brown, "the congeries of bodies exist as separately in glass as they existed before they were formed into glass."

This is more mysterious! We in vain strain our eyes to discover the bodies. The glass still appears uniform. After our astonishment shall have progressed sufficiently, it may be allayed by learning that the declaration of Mr. Brown means only that chymists can reduce glass to its pristine materials. That men can compose from materials so unseemly as sand and alkali the beautiful fabric of glass, and that they can again transform glass to its pristine rudeness, are facts sufficiently admirable without the heightening of any verbal delusion.

shall find that the simplicity which his description affords, arises from an ignorance of the fact, that the sensible meaning of words is the sensible phenomena to which the words refer. That the sand is present in glass, and would be visible were our eyes sufficiently acute, means not the same as when I say this table is present. The word present, as used by Mr. Brown, means the ability to reproduce sand by an analysis of glass. We can arrange words into such propositions as we please, but the sensible realities to which words refer, and which alone give words a sensible signification, are not affected by our phraseology. To these realities, as revealed by our senses, we must refer for the signification of language. To refer to words for the signification of what our senses reveal, is to err as grossly as to refer to a picture of the moon for the purpose of ascertaining whether the moon, which we see in the horizon, possesses its true colour, shape, and other appearances.

§ 21.—*Philosophy often expends itself in a contest about phraseology, from not knowing that the meaning of words is controlled by the sensible existences to which the words refer.*

"When a spark," says the same philosopher, "falls on gunpowder, and kindles it into explosion, every person ascribes to the spark the power of kindling the inflammable mass. But," continues he, "let any person ask himself what he means by the power which he imputes to the spark; and without contenting himself with a few phrases which signify nothing, let him"— What? Shall he content himself with no phrase, but deem the word power significant of precisely what his senses discover in the spark and explosion? No:—he must content himself with some phrases which Mr. Brown prescribes. Such has always been the advice of philosophers, and such will be their advice, till they know that the sensible signification of every word is neither more nor less than the sensible existence to which the word refers. Every philosopher gives us a new phrase, and like a quack with a new nostrum, desires us to be content with no other. In the present case, Mr. Brown advises the person to answer, that by the power imputed to the spark, he means only, "that in all similar circumstances, an explosion of gunpowder will be the immediate and uniform consequence of the application of a spark."

§ 22.—Admit that the person shall answer thus, what is the sensible signification of the answer?—precisely what our senses reveal to us in the spark and explosion:—precisely what the word power refers to. You may suppose that the occurrence is vastly simplified by the new phraseology, but the supposition is founded on the errour of employing the phrase to interpret a revelation of your senses, instead of employing the revelation of your senses to interpret the phrase.

Lecture VIII

EVERY GENERAL PROPOSITION POSSESSES AS MANY SIGNIFICATIONS AS IT POSSESSES REFERENCE TO DIFFERENT PARTICULARS

NATURALISTS assert, that the oak, with its towering trunk, its gigantick limbs, and its diffusive roots, is originally compressed within an acorn. They make this discovery by vision, and trace in microscopick lineaments the sylvan monarch. So an author can indite a few propositions, which shall comprehend a system of philosophy; but knowledge, thus compressed, is as undiscoverable to every understanding except the author's, as the oak is undiscernible to every eye but the naturalist's.

In detail then we must proceed. The oak must be suffered to issue from its imagined nucleus, to enlarge gradually its stem, to protrude successively its branches, and to indurate by alternate suns and tempests, before it can serve any useful purpose; so an author must be permitted to unfold gradually his premises, frame his propositions, accumulate examples, and evolve slowly his conclusions, before his labours can impart any beneficial instruction. Patience, then, must be *your* characteristick and *my* motto.

§ 1.—In our last lecture, I endeavoured to show that every word possesses as many significations as it possesses references to different phenomena. The same rule applies to propositions. Every proposition possesses as many significations as it possesses references to different particulars.

§ 2.—*Every proposition signifies some particular that the speaker refers to; but the proposition is interpreted by something that the hearer refers to.*

We are, however, constantly prone to errour in the interpretation of propositions. I lately heard a gentleman exclaim that his situation was unhappy. Another rebuked the speaker, and insisted that his situation was peculiarly happy.

In these conflicting propositions, each speaker alluded to different particulars; and if he had stated them, no disagreement would have occurred; the first speaker would probably have admitted that he was desirably situated in the cases enumerated by the second, and the second would have admitted that unhappiness existed in the particulars enumerated by the first.

§ 3.—*One particular may constitute the meaning of numerous propositions.*

If I have been hurt by riding a vicious horse, I may construct numerous propositions, for which I may possess no signification but the above accident: thus, things which are very valuable when good, are frequently worse than worthless when they are not good.

Brute animals are so destitute of gratitude, that the more you pamper them, the more inclined they will become to injure you.

What in animals we call a vicious practice, is probably performed without any vicious intention.

§ 4.—*General propositions produce often an apparent conflict of opinion where no disagreement exists.*

To a person who is ignorant of the accident to which I refer, the propositions will be applied to other particulars. Such an application may induce a denial of my last position; he may insist that animals are conscious when they perform a vicious action. He alludes to his dog, who, after killing a sheep, exhibited symptoms of fear. My proposition was not intended to controvert this. I meant only that starting at his shadow, a practice by which my horse threw me from his back, was performed without any intention of dismounting his rider.

§ 5.—*Propositions possess not always a determinate meaning.*

But suppose I assert that "infancy is a state of dependance." I may refer to no particular infant, nor any determinate acts of dependance. This will arise from my familiarity with the proposition. When I used it first, I referred to some particular case; but now, I employ it without thinking of any; and were you to demand of me some example, I should state one which I did not think of when I uttered the declaration.

§ 6.—*We often involve our actions in general propositions.*

The Scripture says, "judge not lest you be judged." Our mode of framing propositions furnishes this text with a popular construction, which implies that the judgments we pronounce are frequently an enunciation of our own practices; thus, I may say, "no man is proof against all temptations." I mean no more than a particular case in which I was vanquished. If the hearer can recollect no occasion in which he was overpowered, he will not assent to my position; and if he can recollect an instance in which he resisted a strong temptation, he may form a new proposition: "some persons are proof against every temptation."

§ 7.—A man who picked up a dollar which he saw fall from a traveller, went to a tavern, and in conversation with the landlord, made this proposition: "Men are more honest in great matters than in small." He meant that he acted dishonestly in not restoring the dollar, whilst in his more extensive intercourse with mankind he was honest. The innkeeper (who had a week previously found in one of his chambers a pocketbook with bank notes, which he intended to keep, though he frequently corrected errours when his guests gave inadvertently some trifle too much) replied, that he thought "men were more honest in small matters than in great."

§ 8.—*Universal gravitation signifies the particulars only to which it refers.**

Most of the phenomena which are adduced in proof of universal gravitation, were discovered after the establishment by Newton of the proposition. Of these subsequent discoveries we may enumerate the experiment of Dr. Maskelyne in Perthshire, which, by ascertaining that a mountain would so attract a plummet as to prevent the plummet from falling perpendicularly, confirmed, says the Encyclopedia, "beyond all doubt, the doctrine of universal gravitation." "But," says the writer, "in establishing a law of nature, we should multiply experiments": accordingly, he relates an experiment made with two leaden balls in 1788, by Mr. Cavendish. "The facts thus adduced, combined with the former, prove," says the Encyclopedia,— what? The phenomena exhibited? No—"they prove," says the writer, "that every particle of matter gravitates to every other particle." And this is correct; for the proposition, how general soever, signifies the experiments only to which it refers. Tradition says, that the law was originally suggested to Newton by the fall of an apple from a tree; and if he alluded to no other phenomenon, the proposition meant originally no more than that simple occurrence. I mean not to enumerate the phenomena to which the proposition refers, nor to restrict its application; I wish to show only the qualities which render propositions significant, and which limit their significancy.

§ 9.—*The sphericity and motions, &c., of the earth, signify the phenomena only to which the propositions refer.**

To say that the earth is a sphere, that it revolves round the sun, and round its own axis, and that we possess antipodes, are truths so long as we consider the expressions significant of certain phenomena to which the propositions refer. If you inquire

---

* See Lecture IX, § 10.

of an astronomer whether the earth is a sphere, he will desire you to notice what he terms the earth's shadow in an eclipse of the moon, the gradual disappearance of a ship as it recedes from the shore, &c. After hearing all that he can adduce in proof of the earth's sphericity, consider the proposition significant of these proofs. If you deem it significant beyond them, you are deceived by the forms of language.

§ 10.—*Till we know the particulars to which a proposition refers, its meaning is unknown to us.*

"Nature," says an astronomer, "has drawn an impenetrable curtain between the inhabitants of the sun and the worlds which circulate around them. She has doomed them to the most solitary dwelling in creation, and has marked them as either unfit to enjoy the noble privileges of intelligent beings, or as unworthy. The planets and the stars are invisible from the surface of the sun, unless a transient glance is obtained through an accidental opening in the solar atmosphere. From the year 1676 to 1684, no such opening occurred; consequently, the inhabitants of the sun never, during eight successive years, obtained a view of the starry firmament."

Not to waste our commiseration at this tale of wo, the writer has happily furnished us with his meaning. It is very simple: "from the year 1676 to 1684, not a single spot was discoverable in the sun's atmosphere."

§ 11.—*Ignorance of the true method of interpreting propositions causes controversy.*

The knowledge possessed of the sun by the learned, differs not essentially from that enjoyed by the illiterate. The learned are acquainted with more telescopical appearances than the illiterate; but the principal phenomena are known to both, and appear alike to all. The sun has been successively called a demon, a heated stone, a body of glass, a mass of fire, and an inhabited globe. At any period, if a philosopher had enumerated the sensible revelations which constituted the meaning of his language, no skepticism would have been exhibited; but the employment of such language, without this explanation, has ever encountered opposition. This alone ought to have made philosophers suspect either that some defect existed in their speculations, or in the interpretation which was applied to them.

§ 12.—*Medical science has suffered by a misconstruction of general propositions.*

The science of medicine has suffered more than any other, by an ignorance of the nature of general propositions. Physicians can seldom see the seat of a disease, or apply direct remedies to it. They are but little more favoured than a clockmaker, who should be bound to discover the defects of a clock, and to repair them by operating through the keyhole. Embarrassed thus by nature, they augment every difficulty by speaking in general propositions. Doctor Parry in his Elements of Pathology says, "the sanguiferous system is the source of almost all diseases, partly in consequence of the natural constitution of the body, and partly from the habits of civilized society." Diseases proceed generally, he supposes, from an excess either in the quantity or momentum of the blood.

§ 13.—*The illustrations of a general proposition constitute often all its meaning.*

The above speculation refers undoubtedly to some sensible particulars; but, as I know them not, the language is to me insignificant. Still, if Dr. Parry had adduced the particulars to which he alludes, the difficulty would yet exist; for his disciples would estimate particulars as the mere explanation of his propositions, and suppose that the propositions had a meaning independent of the particulars.

§ 14.—*Conflicting general propositions often harmonize when we know the particulars to which they refer.*

Cullen asserts, that when an external cause produces in us a morbid action, nature exerts an opposite process to counteract the evil: thus, an excessive load of food forced into the stomach possesses a tendency to destroy life, but the stomach resists the evil, and disgorges its contents. Some medical writers assert a conflicting proposition. They say, that every morbid change which occurs in our system is essentially injurious, and must be opposed by medicine; if the stomach is discharging its contents, the physician must endeavour to prevent the discharge.

§ 15.—Two physicians, who should severally enforce the above propositions, would employ opposite remedies. But to act thus proceeds from an erroneous belief that the propositions are significant of more than certain particulars. A person who knows the particulars to which each proposition alludes, will probably find that both positions are correct.

§ 16.—*No general proposition is significant of more than certain particulars.*

A father said once, "My son, in water exists a principle which is destructive of life, and in brandy a principle preservative of life." The father meant, that immersion in water would produce death, and that a small quantity of brandy was occasionally salutary. The proposition was correct while confined to the particulars to which the father alluded; but the son, supposing its application universal, refrained from the use of water, and substituted brandy. We all err in a similar manner, though not always in a like degree, when we consider any proposition significant of more than certain particulars; and if those who promulge general propositions, will not announce the particulars to which they refer, we have still every thing to learn.

§ 17.—Physicians have employed much controversy on the origin of yellow fever, some asserting that it is indigenous, and others exotic. Were each partisan to detail the particulars to which he refers, no disagreement would probably exist; but while he deems his proposition significant of more than certain particulars, endless controversy ensues. Each thinks justly that the other errs, for the same ignorance of the nature of language misleads both.

[When we obtain all the facts which relate to any subject, we obtain every thing that is essential. Convenience requires that the facts should have a name; but we may employ exotic or indigenous, or any other word, and the only profitable controversy is, whether we have selected an appropriate name. The controversy may be important in lexicography, but to suppose it essential to either medicine or philosophy, is to reverse the order of nature, and to consider the name more material than the phenomena named; or rather, it is to mistake the nature of language, by supposing that a general proposition signifies more than the particulars to which it refers.]

§ 18.—*We should never contest general propositions, but the particulars to which the propositions refer. Men cannot be forced to adopt but one phraseology.*

"Suppose," says Dr. Francis, "A to be ill of dysentery in a small confined apartment, his person neglected, the atmosphere around him impure and offensive; B visits him, and becomes sick with the same disease. Doctor Bayley, and others who adopt the doctrine of infection, as opposed to contagion, insist that the disorder of B proceeds from the impure air of A's chamber, and not from any thing emanating from the body of A; but," says Doctor Francis, "as we may without hazard visit an equally filthy chamber where C lies ill of a broken limb, I ascribe the disease of B to a peculiar virus generated in the system of A by the disease under which he labours, and communicated by his excretions to the surrounding atmosphere."

§ 19.—Now, what is the controversy between Doctors Francis and Bayley? Whether the disorder of B proceeds from a peculiar virus generated in the system of A, or from the impurity of A's chamber. They brandish at one another these propositions, without knowing that no proposition is significant of more than certain particulars. The moment they appreciate this fact, they will discover, that instead of contesting each other's general propositions, they should contest the particulars to which the propositions refer. For instance, let Doctor Francis say that B will not become diseased if he visits the impure chamber of C, who lies ill of a broken limb. If Doctor Bayley denies this assertion, the controversy becomes a question of fact, which is terminable by an experiment, and not by debate.

§ 20.—*Nearly every proposition is true when interpreted as the speaker interprets it. This results from the nature of language, and not from conventional agreement.*

To compel all men to employ the same collocation of words is impracticable. The attempt has filled the world with controversy, and not brought us to the desired uniformity. We, however, greatly aggravate the difficulty by not knowing that every proposition possesses as many different meanings as it refers to different particulars. This arises from no conventional law of language, but from its natural dependance for all its sensible signification on the sensible particulars to which it refers. Two men may employ different propositions, while the speakers refer to the same fact; and they may employ the same proposition, while they refer to different and even opposing facts. I am so confident that nearly every declaration is true, in the manner intended by the speaker, that I rarely contradict. If a man tells me in the middle of a delightful day, that the air feels as if we are shortly to have rain, I conclude that his assertion announces something unknown to me—perhaps the recognition of a feel which he once experienced antecedently to rain: hence, his prediction is true in the manner that he intends; and a denial he would construe into an assertion that he does not experience the feel which constitutes the meaning of his prediction.

§ 21.—I heard a man contend that no degree of heat could melt diamonds; whilst another was positive that they would melt. He who asserted their fusibility, referred to nothing but an article which he had read in a Cyclopedia; and he who maintained their infusibility, referred to an assertion of his father. Both persons were positive, because they intended no more than the above facts. If, however, each had discovered the other's meaning, the controversy would probably not have terminated. It would unconsciously have changed to another question, whether the Cyclopedia was entitled to more credence than the father; the discussion of which would have produced an altercation as virulent as the former, and with as little understanding by each disputant of the facts referred to by the other.

§ 22.—*General propositions are unintelligible till resolved into some known particulars.*

General propositions are often found in books, unaccompanied with any explanatory particulars.[1] Such propositions are unintelligible, unless we apply some particular to them. For instance: "We are," says Professor Stewart, "enabled, by our instinctive anticipations of physical events, to accommodate our conduct to what we perceive is to happen." This is followed by no example; hence, it will be insignificant to every person who cannot attach to it some incident. The event which it caused me to think of, was the falling of a tree. Instinctive anticipation would enable me to perceive, that I should be crushed if I did not accommodate my conduct to what was to happen; that is, if I did not change my position. Probably Mr. Stewart thought of something different. The event to which I allude may never have occurred to his observation.*

---

* The inexperience of children tends to make general propositions unintelligible to them; hence, books intended for children should speak of individual incidents, and avoid general propositions.

[1] In Johnson (I) the passage reads:

From an ignorance of the nature of general propositions, we often find them in books and conversation unaccompanied with any particulars. Such propositions are unintelligible, unless we can apply some particular to them. For instance, the above is a general proposition. What can you understand from it? I have elucidated it by no example, and if you can think of none, the proposition will be insignificant. If, however, you can think of an example, it will probably be different from any thing that has fallen under my observation; hence we may verbally possess the same information, while it is wholly dissimilar.

§ 23.—Plato explained the gradual decay of the human system by saying, "matter was first converted by Deity into bodies
of triangular shapes. Of these the elements were constituted,
and they assumed regular geometrical figures. Fire became a
pyramid, the earth a cube, the air an octahedron, and water an
icosahedron. The human frame is composed of these elements,
and as their angles become by time blunted, and unable to retain
their hold, the fabrick gradually dissolves."

§ 24.—This is the laboured production of a wise man. He
doubtless had some particulars to which his propositions referred; but as we know them not, his language is as insignificant
as the disconnected prattle of infancy.

§ 25.—*Some writers commit a species of tautology, by involv-
ing in general propositions the facts which they subsequently
particularize.*

Other writers avoid the above errour. If they involve any
fact in a general proposition, they subjoin the fact by way of
example, though it truly constitutes all the meaning of their
proposition: thus, "the more," says Saint-Pierre, "temples are
multiplied in a state, the more is religion enfeebled."

§ 26.—What did Saint-Pierre mean? You will find in his
succeeding paragraph. "Look," says he, "at Italy, covered with
churches, yet Constantinople is crowded with Italian renega-
does; while the Jews, who had but one temple, are so strongly
attached to their religion, that the loss of their temple excites,
to this day, their regret."

§ 27.—His general proposition means but the above particulars, therefore you need not controvert the position, and show
that in your country the increase of temples increases the number and zeal of worshippers. If you argue with Saint-Pierre,
blame him for using words in a way which you do not approve,
but not for denying facts to which he never alluded.

§ 28.—Malebranche, in accounting for the phenomena of
memory, says, "in childhood the fibres of the brain are soft and

flexible; but time dries and hardens them, so that in old age they are gross and inflexible."

§ 29.—Malebranche is not enumerating any phenomena discoverable by inspection of the brain. What then does he mean? It follows in his own words: "flesh hardens by time, and a young partridge is more tender than an old one." You may wonder how this concerns memory. I know not. It, however, concerns his theory, and probably constitutes all he means by the hardness and inflexibility which he makes age inflict upon the brain.

§ 30.—Mr. Hauksbee asserts that the aurora borealis is the effect of electricity on a vacuum. What does he mean? He states subsequently as follows: "the excitation of electricity in an exhausted Florence flask produced a light which resembled the aurora." Another person who shall find that all the phenomena of the aurora borealis cannot be thus imitated, will insist that Mr. Hauksbee is wrong; but in truth both are right, for they mean severally no more than the facts to which each refers. The difference between them is in their language, apart from which they will agree.

§ 31.—*General propositions bring often unmerited honour on their authors.*

We are prone to award unmerited commendation to the authors of general propositions: thus, the assertion attributed to Pythagoras, that the earth revolves round the sun, is supposed to imply a knowledge by him of the Newtonian theory; while probably no feature of it was ever imagined by Pythagoras. He may have intended some particulars that have long been exploded from science.

§ 32.—Lord Bacon asserts that reason is supposed to govern the words of men, but that words often possess power to react upon reason. "This aphorism," says Professor Stewart, "may be considered the text of the most valuable part of Locke's Essays, the part which relates to the imperfections and abuse of words; but till within the last twenty years, its depth and importance were not perceived in their full extent."

§ 33.—Mr. Stewart alludes to what has been written since the time of Bacon, by Mr. Prévost and Mr. Degérando; but Bacon is no more entitled to credit for the observations which have subsequently been marshalled under his aphorism, than the man who first formed the word Napoleon is entitled to the renown that has lately been connected with that appellation. The aphorism, when invented by Lord Bacon, was significant, as we find by a reference to it in his Novum Organum. What he intended, he there expressed, and further than this the proposition possessed probably no signification in his understanding.

§ 34.—*We must interpret every general proposition by the particulars to which it refers; and not interpret the particulars by the general proposition.*

We are informed by phrenologists, that various prominences on the skull conform to certain protuberances which exist in the brain; and that a man's piety, courage, memory, endurance, with all his other moral qualities which either exalt the individual or degrade, conform, in their degree, to the magnitude of the said protuberances. No person can read Spurzheim's treatise on phrenology without discovering that the above assertions refer to many interesting particulars, which hence constitute the meaning of the assertions. To believe, however, that the assertions signify more than all the sensible particulars to which they refer, is to interpret our experience by the language that we apply to it; instead of interpreting our language by the revelations of nature. Such an interpretation subordinates nature to language, instead of subordinating language to nature.

§ 35.—We are told that the tides are caused by the influence of the sun and moon. If you would know the external meaning of the proposition, (the meaning which relates to the realities of the external universe,) you must ascertain all the sensible information to which the proposition refers. The sensible particulars prove not themselves, and, in addition, that the tides are caused by the sun and moon; but they signify all that the proposition means. I intend not to say that the proposition is improper, but I wish to designate its meaning. The proposition is usually deemed far more important than all the particulars to which it refers. The particulars are estimated as the mere indications by which the sagacity of Newton was enabled to discover the more comprehensive truth that is involved in the general proposition.

§ 36.—*Some sensible particulars imply others, by virtue of our experience.*

When a jury pronounces Thomas guilty of murder, they may possess no other particulars than that the cry of murder proceeded from a house out of which Thomas, covered with blood, was seen to issue. On entering the house, a man, recently killed, was lying on the floor, with the sword of Thomas in his breast. You may ask whether the verdict of the jury, which pronounces Thomas guilty, must not signify the above particulars, and also, that Thomas was the perpetrator? Yes, but this result is included in the particulars which are proved. The particulars testified to are experimentally connected with the further fact, that Thomas was the perpetrator; precisely as I know that a piece of gold is round, when you tell me that measure it where I please, from the centre to the extremity, the length is just an inch. The implied roundness is a result of my experience with round bodies; and the implied agency of Thomas, is a result of our experience with men, their motives, and actions, &c. In both cases, therefore, we refer to sensible particulars, which are as comprehensive as the general propositions.*

§ 37.—Finally, then, if we would appreciate the nature of general propositions, we must remember that each possesses as many sensible significations as it possesses a reference to different sensible particulars; that no general proposition possesses any significance, if it refers to no particular; and that no proposition can signify more than the particulars to which it refers.

* See Lecture IX.

Lecture IX

WHEN THE NEGATION OF A PROPOSITION REFERS TO NO PARTICULAR, THE
NEGATION IS INSIGNIFICANT; AND THE PROPOSITION POSSESSES AN UN-
LIMITED AFFIRMATION, WHICH MAKES THE PROPOSITION SEEM TO
SIGNIFY MORE THAN A LIMITED NUMBER OF PARTICULARS

§ 1.—*That the sensible signification of a general proposition
is limited to the sensible particulars to which the proposition
refers, proceeds from nature and not from convention.*

IN MY last discourse, I attempted to show that the sensible
signification of every proposition is limited to the sensible particulars to which the proposition refers. The limitation proceeds from the nature of language,—every word being a sound
inherently insignificant. The principle seems to be controverted
by propositions which assert that all men must die;—that every
unsupported stone will fall towards the earth, &c.; for if a
proposition is significant of nothing but the particulars to
which it refers, the proposition that all men must die seems
equivalent only to the proposition that all men have died.

§ 2.—*Affirmative propositions possess a universal application, when the negation of their universality refers to no sensible particular.*

The proposition that all men will die, possesses a universal
application for the reason that to say, some men will not die,
refers to no sensible particular, and hence is insignificant.*

§ 3.—*Uninterrupted experience excites a feeling of expectation which enters into the meaning of some propositions that
allude to futurity.*

To assert that the sun will rise to-morrow and daily for
ever,—that the moon will continue to wax and wane,—that the
seasons will continue to alternate,—that the winds will continue
changeable,—are highly significant propositions. You may say
that the assertions, (so far as they are prospective,) refer to

* See Lectures VIII and X.

nothing. This is not true. They refer to an internal feeling of expectation, which is excited in us naturally by our uniform experience. But the assertions are especially significant illimitably, from the fact, that though they can be denied verbally, the negation will refer to no sensible experience, and hence will possess no sensible signification.*

§ 4.—*A universal proposition that speaks of futurity, cannot be invalidated by a negation that refers to no sensible particular.*

To assert that food will not always be necessary to support life, refers to no sensible experience; hence, it cannot invalidate the significant proposition that food will always be necessary to sustain life. A universal proposition, when it speaks of futurity, may therefore be significant, from the mere fact that a negation of the proposition is insignificant.

§ 5.—*If a negation refers to no sensible particular, the negation is insignificant.*

When I assert that every unsupported stone possesses a tendency to fall towards the earth, you may say that millions of stones exist with which the experiment has never been tried, and that they may not possess any tendency towards the earth. The difficulty with this potential objection is, that as it refers to no sensible experience, it possesses no sensible signification.

§ 6.—*All affirmations and all negations refer for signification to our experience.*

That light and darkness succeed each other over the whole earth within every twenty-four hours, and that every stone possesses a tendency to fall towards the earth, are positions equally consonant to all my experience. Still, a negation is significant when applied to the first position, but insignificant when applied to the second position; because the negation of the first position refers to the sensible experience of many men, while a negation of the second position refers to no experience.

* See Lectures VIII and X.

§ 7.—*Propositions are neither significant nor insignificant, but as they refer to our sensible experience.*

Thousands of human beings exist who never heard that light and darkness intermit their daily alternations; hence I may insist that your belief in the universal gravitation of stones may arise from only a like defect of experience. The cavil, however, refers to no sensible particular, and therefore possesses no sensible signification. I may as well talk of the possibility of hot ice and cold fire. The assertions are insignificant, because they refer to no sensible particular.

§ 8.—*Though the absence of a sensible negative will make an affirmative proposition universal in its meaning, yet the affirmative proposition will signify the sensible particulars only to which it refers.*

To an uninformed man within the tropicks, no proposition can be more universal in its application, than that which affirms a diurnal succession of light and darkness; yet we know that the proposition is significant of nothing but the experience of the uninformed man. The universality of the proposition depends upon his unacquaintance with any sensible exception; but his inexperience cannot enlarge the signification of the proposition. It will still signify the sensible particulars only to which it refers when he employs it.

§ 9.—*The universality of a proposition relates to the absence of a sensible negative particular, and not to the number of the affirmative particulars.*

I have heard of a child in England, who had seen but two negroes, and each of those happened to possess but one arm. The child was heard to speak of negroes, and among their peculiarities he enumerated that negroes possess only one hand. The universality of the proposition was true according to the knowledge of the speaker, and hence we see that the universality of a proposition relates not to the number of particulars to which the proposition refers, but to the absence of a negative instance. In like manner, the small number of comets which we have seen or heard of, disenables us not from applying universal propositions to comets.

§ 10.—*Many scientifick propositions owe their propriety to the absence of a sensible negative.*

The roundness of the earth, its diurnal and annual motions, &c., refer for signification to numerous sensible particulars, which constitute all the sensible signification that the assertions possess. Still, if any person chooses to say that the earth is not round,—that it possesses no motion, &c.,—the negations will possess but little if any sensible signification. The negations may mean that I cannot feel the motion as I can feel the motion of a coach;—that I cannot feel the roundness as I can feel the roundness of an artificial globe. But the affirmative propositions do not include within their signification that the roundness and motions can be felt; hence the roundness and motions which are affirmed, remain without a sensible negative.

§ 11.—Similar to the foregoing are the assertions that the moon and sun cause the tides; that every fixed star is a sun, and the centre of a planetary system; that beyond all telescopick vision other stars exist, which also are the centres of more remote systems; that the earth appears like a star to the inhabitants of the planets, &c. These assertions are all significant of some observations, some calculations, or of at least some thing; whilst a negation of them may refer to nothing, and hence be insignificant. The propositions, instead of being negatived, require to be limited in their signification to the sensible particulars to which they refer.

§ 12.—*A doubt or salvo which refers to nothing sensible, is verbal only and sensibly insignificant.*

An Esquimaux Indian will be as positive that water every where freezes during the winter, as I am that a piece of gold will every where exhibit the sight round, and the feel round, when the piece is so formed that a line drawn any where from the centre of it to the surface, will measure just one inch. Now, I know that the Esquimaux is mistaken. Countries exist in which water never freezes, and why may not some countries exist in which the principles of nature are so different from those with which I am acquainted, that a piece of gold may possess the proportions that I have stated, and still not be round? The two cases are radically different. That countries exist in which water never freezes, is a significant declaration, for it refers to the sensible experience of many credible witnesses; but the doubt in relation to the gold is merely verbal. It refers to no sensible experience, and hence is as sensibly insignificant as any story of giants or fairies that amuses infancy.

§ 13.—That the dead exhibit neither sensation nor consciousness, &c., is all we mean when we assert that the dead are void of feeling and consciousness. We cannot know experimentally that the dead suffer no pain on a funeral pyre, or under the knife of an anatomical demonstrator, or under the process of decomposition. You may deem this reflection full of horrour, and deprecate for the dead some attention to the possibility of their latent sensibilities. But you will deprecate in vain. The anatomical demonstrator will proceed in his operations as unconcernedly as before. He may not be able to state why he disregards your remarks; but the reason lies in his practical acquaintance with the nature of language. Your remarks refer to nothing sensible, hence he knows them to be sensibly insignificant.

Lecture X

LANGUAGE CAN EFFECT NO MORE THAN REFER US TO THE INFORMATION OF OUR SENSES

THE EARTH possesses gradations of temperature, from the frigidity of a polar winter to the intensity of an equatorial summer. With the Esquimaux we may dwell in houses of undissolving ice, repose on ledges of everlasting snow, and pierce the huge walrus amid an accumulated frost of ages: or with the Ethiopian we may bask in a tropick sun, repose in scorching groves, and press the gushing lusciousness of spontaneous fruits. We may avoid both extremes. We may enjoy a sky that never clouds, a herbage that never fades, a cold and heat so attempered that the thought of either is unnatural.

This is poetry, but not fiction. It is the romance of nature: yet, with this diversity before him, and sensitive to its effects, man scarcely ever changes his location with a view to climate. As a tree falls it lies; and where Providence decrees our birth, we also are stationary. This trait in the human character may be heightened if we reflect on the power of our appetites, and the turbulence of our passions. To satiate his appetites, a man will dissipate suddenly the labours of his ancestors; and to gratify his passions, he will renounce reputation and hazard existence. Still, no luxury exists of flood, field, or air, but in some regions it is the banquet of peasants; and no passion is so irregular, but in some countries its object is lawful enjoyment. But again these temptations fail to allure. The most rigid moral discipline, and the coarsest of nature's caterings, remove not even the sensual from the land of their nativity.

A similar inconsistency is apparent when we select our occupations. We should determine theoretically that when a man possesses no higher object than a subsistence, he would select the least offensive employment that will compass his object; still the most laborious pursuits, and the most noxious, are supplied with followers as readily as the most easy and healthful, and without the poor consideration of being more pecuniarily profitable.

Literature presents the same peculiarity. We might reasonably imagine that a man who devotes his life to literature, (a devotion in itself perverse,) would select subjects in which the playfulness of fancy, or the vivacity of wit, would relieve the irksomeness of composition; at least, that he would avoid the labyrinths of metaphysicks, and the straits of logick: toils which seldom can supply even the consolation that a French authoress extracted from an assimilation of herself with a lamp; that she consumes to enlighten others. Yet in literature also the rugged walks are voluntarily thronged equally with the most agreeable. This thought is gloomy, but it happily suggests the subject of our lecture.

§ 1.—*Words can supply the place of no sense. They can simply refer us to what our senses have disclosed.*

I have heretofore stated several fundamental principles of language. A principle as fundamental as any of the former, and more essential than all of them to a just apprehension of human knowledge, is this,—language can effect no more than refer us to the information of our senses.* The most forcible language, and the most fluent utterance, are inadequate to infuse into the blind a knowledge of colours. Why? Because colours are sights, and nothing can reveal to us sights but seeing. We may apply the same conclusion to every other item of our knowledge. Words can supply the place of no sense;—they can simply refer us to what our senses have disclosed.

§ 2.—*No sight which I have not seen, can be revealed to me by words.*

Truth possesses generally two aspects—one so gross that every person sees it; the other so subtle that the most acute pass it unnoticed. For instance, that words cannot reveal colours to the blind, is obvious; while the kindred fact, that no sight which a person has not seen can be known to him, has been denied by even the sagacious Hume.

He says, "suppose a man is acquainted with every colour except a particular shade of blue. Let now all the shades of blue, except the above, be placed before him in an order descending gradually from the deepest blue to the highest; will he not be able, by his imagination, to acquire a knowledge of the absent shade?"

---

* See Lecture XI.

§ 3.—Hume asserts that he can. He is wrong. The absent shade is a sight, and nothing can reveal it but his eyes. The law which prevents blind men from knowing any colour, disenables him from knowing the absent shade.

§ 4.—But, if we cannot thus learn a new appearance, can we not by some mental elaboration commix known sights, and discover the effects?[1] No. A change of appearance is a new sight,

---

[1] In Johnson (I) this reads:

But, if we cannot thus learn a new appearance, can we not by some mental elaboration compound our ideas; commix known sights, and discover the effects which result from juxtaposition or separation? Whatever produces a change of appearance, is essentially a new sight; and irremediably unknown till disclosed by our eyes. It happens often that a drowned man, who is found after some mutilation, is not recognized by his intimate friends. Many features may be unchanged, but they are seen in a new connexion. If the body is eventually recognized, it is by looking singly at some part which is unchanged.

To speak of a less revolting calamity, suppose some of us should grow old, and being anxious to linger in the precincts of youth, should change his grizzled and scanty locks for glossy and exuberant ringlets. Need we an actual glance to teach us how this new combination of familiar sights will affect the appearance of our father or brother? Let language be exhausted in describing the new appearance. Let feeling, and every other sense exert their powers to inform you, and then direct your eyes to the metamorphosed individual, and you will receive an instantaneous communication which no other means can yield.

If I have seen the change produced by such a process in A, I do not assert that language cannot inform me that C is similarly transformed; and thus teach me the appearance of C, without an inspection. Language can refer me to any phenomenon that I have experienced;—but in the slightest particular that discriminates the appearance of C from A, words can avail nothing. They can apprise me that there is a difference, and may inform me what the difference is like, (so far as they can refer me to any thing I have seen;) but beyond this, their most eloquent efforts fall upon my ear as upon the ears of the blind:—nature renders them powerless to us both.

When a milliner wishes to know how a ribbon which lies before her will appear on a hat, she does not trust to her ability to compound

and irremediably unknown till disclosed by our eyes. When a milliner wishes to know how a riband which lies before her will appear on a hat, she trusts not her ability to compound ideas; but, from a practical acquaintance with the limitation of her faculties, applies the riband to the hat.

§ 5.—*Pictures can reveal no sight but themselves.*

From the known inadequacy of words to reveal new sights, we employ pictures. But a person who never saw the original, will receive from its representative no sight except that of the painting. Let a youth study geography, and be competent to designate on a map or globe every kingdom, and to tell its latitude, climate, soil, productions, and appearance; his knowledge is precisely what he displays: various appearances on maps, globes, and pictures, together with words and phrases which he has learnt to associate with them. If he thinks he knows any sight which he never experienced, a visit to the countries he has been taught to speak of will undeceive him. He may recognise names of places, names of customs, and names of natural productions; but the sights will be new. All the ingenuity of man, assisted by painting, sculpture, and eloquence, cannot teach the brightest understanding the exact appearance of even a pin, except by presenting to his eyes what will produce a sight that in every respect is a pin.

§ 6.—*No taste which I have not experienced, can be made known to me.*

I shall not press this point. That language can reveal to me no sight that seeing has not informed me of, is a physical truth which experience will substantiate. But the position is equally true of the information furnished by our other senses. Let an

---

ideas; but, from a practical acquaintance with the limitation of her faculties, applies the ribbon to the hat. I have known a good housewife view with much curiosity a little bauble in the hands of her child; till by going to her sideboard she discovered that it was broken from an urn from which she has daily drunk for years.

epicure prescribe some unusual mixture of known ingredients, and after his imagination has feasted on the compound, let him present it to his taste, and he will discover the inefficacy of his foreknowledge.

§ 7.—*No sound which I have not heard, can be made known to me.*

If I have never heard a cataract, you may inform me what the sound is like; and if I have heard a similar sound, I shall be instructed; but language can effect no more than such an approximation. Should you wish to acquaint a child with the sound of a cataract, his conception of it will probably be very erroneous; not because his faculties are less acute than yours, or language less operative on him than on you; but because his experience is less than yours, and language can be significant to him of his experience only. If he has heard no sound more consonant, you must refer to even the lowing of an ox. You may qualify the comparison, by saying the cataract is awfully louder; but if he has heard nothing louder, the qualification will not add to his instruction, except that it may teach him he is still ignorant of the correct sound of a cataract.

§ 8.—*Brilliancy of imagination and acuteness of intellect cannot perform the office of any of our senses.*

But cannot the letters of the alphabet be combined so that by looking at the combination, seeing can teach me a sound that hearing has never informed me of? I may combine letters so as to denote a new sound; but the sound, so far as it is new, will be unknown to me, till my organs of speech have read the combination, and thus made my hearing acquainted with it. Seeing the letters can of itself teach us a new sound, no more than it can teach a deaf mute. The same inability is common to all; nor let any person suppose that he can compound known sounds, and thus acquire a sound which he never heard. Brilliancy of imagination, and acuteness of intellect, cannot pass the barriers erected by nature. The most practised musician can, no more than the most unskilful, know the sound which will be produced by a new combination of familiar notes. So far as the combination will produce a sound that he never heard, so far the effect of the combination must be unknown to him.

§ 9.—*No feel which I have not felt, can be known to me.*

A person who has never felt pain, (if we can conceive such a being,) will possess no correct meaning of the word; and he who has felt no greater pain than a toothache, may be told of the superior agonies of the gout, but he will not be able to divine the feeling. Language cannot perform the office of any of his senses. It can record phenomena, but not reveal them.

[Our knowledge of each other's feels is probably more imperfect than of each other's tastes, sights, sounds or smells. The gout, consumption, dropsy and other diseases, are feels which are known to only a small portion of mankind, and collectively to no man.]

§ 10.—*No muscular effort which I have not experienced, can be made known to me by language.*

From the inadequacy of language to effect more than a reference to our experience, arises the inefficacy of verbal instruction. A writing master may direct a child how to make a perpendicular mark; but in every particular in which the directions refer to some motion which the pupil has never produced, or to some muscular effort that he has never made, the directions are as impotent as a discourse on colours is to the blind.

§ 11.—*Nearly every word possesses a verbal meaning as well as a sensible meaning.*

That the significancy of a man's language is limited to his sensible experience would be readily admitted, were we not embarrassed with one difficulty. Bonfire names a sight, and melody a sound. If these words possessed no other signification, we should immediately understand that the import of bonfire must ever be unknown to the blind, and the import of melody unknown to the deaf. But these words, and nearly all others,

possess a further signification: they name words also. This is
an important distinction, and till you understand it, you will
be liable to delusion.

§ 12.—*The sensible signification of a word nothing can reveal but our senses;—the verbal signification can be disclosed
by words.*

Recollect, then, that nearly every word possesses a signification which refers to our senses, and another which refers to
words.[1] The sensible signification is the sight, sound, taste,
feel, and smell, to which the word refers; therefore, nothing
but our senses can reveal to us this signification; but the verbal
signification of a word may be known to any person who possesses hearing, and even to those who are void of hearing, if
they have acquired the art of reading.

[It is curious that so simple a distinction in the meaning of
words should be unknown in the disquisitions of our most acute
metaphysicians. They constantly disregard the simplicity of
our knowledge, and look for truth either above the surface of
things or below it. They have therefore again attributed to nature a property which exists in language only; that is, they have
observed that some words are reducible into other words, while
some cannot be so reduced: for instance, murder can be translated into a sentence; "a felonious killing with premeditated

---

[1] In Johnson (I) the passage reads:

Recollect, then, that nearly every word has a signification which
refers to our senses, and another which refers to words. The verbal
signification is usually termed a definition. It is regulated by principles wholly different from those which govern the sensible signification. The sensible signification is the phenomena to which the word
refers, and therefore nothing but our senses can reveal to us this signification; but the verbal signification of a word may be known to any
person who possesses hearing, and even to those who are void of hearing, if they have acquired the art of reading. The blind may discourse
eloquently about fires and illuminations; and the deaf mutes in our
asylums may write pertinently about melody; but it is only the verbal
signification of these words of which either have any knowledge.

malice." The word white cannot be thus translated; it names a
sight only. This difference, which is purely an artifice of language to condense a sentence into a single word, has been
supposed a mysterious mental process; and the words which
effect such condensations, have been termed complex ideas,
abstractions, &c.

[Perhaps no language is so uncultivated as not to possess
words of both the above classes; but rude languages are chiefly
composed of words that name sensible phenomena only, that is,
words which are undefinable. If we examine the English language we shall find that our Saxon words are principally of
the above character. Indeed, a large portion of our undefinable
words are Saxon: as fire, water, black, sun, earth, ground, &c.
And when we find an undefinable word that is not Saxon, we
may generally discover that we have a Saxon word that is
synonimous; for instance, infant is Latin; but we have the
synonimous word child, which is Saxon.

[When men acquire a knowledge of foreign languages, they
enrich their own. A foreign word supersedes gradually the
words which constitute its interpretation; instead of saying, "an
arm of the sea," we now use the word estuary, and thereby condense a sentence into a word. Native words are frequently
compounded, so as to condense into one word the signification
of several words:—shipwreck refers to what was expressed
originally by a sentence.

[I do not mean to enumerate the ways by which definable
words are introduced into language and periphrases avoided;
but merely to illustrate, by a few examples, my view of language. Definable words, though generally the name of other
words, become occasionally the name of phenomena: thus, if
I have never seen a shipwreck, the word will signify to me the
words that constitute its definition, conjoined perhaps with some
narratives and graphic representations. With another man, shipwreck may signify a sublime spectacle which he has seen.

[The meaning of definable words is not only thus different with different individuals, but it varies in the same individual at different periods. Shipwreck signifies to me at present no more than some words and paintings; but hereafter it may unfortunately name a sight.

[I have now shown that we possess words which signify phenomena only, as white, sour, pain, loud, &c. and that we have other words which sometimes signify phenomena and sometimes words; as estuary, shipwreck, murder, &c. We have still another class: words that never signify phenomena, but words only. These are not numerous in any language, though they probably exist in all languages. Infinity is an example of this class. It is never a sight, feel, taste, or smell; nor is it a sound, except as it names other words. Angel, paradise, eternity, hell, and many other words of the highest importance, are also of this class. They name no sensible phenomenon, but refer for signification to some gracious declarations of scripture.

[From this glance at the construction of language, we may easily see why some words are definable, and others not. Words are definable when they signify other words. Definable words have therefore two significations; a phenomenon and a phrase. To this distinction I wish to direct your particular attention. It has never been noticed, and produces dire confusion in every disquisition that relates to human knowledge. We find Locke, and his most acute metaphysical successors, asserting constantly that the meaning of definable words can be discovered by some process distinct from sensation. Green, violet, red, &c. are undefinable words, and their meaning cannot be known except by vision; but rainbow, he says, is a definable word; and its meaning can be distinctly revealed to any person who has seen the colours of which it is composed.]

§ 13.—*We rarely discriminate between the verbal significa-tion of a word and its sensible signification.*

When Locke says that the meaning of rainbow can be revealed to a person who never saw one, provided he has seen red, violet, green, &c., Locke is alluding to the verbal meaning of rainbow. This meaning can be known to the blind, and I once saw a company surprised when a blind youth was exhibiting what was esteemed a triumph of education over natural defects, by giving an explanation of the appearance of rainbows. The company knew not that rainbow possesses two significations;—one a sight which nothing can reveal but seeing, and the other words that can be learnt by hearing.

§ 14.—*Words and definitions can disclose only the verbal meaning of words.*

You may suppose that we differ from the blind; and that an enumeration of the colours of a rainbow, and of their figure, size, position, and arrangement, to us who know the sights which the words signify severally, would reveal to us a rainbow, not verbally merely, but visibly.

§ 15.—The premises are, however, impossible. No person can have experienced the colours which compose a rainbow, and their figure, position, and arrangement, without having seen a rainbow. Take any one of the colours, say red: it names not one sight only, but numerous sights. Fire is red, blood is red, my hand is red, bricks are red, and an Indian is red;—which of these is he to imagine, when you speak of the red of a rainbow? The same remark will apply to the other colours, and to their figure, position, and arrangement.

§ 16.—But admit that a person who has never seen a rainbow, shall still have seen all its colours. Admit further, that when you enumerate the colours, he shall guess the precise red, orange, yellow, &c., to which you refer; yet, for the person to know how the colours will look when they are combined, will be impossible; much less, how they will appear when drawn into the shape, size, and position, of a rainbow. If he has seen such a combination, he has seen a rainbow; but if he has not seen the combination, language is inadequate to reveal it. After the most copious definition, and the most familiar acquaintance with the sights separately that are referred to by the defining words, a person will be conscious of a new sight the moment he sees a rainbow.

[Another common illustration of the power of definitions, is furnished by the word centaur. We are told that a person who has seen a man and a horse, may, on hearing the definition of centaur, fantastically combine the head of the man with the body of the horse, and thus acquire the complex idea signified by the word defined. The error lies in supposing that the definition effects more than to teach us the verbal signification of centaur. If hearing the definition could teach me the sight centaur, hearing can perform the office of vision; a position which experience will momentarily refute. So rigid is nature on this subject, that the most intimate acquaintance with two sights will not enable me to know the appearance which they will present when blended. The same law regulates all our senses: after drinking two liquors, endeavour to combine their flavour, and when you think the mental combination is complete, mingle the liquors, and the moment you taste them you will be conscious of a new taste.

[If then the object of definition is to reveal any sight, sound, taste, feel or smell, that our senses have never experienced, the attempt is vain; and it is not more vain in simple ideas than in complex; in the word white, than in the word rainbow. But if the object of a definition is to teach us the verbal signification of any word, the instruction is useful and adequate.

[I hope you are now proof against the delusion, that definitions can reveal to you existences which your senses never disclosed. Verbal significations only, can be revealed by definitions. The position remains unshaken and immutable, that language can effect no more than to refer us to such phenomena as our senses have revealed to us.]

§ 17.—The opinion that definitions can teach us more than

the verbal signification of words, has descended from antiquity. The ancients, however, thought that definitions are applicable to all words; while the moderns see that this involves an admission, that we can acquire a knowledge of sights without the agency of seeing, &c. Hence, the moderns exclude from the power of definition all such words as white, loud, &c., that signify sensible information only. They perceive not that other words are definable only because they possess a verbal signification; and that so far as the object of a definition is to reveal a new sight, taste, feel, smell, &c., all words must be equally undefinable.

§ 18.—*A knowledge of the two-fold character of words useful in the instruction of deaf mutes.*

If the instructors of the deaf will study the difference that has now been stated between the verbal signification of a word and the sensible signification, they will find the discrimination important: for instance, suppose they wish to teach a deaf mute the signification of joy, they must teach him two significations; the verbal signification, and the sensible. The verbal is easily taught, after you determine the form of words into which joy shall be resolvable. The sensible signification no words can teach—it is a feel, and can be disclosed only by making the mute know (by any method you can) the feel to which the word alludes. Every mute should be taught this difference in the character of words, and his knowledge will be definite, and his progress in learning agreeable.

[I beg you to remember I am not writing a treatise on definitions, but was compelled to show that language can effect no more than to refer us to known phenomena. Definitions can teach me the verbal signification of a new word; but it can teach me no new phenomenon. Before I dismiss definitions, I will remark, that the meaning of angel, immortality, eternity, and such other words as signify words only, must be incurably unknown to any person who possesses no language: hence the difficulty which is experienced in conveying to deaf mutes any instruction on subjects connected with eternity. To mutes who learn to read, the difficulty is obviated; for they acquire the meaning of definable words in the same way as we. There is, however, this curious difference—with us, definable words signify oral words, that is, sounds; but with the deaf mute, they signify written words—that is, sights.

[I shall conclude this Lecture with one observation: in every case in which language seems to effect more than a reference to known phenomena, it refers to words only. I will illustrate this doctrine with the most solemn application I can adduce—its application to our knowledge of death. Confessedly we know but little of death; but that little is much beyond what is actually known. Death, say we, is at least a state of rest. If the dead feel no pleasure, they are free from pain. Be they buried or unburied, cast on a funeral pyre, or laid on a bed of roses, is alike to them. These expressions are significant and true; but not to the extent that is generally imagined. They are significant and true, so long as they refer to the phenomena exhibited by death; but the moment we extend, in the least, the signification,

> be it so much
> As makes it light or heavy in the substance,
> Or the division of the twentieth part
> Of one poor scruple; nay, if the scale turn
> But in the estimation of a hair,—

our words refer to no archetype in nature, and are insignificant—except as they may refer to declarations of holy writ. We cannot increase our knowledge of death by employing language upon it; but by resorting either to revelation or our senses. One sight may be referred to by a thousand words, but the sight will be neither enlarged nor multiplied. Copiousness may increase the bulk of our dictionaries, but not our knowledge of nature.]

PART SECOND

OF LANGUAGE WITH REFERENCE TO PHENOMENA
INTERNAL OF MAN

Lecture XI

§ 1.—*Language refers to our internal feelings.*

IN MY last discourse, I state that language can effect no more than refer us to the information of our senses. Language, however, refers to a large class of existences, which are not usually deemed the objects of our senses:—for instance, the phenomena that we designate by the words love, anger, joy, hope, faith, hunger, pity, sympathy, judgment, reverie, &c. These I call internal feelings; hence, I class them among the information that we derive from our senses. I will not defend the propriety of this classification. The sense of feeling is usually restricted to external information; but I adopt the term internal feelings, as it will probably indicate the phenomena which I wish to designate.

§ 2.—*Language would lose a large portion of its meaning, to a person destitute of internal feelings.*

To a person who should be destitute of internal feelings, love, hope, fear, &c., would be words of very little meaning; as also joy, sorrow, anger, anticipation, expectation, jealousy, hunger, thirst, sleepy, weary, health, vigour, lassitude, &c. The words would not be destitute of meaning to him, because nearly every such word includes within its signification some external action or appearance, which enables us to determine by looking at a man, that he is sleepy, faint, angry, jealous, envious, hungry, &c. By means of these external exhibitions, a man who should be void of internal feelings, might discourse about love, anger, envy, &c.; as a man who should be void of the sense of taste, could talk of the deliciousness of peaches, oranges, grapes, &c.—his words referring to the appearance of the fruits.

§ 3.—*Internal feelings enter largely into the signification of words that relate to religion.*

The words eternity, heaven, hell, angel, redemption, resurrection, faith, and many other words of sacred import, are connected, in religious men, with certain internal feelings which give to the words a pungency and unction. With irreligious men, the words are connected with no such feelings, and are perhaps deemed significant of nothing but certain verbal definitions. An inattention to this difference in men produces much of the disagreement which exists on religious subjects.

§ 4.—The words Jupiter, Juno, Mars, &c., were associated with feelings which probably made the names awful to the Greeks and Romans; while, to us, the words are significant of nothing but historical narratives, or connected with feelings of derision. The word Jehovah was connected with such feelings in the ancient Jews, as made them refuse to utter it under any inducement. I am told, it is still thus esteemed by existing Jews.

§ 5.—*Religious feelings seem a part of the human constitution, like hope, fear, &c.*

Religious feelings seem as much a part of the human constitution as sympathy, hope, fear, doubt, uncertainty, confidence, &c. Religion may change its modes of worship, and the nominal objects of its worship; but the internal feelings which alone give urgency and vitality to the worship, must always make every man liable to religion;—though he may not be always religious, any more than he is always under the influence of love, sympathy, hope, fear, doubt, &c.

§ 6.—*Religion, from its connexion with our internal feelings, is but little affected by adverse logick.*

Infidels, when they seek to subvert Christianity, deem nothing necessary but to refute logically the tenets of revelation. Logick can, however, effect nothing, till it can prevent the Scriptures from exciting religious feelings. You may endeavour to convince a man that his wife is neither handsome nor lovely; but if she produce in him the feelings of love, your logick can effect but little, though he may be unable to refute it, or to discover that your arguments are untrue.*

§ 7.—*Internal feelings enter largely into words that are not religious.*

Ghost, witch, spectre, fairy, sorcerer, and a multitude of other words, derive their principal signification from the internal feelings with which they are associated. In children often, and in adults frequently, such words are highly significant and terrible.

§ 8.—*The whole universe can be nominally analyzed into sights, sounds, tastes, feels, smells, internal feelings, thoughts, and words.*

In our second lecture, when I resolved external existences into sights, sounds, tastes, feels, and smells, I avoided any reference to existences which are not external, because I feared that they would complex a classification which was already abstruse. I should else have said, that all existences which are not external can be characteristically designated as internal feelings, thoughts, and words:—hence, that the whole universe can be nominally analyzed into sights, sounds, tastes, feels, smells, internal feelings, thoughts, and words.

§ 9.—*Our analysis is artificial; the universe can be correctly expounded by itself alone.*

You must remember that the object of my analysis is to teach you to subordinate language to nature. To effect this instruction, I must possess some mode of referring to natural existences; but if you desire to know what the universe truly is, you must dismiss my names, as well as all others, and contemplate the universe externally with your senses, and internally with your consciousness. The information thus obtained is the universe. The moment this information is clothed in language, either ar-

---

* Many men, as well as children, may be speculatively convinced that a corpse is harmless, and yet be prevented by fear from remaining alone with it at midnight.

ticulately or in thought, you are wandering from the substance
of the universe to the shadow,—from the realities of creation to
the artificial and conventional terms by which men communicate with each other; and you will infallibly become entangled
and confused with the sophistries and errours which have been
created by a long habit of estimating nature by language.

§ 10.—*Words that refer to our internal feelings are subject to
all the rules of interpretation which are enumerated in the preceding lectures.*

All that has been said in relation to the oneness and identity
of external existences (as compared with the oneness and identity of their names), applies even more violently to internal
feelings than to sights, sounds, tastes, feels, and smells. In
treatises, for instance, which have been written on our passions, appetites, emotions, &c., the internal feelings, &c., which
give significancy to the word love, are enumerated not as the
meaning of the word love, but as the acts and propensities of a
mysterious unit love, who holds his seat in the heart. Wisdom,
reason, judgment, conscience, instinct, and numerous kindred
units, are crowded into the head, where, on invisible tripods,
they sit, and hold divided dominion over the conduct, thoughts,
and feelings of the man in whom they are situated.

§ 11.—*The identity of love is as fallacious as its oneness.*

I love my dog, horse, children, property, country, &c. In each
of these applications of the word love, it refers to a feeling
which I experience; but the feelings that are thus referred to
are not as identical in nature as in name. They possess a sufficient homogeneity to make the word love appropriate to them
all; just as I discover in a whale, an anchovy, and an eel, a
sufficient homogeneity to make the word fish appropriate to
them. In both cases we should estimate the verbal identity by
the revelations of nature; but we reverse this principle, and
in both cases make the verbal identity authoritative over the
natural diversity.

§ 12.—*We subject our internal feelings to fewer verbal distinctions than our sensible information.*

The remarks which I have made on the identity of love and its oneness, apply to pity, and every other word that refers to internal feelings. Indeed, the identity which we impute to the internal feelings that are designated by one name, is responded to by nature with less strictness than the identity which we impute to the external existences that we designate by one name. If, for instance, your child should hurt itself grievously, you will be said to pity it; and if you see a wounded fly, you may pity the fly. The two feelings in you will differ much; yet, from the difficulty which men experience in indicating to each other the precise internal feeling that any event excites, we apply the word pity to both the above cases, and to a multitude of other varying cases. We are more definite with external differences. The words scarlet, red, pink, crimson, &c., designate sights which vary less from each other, than the pity which you felt for your child varies from the pity which you felt for the fly. The divisions to which we have subjected our internal feelings are gross and general. They are like the division of external objects into fish, birds, and insects; rather than like the nicer discrimination to which we refer by the words whale, grampus, porpoise, &c.

§ 13.—*Language is significant of what our senses inform us of, what we are conscious of experiencing within ourselves, and of words.*

I have now shown that words derive their signification from external existences and internal consciousness. An item of either will render a word significant, and the item will constitute the signification of the word. I stated also in my last discourse, that words themselves constitute another source of signification to words. We are so accustomed to a captious verbal philosophy, which interprets creation by words, instead of interpreting words by the realities of creation, that some person may show language to be significant of many objects, &c., which cannot be embraced by my classification. I cannot avoid this difficulty; for should I adopt his classification, another person may show still further omissions. No power exists to make all men employ the same language, and contention will continue in relation to phraseology, till men shall know that the meaning of a phrase is to be sought in the revelations of nature; and, that no diversity of phraseology is important, (except philologically,) so long as we can ascertain the natural phenomena, &c., to which the phraseology is intended to refer. Language is significant of every thing that we discover it to be significant of; but a description so general as this would fail in enabling you to individuate the signification of words to the extent which my design renders necessary.

§ 14.—*Words are significant of other words.*

We find by our dictionaries that every word may be resolved into other words. Words often possess no signification but as representatives of other words. When an Englishman first learns the French word *oui*, its signification consists in its representing the English word yes. A portion of the words which every man uses is significant on the above principle only.

§ 15.—*A word which at one time signifies a word, may, at another time, signify a sight, &c.*

Decapitate signifies to me nothing but the phrase "to cut off a head." Should I unfortunately see a person guillotined, the word decapitate might thereafter signify the sight. To circumnavigate the globe, possesses with me no meaning but certain words and phrases; but with Anson or Cook, the meaning consisted of the revelations of their senses. The word gout, which to one man is significant of words only, is to another significant of excruciating feels, &c.

§ 16.—*Some words never signify any thing but other words.*

We possess words which never signify any thing but other words. Infinity, eternity, are of this class, and antediluvian,

millennium, fairy, and Mahomet. When I read a treatise on
eternity, the whole treatise becomes in a manner the signification of the word eternity. What I read in the Holy Scriptures in
relation to it, becomes also a part of the meaning of the word.

§ 17.—*Some words of the above class, when connected with
an internal feeling, are of the most sacred character.*

God, heaven, hell, immortality, angels, and many other words
of the most awful import, are principally significant of scrip-
tural declarations, and of various other words, sentences, and
treatises; except that they are significant of certain internal
feelings also, which constitute a vivifying and essential part of
their signification to persons who happily possess such feelings
in association with the words.

§ 18.—Much errour occurs in our speculations from our not
discriminating whether we allude to the verbal meaning of a
word, to its sensible meaning, or to its meaning with reference
to our internal feelings. The malignity of the errour is increased when the diversity of meaning is deemed an ambiguity
of nature, instead of an ambiguity of language. This topick
deserves a separate elucidation, hence I shall defer it till our
next meeting.

§ 19.—*The present lecture is only introductory to succeeding
ones, which will show that speculative writers fail to discriminate between the verbal signification of a word,—its sensible
signification,—and its signification with reference to our internal feelings. They deem the variety of meaning a duplicity of
nature, instead of a property of language.*

From even the rapid glance which we have taken, we may
readily apprehend the confusion which must occur in philosophical and all other verbal speculations, if a writer fails to
discriminate between the verbal signification of a word,—its
sensible signification,—and its signification with reference to
our internal feelings; and especially if he deem the variety of
meaning an ambiguity of nature, instead of a property of lan-

guage. This topick is important, and the present discourse is merely a necessary introduction to it. I shall however defer entering on the subject till our next meeting.

Lecture XII

MUCH ERROUR OCCURS IN OUR SPECULATIONS WHEN WE OMIT TO DIS-
CRIMINATE BETWEEN THE VERBAL MEANING OF A WORD, ITS SENSIBLE
MEANING, AND ITS MEANING THAT REFERS TO OUR INTERNAL CON-
SCIOUSNESS

§ 1.—*We should discriminate between the verbal signification of a word, and the sensible signification.*

PROFESSOR BROWN says, "power is nothing but invariable antecedence." Is it nothing but those words? If he is speaking of the verbal signification of power, it may be what he says. The sensible signification I will designate algebraically, (as an unknown quantity,) by the letter x. Power is, therefore, x. But Mr. Brown says it is invariable antecedence; therefore, invariable antecedence is the same x. The like may be said of every phrase into which you may resolve the word power. The sensible signification (x) remains independent of our language, and unaffected by it. It is known alike by the savage and the philosopher. They differ widely in their theories, and verbal signification of power; but when their senses reveal to them x, their sensible knowledge is identical. A deaf mute may possess the sensible signification of power as fully as either of them.

§ 2.—*The senses alone can reveal to us the sensible signification of words.*

What then is x? Your senses alone can yield the answer. Words may direct my attention to what I should not have other-wise noted in x, but they cannot reveal to me any part of x,— they cannot perform the office of the senses. A philosopher may write a volume in simplifying power, or in complexing it; but his treatise will (however he may intend) constitute nothing but the verbal signification of power. A boy who fires a squib to show you that a spark possesses power to ignite gunpowder, differs verbally only from Professor Brown, who insists that what the boy calls power in the spark, is only an invariable antecedence. All that is sensible is alike to both, and all that is not sensible is verbal only; and cannot be thought of even, except in words.

§ 3.—*Words can yield us nothing but the verbal signification of words.*

"What we denominate form is nothing separate from the elementary atoms of a mass, and merely the relation of a number of atoms coexisting in apparent contact."[1] Thus speaks Professor Brown. We may ask, however, whether form is merely the above words. Something is ulterior to the words, if we are alluding to the sensible realities of the universe. The words can yield us but the verbal meaning of form. The sensible reality is x. The girl who in rolling up her handkerchief tells you she is forming a doll, and Professor Brown with his elaborate definition, mean the same x, if they refer to the sensible signification of the word form. The professor may laugh at the simplicity of the child, and she may laugh at the abstruseness of the professor, but they differ only verbally;—and the child is probably less in errour than he.

---

[1] In Johnson (I) the quotation is followed by:

This degradation of form is in revenge of the estimation which, under the name of substantial forms, it received from the Peripatetics: for it is with words as with men, among whom, when one has been unduly honoured, there is excited a malicious desire to withhold even the consideration which he can justly claim. We may now consider shape or form much more simple than we have heretofore supposed. Form is only the relation to each other of a number of atoms. If, however, we estimate correctly the phraseology, we shall find that we gain by it nothing. The phenomenon will not change its nature to conform to our new phraseology; but the phraseology will change its signification to conform to its new application, and mean neither more nor less than the phenomenon.

§ 4.—*We strangely confound the verbal signification of a word with the sensible signification.*

Professor Brown speaks also of a statue; thus, "the sculptor alters the form of a block of marble, not by communicating to it any new qualities, but by detaching from it a number of the corpuscles, which were included in our conception of the whole." Are these words the process by which the sculptor produces the statue? The words are but a narrative of the process. The sensible process is x. The same to which another person may refer by saying that the sculptor, by elaboration, produces the statue out of a block of marble. One expression may be more descriptive than another, and more appropriate; but nature, sturdy and unaffected by our phraseology, is known as fully to a deaf mute who has seen a statue sculptured, as to Professor Brown. Hence, we need not be surprised when Professor Brown adds, that the sculptor, "after he has given the last delicate touches that finish the Jupiter, the Venus, or Apollo,—the divine form which we admire, (as if it had assumed a new existence beneath the artist's hands,) is still the same quiescent mass that slumbered for ages in the quarry."

§ 5.—*The sensible signification of a sentence is the sensible existence to which the sentence refers.*

Is the Apollo the same quiescent mass that slumbered for ages in the quarry? This is the verbal account of its sameness. The sensible sameness is x. The same to which I may refer by saying, that the statue is transformed from what it was in the quarry. We may debate the propriety of our respective phraseology, but let us not confound verbal disquisition with the realities of creation. The sensible reality is just as we discover; and when we divest it of all names, we shall understand it better than by the most laboured verbal description.

§ 6.—*Phraseology is controlled by custom, but the sensible signification of phrases is controlled by nature.*

"Ice," says the same philosopher, "differs from water only

in this,—the particles which formerly were easily separable, now resist separation with a considerable force." Is the difference between ice and water nothing but the above words? The words may constitute the verbal difference, but a difference exists which is independent of words. The sensible difference is x. We may refer to it by the words of Professor Brown, or by the words of some other philosopher, who may deem that he is greatly improving philosophy by the introduction of some new phrase; but if we would truly understand nature, we must turn from words to the mute revelation of our senses.

[An Emperor of Siam disbelieved a Dutch embassador who related that in Holland water becomes so hard that men walk on it. Possibly, if the embassador had employed the language of Mr. Brown, the phenomenon would have seemed more probable. Hudibras says of glass, that it is only the ice of fire:—a simplification which, though used in ridicule, is like that of Mr. Brown. Both seem to give an easy reason for the phenomena to which they refer; but the ease arises from not knowing that every word has as many meanings as it has applications to different phenomena. The word ice, in the description of Hudibras, and the resistance of the particles of water in the description of Mr. Brown, mean not what they signify when employed ordinarily, but what are discoverable in ice and glass; and what we speak of with language more seemingly inexplicable.]

§ 7.—What is lightning? An old dictionary says, "it is the flash which attends thunder." The moderns laugh at this simple explanation of lightning. They call it a discharge of electrick fluid. But would we know the sensible signification of the word, we must dismiss both of the verbal meanings. The modern may be better than the ancient; but neither is lightning, except in the verbal signification of the term. Lightning, in its sensible signification, is x. The sensible signification is known to a deaf mute, as fully as to persons who can repeat a definition. The revelation of our senses can alone teach us the sensible signification of words.

§ 8.—*We cannot transmute sights, feels, &c., into words.*

What is a point? Mathematicians say it is something which possesses neither length, breadth, nor thickness. Mathematicians are right, but they are describing a verbal point. The distinction is nowhere admitted. They are attempting to resolve into words a sensible existence. The process is a delusion. Natural existences cannot be transmuted into words. Words may refer us to sensible existences, but words cannot become something that is not verbal.

§ 9.—A sensible point is wholly different from the above definition. It is x, and nothing can reveal it but our senses. So far from its possessing neither length, breadth, nor thickness, you will discover it to possess visible length and visible breadth. A visible existence without length and breadth is impossible.

§ 10.—*Logick relates to the verbal meaning of words, and its conclusions must not be confounded with sensible existences.*

Assuming that the definition is a point, and not discriminating that it is a verbal point merely, mathematicians deduce from the definition that no number of mathematical points, however congregated, can obtain either length, breadth, or thickness;— for what possesses no length, cannot acquire length by adding to it what also possesses no length, &c. The logick is incontestable, but let no man suppose it relates to more than a verbal point:—let no man mistake a process of language for the realities of the external creation.

§ 11.—Again, every material sensible substance is said to be formed by an aggregation of certain insensible atoms. But are substances formed by those words? Yes, verbally they are thus formed, and the following are some of the verbal consequences which are deduced from the premises, and mistaken for physical investigations:—"As atoms are the first matter, they must be indissoluble, or they would be corruptible; and," adds Sir

Isaac Newton, "they must be immutable also, in order to the world's continuing permanently in the same state, and of the same nature: hence," continues he, "God, in the beginning, created matter in solid, massive, hard, impenetrable, moveable atoms, incomparably harder than any of the porous bodies compounded of them;—nay, so hard as never to wear or break in pieces;—no human power being able to divide what God made one at the creation. While these particles continue entire, they may compose bodies of one and the same texture in all ages; but if they were liable to wear or break, the nature of things depending on them would be changed."

§ 12.—But now arose a difficulty: these atoms become visible and tangible when numbers of them aggregate together; hence, they cannot be as small as mathematical points,—no aggregation of which can obtain length, breadth, or thickness. Atoms, therefore, must possess length, breadth, and thickness. But whatever possesses length, breadth, and thickness, can be divided into parts; where will you begin, then, to find the elementary atoms? Begin at what fragments you please, the fragment will be composed of parts, and can be divided. Pursuing this process, you never can arrive at the constituent particles which form the elements of matter. This difficulty is as old as Aristotle, who hence denied the existence of such particles. Modern ingenuity has removed the difficulty. God, at the creation, made the atoms sufficiently small to answer his purpose, and constituted them indivisible, not from lack of parts, but from lack of penetrability; and truly when we consider that the light which a candle emits every moment consists of a greater number of these native particles than the number of all the sands on the sea shore, we may reasonably leave them without further diminution. Alas! alas! that these verbal disquisitions should be confounded with the sensible realities of creation! The disquisitions are logical and ingenious I admit. They may be scientifick and useful; and, like some other propositions, they may refer enigmatically to sensible particulars, which give them more significancy than is known to me; but we shall gain nothing by confounding verbal speculations with sensible realities.

§ 13.—If you learn by my remarks to estimate correctly the above propositions only, you will have listened to me with but little benefit; for the above positions are so glaringly discordant from sensible realities, that without any elucidation you may be willing to dismiss them as fallacies. To disclose the principles which make the propositions defective is my object; that you may estimate correctly other propositions, which, though less repugnant to sensible experience, are as radically defective as the above.

§ 14.—*We cannot enlarge our sensible knowledge by words.*

We can no more enlarge our sensible knowledge by words than you can enlarge the physical superficies of your farm by words,—or than you can disclose colours to the blind. The revolution, for instance, of the earth around its axis, and around the sun, are significant of many sensible phenomena. These constitute the sensible signification (the x) of the propositions; while all that is not sensible is verbal. The words may be interesting,—they may be logical processes, and mathematical processes; but they are not the realities of the external universe. These our senses alone can reveal to us.

§ 15.—*Sensible existences will not conform to our phraseology, but our phrases will signify the sensible existences to which the phrases refer.*

The distant landscape which we behold from our window is, we are told, a wonderfully small miniature on the retina of our eye. The distant landscape is, however, not these words. So far as your words refer to what I behold, the distant landscape is x.[*] We may talk about it as we please, but the revelation of vision can alone give me sensible information in relation to it. Your language is sensibly significant of all the sensible revelations to which it refers, but all beyond is verbal.

---

[*] For a full explanation of this subject, see Lecture XXIII.

§ 16.—*We must refer to the revelation of our senses for the meaning of words, and not refer to words for the meaning of what our senses reveal.*

But the colour of grass is certainly a sensation in our mind, and not any thing spread over the grass? I answer,—the location of the colour (if you refer to the sensible signification of location) is not words. It is x. To this you must refer for the meaning of any verbal location that you may give to colour.* If we appeal to words to explain the revelations of our senses, we are inverting the order of nature. We must appeal to our senses for the meaning of words.

§ 17.—*All that my senses disclose, and all that I am conscious of experiencing within myself, constitute the realities of nature. The rest of my knowledge is verbal.*

Our almost incessant employment of words tends to confound them with the phenomena of nature. We teach children the names of sensible existences, just as we teach them the names of the characters which compose the alphabet. The sight which we call moon, becomes to a child as much the sign of the word moon, as the sight of the character A becomes the sign of the sound which the character represents. The name and thing named become strangely confounded and identified. All our learning, from youth upwards, tends to confirm the confusion which exists between language and nature. Nothing is, however, more important to a correct understanding of language, than a subordination of it to natural existences; and this subordination cannot be effected till we discriminate between words and natural existences. Nothing is also more easy than to make the discrimination, provided you cease from speaking, both audibly in words, and inaudibly in thought.† The words which we utter in thought are as dependant on natural existences for their signification, as the words which we articulate audibly. To discriminate, therefore, the realities of nature from lan-

* Ibid.　　† See Lecture V, § 39.

guage, we must deem no words as belonging to nature, whether the words be uttered in thought or speech. All else* that your senses disclose to you, or that you can experience within your-self by any means whatever, belong to nature. They are the archetypes of which words and verbal thoughts are but the artificial types.

§ 18.—*As bank notes are the artificial representatives of specie, so words are the artificial representatives of natural phenomena.*

We employ words as though they possess, like specie, an intrinsick and natural value; rather than as though they possess, like bank notes, a merely conventional, artificial, and repre-sentative value. We must convert our words into the natural realities which the words represent, if we would understand accurately their value. Some banks, when you present their notes for redemption, will pay you in other bank notes; but we must not confound such a payment with an actual liquidation in specie. We shall still possess, in the new notes, nothing but the representatives of specie. In like manner, when you seek the meaning of a word, you may obtain its conversion into other words, or into some verbal thoughts; but you must not confound such a meaning with the phenomena of nature. You will still possess in the new words, nothing but the representatives of natural existences.

§ 19.—*When words attempt more than a reference to the rev-elation of our senses, the words may possess a verbal meaning, but not a sensible meaning.*

Every writer who treats of physicks, seems to carry on a game of bo-peep between nature and language. The verbal meaning of a word, and its sensible meaning, are so confounded, (the writer referring at one moment to the verbal meaning, and at the next to the sensible meaning,) that a reader usually ac-quires by his study, a knowledge of the verbal ingenuity of man,

---

* Words also belong to nature in their character of unmeaning sounds.

but not a knowledge of the sensible realities of the universe. I wish not to depreciate verbal learning, but to mark distinctly the boundaries between what is verbal and what is sensible. Our senses alone can reveal to us sensible realities; and the moment words attempt to express more than our senses discover, the words lose all sensible signification, how much soever they may retain a verbal signification.

§ 20.—*The sensible signification of a theory is the sensible phenomena to which the theory refers.*

At one period a philosopher would say, that lightning is the effluvia of sulphureous and nitrous bodies, which meet in the air, and ignite by means of a strong fermentation. This was probably better than to say with the ancients, that lightning is an instrument of vengeance, formed by the Cyclops for the use of Jove. Both theories have been superseded by electricity; hence we may reasonably suppose, that the electrick theory is better than its predecessors; but they all are alike limited in sensible signification, to the sensible particulars to which they refer.* The sensible phenomena to which a theory refers can be revealed by the senses only, and must not be confounded with the theory, except to control its sensible signification. A change of theory is not always founded on an accession of sensible knowledge. While we laugh at the ancients for deeming lightning a manufacture of the Cyclops, the sensible knowledge possessed by the ancients in relation to lightning may have been equal to ours. I believe it was equal, with the exception of some electrical experiments. Persons who are unacquainted with the distinction which exists between verbal learning, and the sensible realities of nature, contrast too disparagingly to the unlearned, the amount of sensible knowledge which the unlearned possess, in comparison with the sensible knowledge possessed by the learned. The amount of sensible knowledge possessed by those who are learned in theories, is not necessarily greater

* See Lecture XVIII.

than that possessed by a man who may be acquainted with no theory.

§ 21.—*We confound theories with the realities of nature.*

In the Polynesian Researches, published lately in London, the author, in speaking of some islands in the Pacifick ocean, says, "The tide is here very singular. If influenced at all by the moon, it is in a very small degree only. The height to which the water rises, varies but a few inches during the whole year. Whatever be the age or situation of the moon, the water is lowest at six in the morning, and the same hour in the evening, and highest at noon and midnight." The writer seems embarrassed by the usual confusion of words with sensible realities. He evidently is seeking in nature for "the influence of the moon," instead of seeking in nature for the sensible meaning of those words. To me, nothing is less surprising than the facts to which he refers, because I know that the sensible signification of those words is nothing but numerous and various sensible incidents which we discover in different seas. If the seas to which the writer alludes exhibit nothing that can yield those words a sensible signification, I shall not deem the circumstance a wonder of nature, but an instance of inapplicability in an ingenious verbal contrivance of man.

§ 22.—*Every theory possesses a verbal meaning as well as a sensible.*

The star α Draconis is 400,000 times more distant from the earth than the sun, or 38,000,000,000,000 miles distant. I object not to this verbal distance. It is, I presume, scientifically and mathematically deduced; but let no man confound it with the sensible realities of nature. The sensible meaning of the alleged distance is not the sights and feels that distance ordinarily designates, but something which, when it shall be disclosed to your senses by astronomers, will be found to consist of but a few very simple celestial appearances. The verbal meaning of the distance is different. It relates to various mathematical processes. So long as the verbal meaning is thus discriminated from the sensible meaning, no astonishment nor incredulity will be excited by the proposition. Astronomers are, however, constantly endeavouring to confound the verbal meaning with the sensible meaning. They seem to glory in the confusion, and to derive an homage to their science from the shadowy misconception.

§ 23.—*We cannot transmute sights, feels, &c., into words, though we strive after the transmutation with an entire unconsciousness that we are transmuting one sentence only into another.*

"When I touch a stone," says Professor Beattie, in his Essay on Truth, "I become conscious of a certain sensation, which I call hardness; but this sensation is not hardness itself, nor any thing like hardness:—it is nothing more than"—what, think you? Nothing more than just what it is. Language can only name it, and naming it will only mislead us. We shall best understand the natural signification of the word hardness by dispensing with all language, and accepting as a signification the mute revelation of our senses. But such a procedure does not suit Professor Beattie. He says, that hardness is nothing more "than a sensation or feeling in my mind, accompanied, however, with an irresistible belief, that the sensation is excited by the application of an external and hard substance to some part of my body."

§ 24.—Let us examine the above:—"When I touch a stone, the sensation is nothing more than a feeling in my mind," &c. Is the sensation nothing but those words? No—it is x, and no words can supply its place. Words can only name it, or refer us to our experience. You may deny Mr. Beattie's definition, and say with me, that hardness is nothing but a name given to designate a feel, &c.; but let us not deceive ourselves by supposing that either of our verbal designations is hardness. We may convert the word into such other words as we deem appropriate, and we may wrangle about the propriety of our expressions; but the sensible signification of hardness is not convertible into words. It is communicable by our senses only.

§ 25.—*Words are sometimes the ultimate meaning of words.*

What is conscience? The dictionary says, "the faculty by which a man judges of the moral quality of his own actions." But conscience is not these words. What is conscience apart from words? It is x. And what is x? What I experience within myself. If I experience nothing within myself; if I employ the word conscience with reference to nothing but the dictionary definitions, or some other words, the x will signify those words. The x will in every case signify the ultimate meaning of the word to which it is applied, whether the ultimate meaning be words, the information of my senses, or an internal feeling, &c.

§ 26.—*In all discussions, we should discriminate whether we are attempting to define a word, or to designate an existence.*

What is the moon? If an infant were to ask me this question, I might tell him to go into the street, and on looking towards the sky, he would discover something that looks like a large round piece of silver. That is the moon. You may say that my designation will not enable the child to find the moon, and you may give him some better description. We probably shall not altercate, because we shall understand that our words are intended to merely point out to the child something that is different from the words. But suppose I were to ask a philosopher to tell me what the moon is; he might say that the moon is an opaque globe of land and water, like our earth. He is not attempting to designate an existence, as I did to the child; but he is defining the word moon. My words were not supposed to be the moon itself; but the philosopher's definition is the moon verbally at least. You probably now understand what I mean by saying, that in all verbal discussions we should discriminate whether we are attempting to define a word, or to designate an existence. The discrimination is seldom made, and the want of it produces much contention and confusion.

§ 27.—What is the human soul? "The immortal part of man," says a universalist. "The living, accountable spirit," says an orthodox divine. "The thinking substance," says a deist. They may contend vehemently; but they should know what they are attempting to accomplish. If they wish to ascertain the best verbal definition of the word soul, they may contend for that object in the above language, or in any which they prefer. But the soul itself, so far as the word names an existence, is not the above words, nor any other. It is *x*. Would you know what it is in nature, you must dismiss all words, (both those of speech and those of thought,) and seek the meaning of the word soul in the mute revelation of your senses, and the equally mute revelation of your internal experience. When you have thus found the meaning of the word soul, you may endeavour to designate to me the phenomena that you have discovered. No man will care what words you employ in this designation, so long as he understands that your object is only to direct his studies or consciousness to some revelations of nature.

§ 28.—*We mistake for sensible investigations, what are only verbal deductions from artificial definitions.*

The Cyclopedia says, "Matter is an extended, solid, divisible, moveable, passive substance, the first principle of all natural things, from the various arrangements and combinations whereof all bodies are formed." But matter is not these words. They constitute the verbal meaning of the word matter. Not, however, noting the distinction, every philosopher resolves matter into a definition, and then reasons about his definition, believing that he is discussing the sensible realities of creation, while he is discussing nothing but verbal consequences deduced from his definition. The Cartesians, for instance, resolve matter into solidity, divisibility, &c., and infer thence that as solidity nor divisibility can exist without extension, extension must exist before any thing can be solid or divisible;—therefore extension alone is the essential property of matter.

§ 29.—Doctor Clarke dissents from the above conclusion of Descartes; for "if extension were the essence of matter, space would be matter; and as space is infinite and eternal, matter would be infinite and eternal, and could be neither created nor annihilated. Besides, the nature of gravity, the motion of comets, and the vibration of pendulums, prove space to be immaterial; hence, extension is not the essence of matter." Nothing can be more acute and logical than these discussions; but to suppose that they are physical investigations, is to confound words with things. So far as the deductions refer to sensible information, they belong to the external realities of nature; but so far as they are verbal deductions from the definition of the word matter, they are mere processes of language. Every definition is analogous to a sum in arithmetick. The figures may be multiplied, subtracted, added, and divided, by virtue of the general laws which regulate numbers; but the result may not indicate any thing which exists in nature: so the words which compose a definition may be ratiocinated by virtue of the general laws that regulate words; but the result may not indicate any thing which exists in nature.

§ 30.—The errour to which I refer, of mistaking verbal deductions for sensible realities, is perhaps sufficiently exemplified in the above instances, but I will state another:—Newton defined all material bodies to be a congeries of corpuscles uniform and alike; and hence inferred that the difference which bodies exhibit in colour, hardness, taste, &c., results from the different arrangement only of the corpuscles of which the bodies are composed. You perceive that the conclusion proceeds from the definition as irresistibly, as that a moon multiplied by twenty becomes twenty moons; but whether nature conforms to either the multiplication or the deduction, depends on nature, and not on the processes of multiplication and logick. The sensible reality is not necessarily connected with the verbal process, or the mathematical process.

§ 31.—*We mistake words for things.*

But after material bodies are all resolved thus into little verbal corpuscles of a uniform size and shape, how came they to arrange themselves together so as to form gross, sensible bodies, of different shapes and sizes? and even how do they adhere together at all? Locke deemed this a great, and even undiscoverable mystery; and nothing is more evident from his remarks, than that he expected no other answer than a quantity of words. How curious a delusion! The object sought is the sensible cohesion of matter into various shapes, sizes, &c.; and the answer is not to be any revelation of the senses, but some sentences of words. What a curious mistake of words for things!

§ 32.—Newton eventually furnished the answer: "Every particle of matter possesses an attractive power, or a tendency to every other particle. The power is strongest in the point of contact, and decreases so suddenly, that it acts not, where any distance is discoverable by our senses. At a greater distance than that which produces attraction, the particles possess a repellent power, and fly from each other."

§ 33.—I will not say that Newton, or any other person, believes that the above words constitute the cement which holds together the particles of matter, and forms them into different shapes, sizes, &c.; but, practically, the words are deemed the cement in the reasoning of philosophers; who, while they are investigating the relation of the words to each other, seem to believe that they are investigating the realities of the external creation: hence, Newton says further, "the smallest particles cohere by the strongest attractions, and compose bigger particles of weaker virtue; and many of these may cohere and compose still bigger particles, whose virtue is still weaker; and so on for divers successions, till the progressions end in the biggest particles on which the operations in chymistry depend, and the colours of natural bodies. The particles, when thus enlarged, still further cohere, till they become sufficiently large to be discoverable by our senses. If the body which they ultimately compose is compact, and bends or yields inward to pressure, (without any sliding of its parts,) and returns to its figure with a force arising from the attraction of its parts, it is hard and elastick;—if the parts slide from one another, the body is malleable or soft;—if they slip easily, and are of a fit size to be agitated by heat, and the natural heat is great enough to keep them in agitation, the body is fluid;—and if it be apt to stick to things, it is humid." These are some of the speculations of Newton—as wise a man as ever lived, but unacquainted with the true character of language. What a waste of effort! and all from not discovering the difference between words and the realities of nature;—from not seeing that the words into which he resolves matter, are not natural matter, but verbal matter; and that his deductions are not physical facts, but verbal consequences of his verbal premises.

PART THIRD

OF LANGUAGE WITH REFERENCE TO THE RELATION
WHICH WORDS BEAR TO EACH OTHER

Lecture XIII

WHEN Agib, the son of Zorader, desired knowledge, he was commanded by a venerable Lama of Thibet, to seek knowledge amid the stones which lie scattered over the peninsula of Guzurat. Agib was discouraged. "Behold!" said he, "the stones are countless; the way is also through the jungle of the tiger, and beset with the ravenous boa." "Ascend, then," said the Lama, "the heights of Caucasus, and seek knowledge among the birds which periodically pass from the Black sea to the Caspian." "Alas!" exclaimed Agib, "the mountain is infested with hostile tribes, and eternal snows disform its summit." "Go, then," said the Lama, "to the beautiful valley which lies before us; penetrate the earth, and knowledge shall be disclosed."

Agib departed. The sun burst from a cloud that had just irrigated the fields. Birds filled the air with harmony. Odours refreshed every breeze, and all nature was animation and beauty. Agib approached joyfully the spot which the Lama had designated. "Now," exclaimed he, "knowledge shall become my possession. Age shall admire my attainments, and youth contend to show me honour." He cast aside a mantle by which his efforts might be impeded, and excavated the earth with activity. Soon, however, the soil became compact, and the strength of Agib less efficient, when the appearance of a mass of stone seemed to preclude all further progress. Agib returned to the Lama, who decided that the stones must be removed. By great labour he removed them, and the cavity was immediately filled with water. In despair Agib again besought the Lama, who commanded that the water should be exhausted. Agib exhausted the water, still nothing was discoverable but a bed of slate. Bruised and dejected, he once more informed the Lama. "Sluggard!" exclaimed the weary priest, "what did you expect to find? You have discovered a ledge of stone that may build temples: you have disclosed a spring which may cherish herds; and more, you have ascertained that though knowledge may be pleasant and profitable, the pursuit of it is laborious and painful."

We probably need not the experience of Agib to teach us that every thing estimable must be costly. Providence seems to impress this law on all the blessings with which we are surrounded. Even health cannot be retained without labour, nor reputation, without a constant warfare against evil enticements. Summon, then, all your resolution to proceed with our investigations, though they should increase your information but a little. If knowledge were attainable without effort, it might possess, like air and water, a theoretical homage; but it would command no practical reverence.

§ 1.—*Reasoning can effect no more than to show us that the conclusion is admitted by the premises.*

My preceding lectures discuss the signification of words. I propose to speak now of the power by which language commands our assent to certain propositions; for instance, why are we forced to admit that a half is less than the whole?

§ 2.—We assent to a proposition when we find that the premises affirm the conclusion. This is the whole process of argumentation. The most elaborate reasoning can effect no more than to show us that the conclusion is admitted by the premises. Why, then, is a half less than a whole? Because the term half admits that it is less:—no other reason exists.

§ 3.—"The table which we see seems," says Hume, "to diminish as we remove from it; but the real table (which exists independently of us) suffers no alteration. What we see is, therefore, nothing," continues Hume, "but the image of the real table."

§ 4.—Why? Because the premises include an admission that the table which we see is not the real table. Those who discover that the premises affirm this conclusion, will assent to the deduction; while others will be unconvinced.

§ 5.—"If we are unable to discover truth, the defect," says Plato, "must arise from one of two causes; either no truth exists, or man's faculties are inadequate to its discovery."

§ 6.—Why are we driven to this alternative? Because, to say that we are unable to discover truth, admits Plato's conclusions. Those only will assent to the dilemma, who see that it is included in the premises; other persons will say that they require further proof.

§ 7.—Carneades held, that the senses, the understanding, and the imagination, frequently deceive us; and therefore cannot be infallible. Why? Because, to admit that they frequently deceive us, implies that they are fallible.

§ 8.—No truth has been more voluminously enforced than the existence of God; still, those who essay to prove verbally this position, (by any other authority than revelation,) must proceed in the manner which I have stated. The arguments generally employed, are the marks of design everywhere apparent, and the impossibility of a creation without a creator. But why can we not suppose a creation without a creator? Because the word creation includes the admission of a creator. In the same way, the word contrivance admits a contriver; the word design admits a designer; and the word paintings admits a painter.

§ 9.—"All the universe," says Hume, "exhibits harmony. Every thing is adjusted to every thing. One design pervades the whole, and this uniformity leads the mind to acknowledge one author."

§ 10.—Why? Because, to say that every thing is adjusted to every thing, and one design pervades the whole, admits an adjuster and a designer.

§ 11.—Again, he says, "the whole face of nature bespeaks an intelligent author, and no rational inquirer can suspend his belief a moment with regard to the primary principles of genuine theism."

§ 12.—But how does the face of nature bespeak an intelligent author? Because it bespeaks intelligence. But how does the face of nature bespeak an author? Because I see in it a design, contrivance, and creation. Before the conclusions of Hume are inevitable, we must admit these premises, which tacitly embrace the conclusions.

§ 13.—The Edinburgh Encyclopedia says: "there must be a self-existent being." Why? Because, if every thing which exists was created by another, we can never arrive at a beginning. If A was created by B, who created B? D. Who created D? E. Who created E? and thus we may proceed illimitably. But every series includes tacitly the admission of a beginning: hence we must eventually arrest our progression, and admit a self-existent being.

§ 14.—*When our conclusions are not obviously admitted by our premises, we explain the premises so as to show that they embrace the conclusion. The explanation is sometimes in the form of proofs, and sometimes a definition.*

Paley's Natural Theology says, "neither the universe nor any part of it can be the Deity." Why? for the only reason that can be given in any argument:—the premises affirm the conclusion. But every person may not see that the premises affirm the conclusion, hence the writer adduces proofs: that is, he teaches us how we may discover that the premises admit his conclusion. He says, "the universe is merely a collective name; its parts are all which are real. Now inert matter cannot be the Deity, nor can organized substances, for they include marks of contrivance; and whatever includes marks of contrivance, carries us to something beyond itself, to a contriver who is prior to the thing contrived, and different from it."

§ 15.—But why cannot the inert parts of the universe be the Deity? Because the term inert negatives such a conclusion. But the organized parts also cannot? No. Because the word organized admits an organizer, and Deity is impliedly self-existent.

§ 16.—"No animal," continues the same writer, "can have contrived its own limbs and senses." Why? Because an implication attaches to the premises, that an animal cannot exist till its limbs and senses have been contrived.

§ 17.—"Nothing," he adds, "can be God which is ordered by a wisdom and a will superior to its own; and nothing can be God which is indebted for any of its properties to a contrivance beyond itself."

§ 18.—Why? For one reason only; the word God excludes from its signification these consequences. Lest we might not know this, and hence not assent to his conclusions, Mr. Paley furnishes the word with a definition: thus, he says, "having in its nature what requires the exertion of no prior being, appertains to the Deity as an essential distinction, and removes his nature from that of all other beings."

§ 19.—He says further: "since something must have existed from eternity, it is frequently asked why the universe may not be that something." He answers, "the contrivance perceived in it proves that to be impossible, for the contriver must have existed before the contrivance." Why? Because the word contrivance implies such a conclusion:—no other reason exists. But why must something have existed from eternity? Because, to say that any thing is produced, admits a producer; to say that any thing is made, admits a maker; to say that any thing exists, admits a cause: hence, how ancient soever the universe may be, something must have preceded it; something must have existed from eternity.

§ 20.—That the earth must be globular, is a conclusion which also language forces us to adopt. In a plane, we tacitly admit that some place exists where the plane terminates, where we may step or fall off. But we discover no such on the earth, hence the earth is not a plane. What shape, then, must the earth possess? Globular. Why? Because, to say that no precipitous termination exists, implies globosity. From a like necessity, we create antipodes, and all the other wonders inculcated by astronomy.

§ 21.—In Gill's Body of Divinity, the author says, "though angels are not endued with bodies, yet, as they are creatures, they must exist somewhere." Why? Because the consequence is included in the meaning which he attaches to the premises, that angels are creatures. He proceeds to ask where they could exist before the heavens and the earth were made, and concludes that they could exist nowhere. Why? Because the somewhere which he deems necessary, is included either in heaven or earth. The object of the author is to prove that angels were made subsequently to the heavens: a conclusion which is but an iteration of his previous admissions.

§ 22.—"Every object, how gorgeous soever its colour in the light, is void of colour in the dark." Perhaps you will not assent to this proposition, though you will admit that colour is invisible in the dark. Natural philosophy proceeds, therefore, as follows: "colour is the reflection of certain coloured rays of light."

Admit this, and objects become remedilessly void of colour in the dark.* If you cannot apprehend this consequence, the following arguments may convince you, for they will show you that the consequence is included in the premises:—thus, colour is nothing but the reflection of certain coloured rays of light; hence, where no light exists, no reflection of coloured rays can exist; therefore, all objects are void of colour in the dark, however they may be endued with the conformation of parts

---

* When a tradesman brings me an account which asserts that I am his debtor, say a hundred dollars, I may be sure that the aggregate is fairly stated, for few men are careless enough to commit an errour in addition. The items of the bill may require examination. So, when a logician tells me the conclusion to which he is arrived by any process of argumentation, I seldom care to investigate his arguments. I assume that he will not make a false deduction, any more than the tradesman will make a false addition. The part which requires examination is the logician's premises;—these are like the tradesman's items. Most people, however, waste all their attention on a logician's arguments, and let him assume what premises he pleases. This is analogous to permitting a tradesman to charge you without restraint, provided he will be honest in his addition of the items.

that adapts them to reflect in the light its most gorgeous rays.

§ 23.—*Propositions are sophistical when the conclusion is only seemingly (not actually) included in the premises.*

Professor Stewart says, "a few moments' reflection must satisfy any one, that the sensation of colour can reside in the mind only; yet our constant bias is to connect colour with external objects."

But why cannot colour be connected with external objects? Because the premises affirm it to be a sensation in the mind. The proposition of Professor Stewart is, however, sophistical. In the premises he speaks of the *sensation* of colour, and in the conclusion he speaks of *colour itself*. A man may therefore say, that the sensation of colour resides in the mind, and yet the colour itself is connected with the external object.

§ 24.—*Sometimes the premises are made to admit very covertly the conclusion.*

"That light, itself a body, should pass freely through solid crystal, is regarded by us," says Professor Brown, "as a physical wonder."

Why? Because, to say light is "itself a body," includes an admission that it should encounter a difficulty in passing through "solid crystal." This is a striking illustration of the indirect method by which premises may be made to affirm a conclusion. To say simply that light passes through solid crystal, would exhibit no reason why it should not pass; but when we add that light is "itself a body," we discover at once that it should encounter opposition.

§ 25.—*Similar principles with the foregoing govern our assent to mathematical propositions.*

Proposition IV, Theorem 1st, in the first book of Euclid, says:—"Let ABC, DEF, be two triangles, which have the two sides, AB, AC, equal to the two sides, DE, DF, each to each; viz, AB to DE, and AC to DF; and the angle BAC, equal to the angle EDF: the base BC shall be equal to the base EF."

That the base BC is equal to the base EF, is evidently admitted by the premises, which affirm that the angle BAC is equal to the angle EDF, and the sides AB, AC, equal to the sides DE, DF. But let us examine if the proof adduced by Euclid changes the character of the process. He says, if the triangle ABC be applied to DEF, so that the point A may be on D, and the straight line AB upon DE; the point B shall coincide with the point E. I would ask why? Because, says

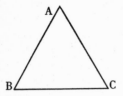 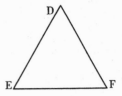

Euclid, AB is admitted to be equal to DE. The proof, then, thus far, is avowedly an admission of the premises.

§ 26.—The process is continued: thus AB, coinciding with DE, AC shall coincide with DF. Why? Because, says the demonstration, the angle BAC is admitted to be equal to the angle EDF; but why does this prove that AC must coincide with DF? It will not prove it to those who do not discover that the coincidence is included in the admitted equality of the two angles. Our assent is governed by this discovery alone.

§ 27.—A process, similar to what we have already investigated, is repeated to show that the point C must coincide with the point F; wherefore, says the demonstration, as the point B also coincides with the point E, the base BC shall coincide with the base EF. Why? Because, says Euclid, if the base BC does not coincide with the base EF, two straight lines would inclose a space. And how do you prove that two straight lines cannot inclose a space? By an admission in the tenth axiom that they cannot. Two straight lines, says the axiom, cannot inclose a space.

§ 28.—In this theorem, then, the proofs are effected by show-ing that the points in debate are admitted either by the premises of the proposition, or by axioms, &c. I have operated on a theorem which is more easily analyzed than any other in Euclid, because the subsequent theorems are demonstrated by preced-ing ones: still, the same principle will be found in all.

§ 29.—*Are the foregoing principles of language conven-tional, or a dictate of our sensible experience with physical bodies?*

I have now shown, that we assent to a proposition when we discover that the premises affirm the conclusion; and that proofs and arguments effect nothing but to show us that such an affir-mation exists. I have investigated this subject too cursorily, but I will leave it, and proceed to show why certain premises affirm certain conclusions: for instance, why the word half implies that it is less than the whole. Perhaps you will say, that the meaning of the word half admits that it is less than the whole; but I ask how it acquires this meaning? If you say, that common consent concurs in attaching this signification to the word, I ask how common consent came to this concurrence? Finally, is the conclusion forced on us arbitrarily by the framers of language, that a half is less than a whole? or does the conclusion depend on some principle which is superiour to any such dictation? The answer to this question will constitute the subject of my next lecture.

Lecture XIV

OUR ASSENT TO ANY PROPOSITION IS FOUNDED ON OUR SENSIBLE EXPERIENCE

FOR THE eccentrick adventures with which it abounds, I occa-sionally visit the valley of imagination. In a recent excursion thither, I noted a young woman who was fleeing, as for her life. Her speed was impeded by an infant, which she held with some tenderness, while her face was suffused with tears. She fled from a monster, whose body was luminous and deformed. He seemed confident of his victim, and pursued her with increasing ardour. She arrived at a river, and turning to ascertain the proximity of her pursuer, plunged the infant in the stream.

When thus disencumbered, whether she succeeded in her retreat I discovered not; for my attention was arrested by two young men, who were preparing to encounter each other in mortal combat. Both would gladly have suspended their intent; but when a relenting thought occurred to either, the monster whom I lately saw appeared, and with threatening gestures frightened the youth from his pacifick contemplations.

Who is this potent being, who can urge a mother to immolate her infant, and terrify two gallant youths to the sacrifice of life? "The monster whom you saw first is SHAME," replied a loiterer like myself; "the second is an impostor, who bears the name only of the former. Shame is the offspring of crime, but false shame is the descendant of folly. The first is justly feared; for whoever falls within his power, he impresses with a mark which burns intensely and durably. The second also affixes his mark on those whom he overtakes; but though it pains for a period, it assuages, and the subject of his malice learns to contemn the monster and his assaults."

This allegory bears but slightly on our subject; but these lectures would long since have yielded to the distractions of business, and the absence of extrinsick impulse, did not the fear of one of these monsters deter me from abandoning a labour publickly undertaken. The motive for perseverance is therefore not very alluring; but, as it is, proceed we with our discussions.

§ 1.—*The incongruity and congruity of any two assertions are the result of our experience.*

Why cannot the same thing both be and not be? Because the proposition contains two assertions which negative each other. How came the assertions by meanings so opposite? By the consent of mankind. But what united on these opposite meanings the consent of mankind? We may proceed thus in an endless train of assertions, without arriving at a satisfactory result. You will, however, remember that I promised to show in this lecture the reasons which compel us to yield our assent to propositions like the above. I proceed to the undertaking.

§ 2.—The necessity for our assent to such propositions is founded on our sensible experience: thus, I can show you a knife, and tell you that the knife is visible. I can remove the knife, and tell you it is invisible. But why cannot the knife be both visible and invisible at the same time? Try if you can effect such a coincidence, and you will discover why. The impossibility is what you will experience. It possesses no other meaning.

§ 3.—*The congruity and incongruity of any two assertions are not the results of the conventional meaning of words.*

Why cannot the same spot be, at the same time, both white and black? Because the word white implies that the spot is not black. But how came white by this implication? Was it arbitrarily imposed by the framers of language? No. The incompatibility of the two colours is a result of experience. If I assert that the same spot cannot be both white and hard, the proposition will be untrue. Why? Because my senses can discover such a coincidence. No other reason exists.

§ 4.—*The axioms of geometry are no otherwise authoritative than as they refer to our sensible experience.*

The axioms of geometry depend for their authority on similar principles. Why are things which are equal to the same, equal to one another? "Because," says Mr. Campbell, "the two expressions are equivalent to each other." But what makes them equivalent? "The latter part of the phrase being a definition only of the former." This satisfied Mr. Campbell; but I ask further, what makes the latter part a definition of the former? We may continue such questions interminably. The axiom means nothing but a reference to our sensible experience. Look,

I can say, at these sticks. Those which are marked A and B are severally equal in height to the stick C. Why, now, must A and B be equal in height to each other? Endeavour to produce a different result, and you will discover that the equality is unavoidable. The necessity is not verbal, nor logical, nor dependant on common consent. It is what you will discover by the experiment. The necessity possesses no other archetype in nature. Independently of experience, we should no more know that A and B must produce the sight and feel that we call equal height, than that they must smell or taste alike.

§ 5.—*A contrivance implies a contriver, because the implication refers to our sensible experience.*

The word contrivance forces us to acknowledge a contriver. Why? Because contrivance contains an admission that it is the effort of some person whom we thence call a contriver. Yet how came the word contrivance to include such an admission? Is it an arbitrary fiat of those who framed the word? No: the admission proceeds from our sensible experience—thus, I can tell you that I am completing a contrivance which will catch birds. What is the contrivance? A trap—behold it! Do you ask why this contrivance implies a contriver? Try to produce such a contrivance without exerting some agency, and you will discover why a contriver is necessary.

§ 6.—*Existence implies a beginning, because the implication refers to our experience.*

Again: to assert that any thing exists, admits a period when the object commenced existing. Why? Because, to suppose an existence which never had a commencement, is absurd. Yet why is such a supposition absurd? We may proceed interminably with such questions, unless we appeal from words to the sensible objects which the words signify; when we shall easily discover the necessity that impels us to admit a commencement. What is an existence? This house is an existence. What is a beginning, when applied to the house? That which I can show you where men are building. Why, then, does this existence imply a beginning? Because the operations which I have exhibited to you must precede the house. Why must they? Attempt to build a house without them, and you will discover. No other reason is effectual.

§ 7.—*Time which is not present must be either past or future, because the position is verified by our experience.*

I can say that time which is not present, must be either future or past. Why must it? Because time is divided into present, past, and future. A negation of the present implies, therefore, that the remainder is either future or past. But whence arises this implication? We may, without end and without instruction, proceed in such inquiries; but if we resort to the sensible phenomena to which the words allude, we shall soon discover why time that is not present must be either past or future. Thus: if the table at which I am standing is not now touched by me, I have either touched it already, or shall touch it hereafter; or I shall never be able to assert with truth that I have touched the table. Why? Make the experiment, and you will discover. When you have found that your efforts cannot controvert my position, you may be told that the results are one meaning of the assertion, that time which is not present is either past or future.

§ 8.—*That ice cannot be hot is an experimental incongruity.*

Ice cannot be hot. Why? Because the name implies that it is not hot. But how came it by this implication? From experience only. The impossibility alludes to what you can discover if you attempt to heat ice: apart therefrom, no incompatibility exists.

§ 9.—*All the implications of language, all its congruities and incongruities, must be interpreted by our sensible experience. They signify nothing more.*

Things which are double of the same are equal to one another. Why? Because, to admit that A and B are severally double of C, is to admit that A is equal to B. But why? Because the words imply the equality. Yet whence the implication? The necessity admits a final explication through our senses only. Endeavour to make both A and B double the length of C, without making A as long as B. You will then discover why A must be as long as B. The necessity is precisely what you will experience.

§ 10.—Again: the whole is greater than a part. Why? The word whole implies that it is greater. How came it by such an implication? After we have bandied questions and answers till we are disgusted with trifling, we may appeal to our sensible experience, and discover readily why the whole is greater. Why, then, must the whole of an orange be greater than a part? Endeavour to prevent it, and you will discover.

§ 11.—But can I not apply the axiom where no existence is discoverable?—Can I not say, that the whole of an invisible atom is greater than a part? You can; and this forms one of the most subtile and common delusions to which language subjects us. The consideration of it will constitute our next lecture. The present discourse shows that a part of an orange is less than the whole, by reason of our finding from experience that the result is inevitable. In my next lecture I shall show that the proposition is wrested from the orange, and other sensible objects, and applied to invisible atoms, &c., where the necessity exists in the forms of language only. This application is the basis of nearly every metaphysical speculation. It is the magician's wand which transports us from a world of grave realities into regions where even our solid and firm-fixed earth revolves in a giddy velocity of many hundred miles during every instant of time; where the inhabitants bear severally fourteen tons of atmospherick pressure; where antipodes exist, whose heads are diametrically opposite to those of other men; and where the smallest line may be divided interminably, becoming less for ever, without extinction. The difference, you perceive, is important, between propositions which experience forces us to assent to, and propositions which the forms of language compel us to admit. The first surprise us with no chimeras or gorgons dire. Every result is precisely what coincides with our daily occupations. It furnishes us with a stable earth, with an erect and congenial position for our heads, and with an agreeable levity of atmosphere. In the midst of these comforts we will end the present lecture.

Lecture XV

AFTER SENSIBLE EXPERIENCE COMMANDS OUR ASSENT TO CERTAIN FORMS OF SPEECH, WE APPLY THE FORMS WHERE NO SENSIBLE PHENOMENA ARE DISCOVERABLE

§ 1.—IN MY last lecture, I showed that when we say the whole of an orange is greater than a part, we admit the position because experience has taught us that the conclusion is inevitable. The same principle governs our assent when we say that every design implies a designer, and every creation implies a creator.

§ 2.—*The implications of language, and the congruities and incongruities of words to each other, though significant of nothing but our sensible experience,* are applied often where nothing sensible is discoverable.*

I said further, that we restrict not to oranges, &c., the assertion that the whole is greater than a part; but we apply it where the words refer to no sensible existence. I characterized this as the most subtile delusion to which language exposes us. The detection of this delusion is to constitute the present lecture.

§ 3.—*The word created owes to our experience its predicability; hence, its predicability is not significant beyond our experience.*

What is the meaning of created? I can see a brickmaker create bricks. I can hear sounds created. You can tell me to place a piece of sugar in my mouth, and it will create a taste; or to press my hand against a needle, and it will create pain. Each of these processes furnishes a meaning of the word created. It is the name of these processes. But what do I mean by apply-

---

* See Lecture XI.

ing the word created to the sun? The bricks are one existence, and the word created refers to something which is different from the bricks; but when created is applied to the sun, I refer to nothing but the sun itself.*

§ 4.—But the sun exists, and must not every existence have been created? The necessity is verbal, and language is a contrivance of men, and significant of their experience only. A creation is necessary to bricks, as we shall experience when we attempt to produce a brick without some creative process; but when we apply the same language to the sun, the necessity refers to nothing, and signifies nothing.†

§ 5.—Still, we discover that a brick must be created ere it can exist; that a boat, house, or basket, cannot exist without a previous creation; and shall we suppose that the sun can exist without a previous creation? I answer, that the word created is merely a name invented by men to refer to some of their operations and actions: when thus used, created is significant; but when we apply it to the sun, where no process is apparent, the word returns to the original insignificance which it possessed before men applied it to the purposes of language; that is, it becomes an unmeaning sound.

§ 6.—*Words possess no inherent signification. Their signification must be interpreted by what we see, feel, taste, smell, and hear. Words possess also no inherent predicability. Their predicability must be interpreted by what we see, feel, taste, smell, and hear.*

This doctrine must be abstruse to persons who have never esteemed language as a collection of mere sounds, that owe all their signification to the objects, &c., to which they refer. That nothing can exist without a previous creation is, besides, a proposition which applies significantly to so many objects, that

---

* Unless I refer to the declarations of revelation. Created has then a signification which is independent of the appearance of the sun. This remark must be remembered in every similar case.

† See Lecture IX, passim.

we cannot wonder it should be deemed universally applicable. The housewife who applies the proposition to her bread, means that the loaf would not have existed had she not wet the flour and kneaded the dough. The miller who applies it to the flour, means that the flour would not have existed had he not subjected the wheat to the operations of his mill; and the husbandman who applies it to the wheat, refers to his seeding the earth, and to various phenomena from seed time to harvest. Suppose, however, we say that the earth could not have existed without a previous creation; we allude to nothing but the earth itself. When we think that we allude further, we mean merely that bread cannot exist without a previous creation; that flour, wheat, bricks, &c., cannot exist without a previous creation.*

§ 7.—But are we not sure that a period existed when the being of the sun commenced? This question is like the former. If I say that a period existed when every brick commenced its being, you may ask what I mean. I shall again show you the operations of a brickmaker, and designate what I mean. But why must the existence of every brick have a commencement? Try to produce a brick without, and you will discover. The necessity is what you will experience. That a house, ship, tree, or an animal, must have a commencement, refers to some sensible operation; but when the word is applied to the sun, it confessedly refers to nothing, and is therefore a sound divested of signification.†

§ 8.—*We do not attribute sweetness to the sun, for the same reason that we do attribute a commencement to the sun. This alone may teach us that the attribution of either is significant of nothing that we know of the sun.*

If all tactile objects possessed a sweet taste, we should consider sweetness essential to the sun, in the same manner as we consider a commencement essential. We now attribute to the sun temperature, gravity, density, and every other property that is constantly associated with the bodies which we can handle.

* See Lecture IX, passim.   † Ibid.

§ 9.—*A negation that refers to nothing is as insignificant as an assertion that refers to nothing. Both must be interpreted by the sensible phenomena to which the words refer.*

You may ask whether I mean to assert that the sun's existence never had a commencement. No. Commenced possesses no signification but as a name of something; and when applied to the sun, the word refers to nothing: hence it is used insignificantly. To apply the word bitter to the sun will not affect the sun, but it will affect the word. It will render the word insignificant. The same principle applies to commencement, whether it be affirmed of the sun or denied. It is equally insignificant in both cases.

§ 10.—*Words are an invention of man to designate his operations and the revelations of his senses. The principle which makes words significant when they refer to these, makes words insignificant when they refer not to these.*

Natural theology assumes credit for the discovery of a self-existent being. How? "Because," says natural theology, "if every existence has been created by a preceding existence, we can never arrive at a commencement." But as much difficulty exists in conceiving a self-existent being, as in conceiving a succession of existences without a commencement.* This dilemma natural theology cannot avoid. Language allows no alternative but to choose between the two equally inconceivable propositions;—a being without a creator, or a succession of creators without a beginning. The dilemma ought to teach us that we are using language insignificantly; that words are invented to designate our operations and experience; and when words refer not to these, they again become sounds which signify nothing.

§ 11.—Even the necessity which impels us to require a creator in the production of objects, shows that the word refers simply to the operations that fall under our observation. Why must

---

* But what is the difficulty in either case? It exists in the absence of some corresponding sensible experience in us. We should find an equal difficulty in conceiving that water can quench fire, or fire consume wood, were the assertions not significant of our experience.

bricks have a creator? Try to produce a brick, and you will discover. The necessity of a creator will be not verbal merely, but what you will experience. But when you ask me why the sun must have a creator, I cannot tell you to produce a sun, and thus discover the necessity. I can only appeal to the forms of language—forms which refer to sensible objects and operations, and which possess no signification where the objects and operations are not discoverable. The ability to predicate a creator in infinitum, is as complete as to predicate it of the sun; and we are compelled eventually to abandon the process, and admit that we are arrived where the process is no longer applicable. This alone ought to teach us that the whole process is insignificant, where it refers to no sensible archetype. It is like the ability to predicate a division of matter in infinitum. Both processes proceed on the same principle, and both are equally fallacious, and merely verbal.

§ 12.—This doctrine is so novel, that I may be accused of saying that the sun had no creator. Such an assertion is no more significant than its converse. The phenomena to which words refer give them significancy; and when we employ a phrase without referring to any discoverable existence or operation, the words are divested of signification. That the sun was created is highly significant, when we refer to the declarations of scripture. The assertion will signify those declarations, &c.; but when we refer to nothing, our assertion signifies nothing.

§ 13.—*Verbal processes may usually be continued interminably; hence they differ characteristically from sensible realities, which are always finite.*

The deity of natural theology is further established by the same process differently applied: thus, matter cannot begin to move of itself. It must have a mover. The conclusion is unavoidable, and this alone may teach us that the words relate to our actions and experience. Why is a mover necessary to give motion to my pen? Try, and you will discover. You will find a perfect quiescence till your hand, the wind, or some other agent, moves it. The necessity is not derived from the nature of the words, but from the sensible facts to which the words refer. Besides, we possess another proof that the necessity, when it refers to nothing sensible, is insignificant; we must either proceed illimitably to predicate a mover, or eventually abandon the necessity, and admit that something moves without a mover: thus, what makes my pen move? My hand. What makes my hand move? A. What makes A move? B. What makes B move?—and so in infinitum. The same necessity exists that the last shall have a mover as the first. This, however, leads to an absurdity. But we do not adopt the obvious conclusion, that we are using language insignificantly; but we adopt the incongruity, that at length something moves without a preceding mover.

§ 14.—Another discovery which natural theology claims, is the existence of a being infinitely perfect. "The maker of any thing must be more perfect than the thing which he makes; hence, the maker of all things must be infinitely perfect." But why? Because the words refer to our operations and experience. The watchmaker must be more knowing than the watch, and the musical instrument maker more knowing than his instrument. When thus applied, the proposition refers to sensible experience; but when we use it without such a reference, the words are unmeaning, and may be (as in all similar cases) predicated in infinitum: thus, B, the maker of a watch, must be more perfect than the watch; but C, the maker of B, must be more perfect than B; and so to the end of the alphabet, without arriving at an infinitely perfect being, unless we arrest the process, and say we have reached a being so perfect that the maker of it is not more perfect. This incongruity can be avoided only by another, which is at least equal; that the being exists without a maker. Consequences so incompatible ought to teach us that language is unfit for such processes, and that we must trust to revelation alone for every external thing beyond the sensible phenomena with which Providence has mercifully surrounded us. To these only, and to our internal experience, words refer; nor can the wit of man devise a word which shall possess a wider reference.

§ 15.—"Since something must have existed from eternity," says Paley, in his Natural Theology, "why may not the universe be that something?" He answers thus: "the contrivance which we perceive in the universe proves that it was preceded by a contriver, and hence it existed not eternally." But why does a contrivance imply a contriver? Because both words refer to our operations. In them only the implication possesses a sensible signification. I would ask (but reverently) whether the appearance of Deity would not exhibit a contrivance as evidently as the universe? If it would, even Deity could not have been eternal: for a contrivance implies a previous contriver. Language is inadequate to such speculations; they are even impious. The heathen make graven images—we make verbal ones; and the heathen worship not more ardently the work of their hands, than we the work of our pens.

§ 16.—*That we are compelled to eventually abandon our verbal processes, should teach us their fallacy.*

But why must something have existed eternally? Because language will not permit the assertion that any thing is produced without a producer. Hence, how remote soever we place any production, the producer must be more remote. But whence this property of language? From the reference which words bear to men and men's operations; and nothing can more explicitly show the nullity of separating language from these operations, than the necessity which occurs eventually of abandoning the process, and admitting that a point is reached beyond which the process is inapplicable; that either something existed without a producer, or a series of producers existed without a beginning.

§ 17.—That something must have existed eternally, may also be deduced from the ancient maxim, that nothing can be produced out of nothing. Why is the axiom true? Because it refers to our operations. Try if you can make a pen out of nothing, a brick out of nothing, a loaf out of nothing, and then you will know the necessity to which the axiom alludes. The necessity arises from no decree of the authors of language, but from what will be revealed to you by the above experiments.

§ 18.—With the above axiom the ancients maintained that the power of Deity extends no further than the arrangement of preëxistent materials. The moderns extend the axiom not so far. We arrive where we say the axiom is no longer applicable: thus, what was the sun made out of? Say A. And what was A made of? B. And what was B made of? We may proceed thus without end. But an end must be found, or matter is eternal; hence we deny the maxim of the ancients, that nothing can be made out of nothing; and we affirm that every thing was originally made out of nothing.

§ 19.—Spinoza, disbelieving the result thus obtained, concluded boldly that Deity himself was the first material out of which all things were fabricated. This, he thought, was a great discovery of reason, by which the maxim, *nihil fit ex nihilo,* was reconciled with the sole eternity of Deity.

§ 20.—*That our verbal processes, when pursued to their ultimate limits, lead to absurdities, should teach us that we are employing language insignificantly.*

When men find that language forces them to admit that all things were originally made either out of nothing, or out of God, we may pause, and at least doubt whether language is applicable to such speculations. The wisdom of the world may well be accounted "foolishness with God." By accumulating and arranging words, we can no more discover any realities which we have not experienced, than we can, by taking thought, add a cubit to our stature.

[To reconcile the free agency of man with the omniscience of God, has also been a desideratum of natural theology. I just drank some water, and antecedently I deliberated whether I should drink water or cider. But if actions are known to God before their inception, it was known that I should drink water; hence though I was deliberating, I could not drink cider, or the foreknowledge of God would have been frustrated. If, however, I could not drink the cider, I was not a free agent. But the dilemma is merely verbal. What is the meaning of the term free agent? It can be explained by some sensible phenomenon only. You may tell me that I can either drink or not the water which is before me. To teach me still more unequivocally, you may show me what it is to be not a free agent. You can withhold my hands, and tell me I am no longer free to drink. Why? Let me try to drink and I shall discover. Hence the term free agent signifies a sensible phenomenon; and if you apply the term to what is not sensible the phrase is divested of signification.

[The controverted expressions have a signification, when they are used in sacred writ; and my comments on them will show the folly of attempting to comprehend their divine archetype. The Holy Spirit has mercifully condescended to reveal that there are realities to which our knowledge has no affinity. This is effected by employing language in a way that is irreconcileable with the phenomena to which we are surrounded; nor can I conceive that any other use of language would accomplish the object.]

§ 21.—*Creation is the interpreter of words, and words are not the interpreters of creation.*

"That matter cannot begin to move of itself, proves," says natural theology, "the existence of something immaterial": thus, I include under the word matter every part which you can feel, see, taste, smell, and hear, of a horse. None of them can begin to move of itself. Then something is in the horse beside matter. Why? I will show you. The horse is now slain. All the matter remains of which he was composed when alive, yet not a particle possesses motion; hence, when the horse could move, something existed in him besides matter. The experiment proves itself, and nothing more nor less. We can refer to it by any expressions we think proper; but the signification of our expressions must be sought in the sights, sounds, tastes, feels, and smells, which we experience. We may contend that in a live horse something must exist beside matter, provided our expression refers to any thing; but the moment the phrase is used to express more than our sensible experience, our words become insignificant even to ourselves. They become mere sounds and archetypes of nothing.

§ 22.—*Nothing can be sustained that is repugnant to revelation. Natural theology is founded on the same fallacy as Zeno's problem of the tortoise.*

But you may contend that my system is subversive not only of natural theology, but of every other. If I thought this, I would never publish these suggestions. Fully impressed with the paramount authority of the Holy Scriptures, I admit that no repugnant doctrine can be true. I have said nothing but what will display the importance of revelation, and show infidels that their deity is a creation of their own; the result of propositions which are precisely like Zeno's problem of Achilles and the tortoise.

§ 23.—I never knew but one atheist, and his unbelief was fortified by the doctrines of natural theology. When you attempted his conversion, by alleging the necessity of a creator for the sun, moon, &c., he would inquire, Who made them? God. But who made God? If you said God is uncreated, he would contend that you abandon the argument by which you seek his conversion; for, if the sun must have had a maker, he considers one equally necessary to the maker of the sun; and so in infinitum. Had this atheist known that language is impertinent to the whole discussion, he would have seen that verbal incompatibilities afford no cause to disbelieve the being and attributes of Deity. [Yet what would induce him to believe in them? Revelation. The same which induces us to believe in the Saviour.

[No heresy is so pernicious as the persuasion that God can be discovered by reason. Science has at various times advanced truths which were thought hostile to revelation; but they all eventually have been confirmatory thereof. A disclosure of the nature of language will result similarly.]

§ 24.—Men must look to revelation alone, not for a Saviour only, but for every part of the Godhead, and every attribute of Deity. Infidels possess no alternative but revelation or entire ignorance. The god whom they acknowledge is a creature of language, and apart therefrom possesses no existence. He is like heathen deities, who probably all originated from verbal deductions like those of natural theologists.

§ 25.—The deity of natural theology is generally moulded to suit the practices of his votaries. The murderer finds that his God is too exalted to regard the conduct of men; the libertine considers the possession of inclinations as a proof that the gratification of them must be an acceptable homage to their maker; and the scoffer of sacred institutions believes that he is evincing a laudable contempt of rites which proceed from degrading views of the being of his adoration. All find not merely an excuse for their sins, but an incitement to sin.

§ 26.—But what proofs have we of the truth of revelation?[1] We possess a testimony within ourselves—the Holy Spirit acting on our feelings, and producing the fervent acquiescence which we term faith. The sacred volume speaks also as never man spake. The happy tendency of its morality; its insight into the

---

[1] In Johnson (I) this reads:

But what proof have we of the truth of revelation? We have all the proof which we ever had, and its sufficiency is continually evinced by the number of believers. When men imagine that God is discoverable independently of revelation, they become proud of what they deem a great effort of reason. They esteem more highly the evidence which substantiates their god, than the evidence which discloses the God of the bible; hence they cavil with the declarations of holy writ, and either believe or condemn them conformably to the dictates of reason.

human character; its adaptation to every period and nation, and to every vicissitude of life; all tend to bow the understanding and the will, not only to admit its doctrines, but to cling to them as the counsellor in the cares and pleasures of life, and the comforter in affliction, pain, and death.

§ 27.—But you may still say, if language can discourse of nothing but our sensible experience and internal consciousness, what can revelation teach? A revelation must necessarily be adapted to our capacity. What we could not understand would be no revelation. It was given for the regulation of our conduct, and not for the gratification of our curiosity. We are told the conduct which is pleasing to God, and the conduct that is displeasing. We are instructed how to obtain His favour, and how to become obnoxious to His displeasure. All that belongs to life is revealed in intelligible language, and what belongs to another life could not be intelligible in any language.

§ 28.—*My remarks on theology possess no object but to show that my views of language are compatible with revelation.*

Recollect that my remarks on theology are elicited incidentally. I once intended to omit them, they being too grave a subject for my discussion; but I preferred to show the adaptation of my doctrines to revelation, rather than to leave the adaptation to other persons, who might misconstrue either my intentions or my tenets. Besides, natural theology afforded a good illustration of the errours to which we are liable, when we consider the conclusions of language applicable, not to the sensible phenomena only from which the conclusions derive their authority, but to cases where our senses can discover nothing: that is, because every thing made implies a maker, we suppose the proposition applicable not only to this house, this table, and the various other objects in which the necessity of a maker refers to our operations and experience, but to the earth and the sun, where the necessity refers to no sensible archetype.

§ 29.—Finally, I have spoken of natural theology not to

detect its errours, but to elucidate the nature of language. With the same view I intend to show some errours in various other departments of knowledge. This, however, would lead me further than your patience to-night will permit; I therefore defer the subject to my next lecture.

Lecture XVI

AFTER SENSIBLE EXPERIENCE COMMANDS OUR ASSENT TO CERTAIN FORMS OF SPEECH, WE APPLY THE FORMS WHERE NO SENSIBLE PHENOMENA ARE DISCOVERABLE. THE SUBJECT CONTINUED, AND FURTHER EXEMPLIFIED BY AN INVESTIGATION OF VARIOUS SCIENTIFICK TENETS

§ 1.—*That an unsupported body will fall to the earth, is an experimental fact. The necessity is physical and not verbal. When the necessity is verbally implied, without referring to any thing sensible, the words return to their original insignificance.*

IN MY last lecture, I gave some examples in natural theology, of the manner in which we continue the forms of language, after the phenomena are withdrawn that give significancy to the forms. In the present lecture, I am to exemplify the same errour in other branches of learning; and when we shall exhibit the conclusions to which this use of language leads us, you will probably be astonished that the fallacy of the process has so long escaped detection:—for instance, the earth is, we say, suspended in space. If the earth rests on any thing, say A, the question occurs immediately, what does A rest on? For the principle which furnishes the earth with a support, forces us to find something on which the support may rest. Hence, if we adopt the Indian tradition that the world rests on an elephant, and the elephant on a tortoise, we must still find something for the tortoise to rest on; and so in infinitum. But this leads to no end, and an end must be found, or no use exists in predicating any supporter; therefore, we discard both Atlas and the elephant, and say, the earth is suspended without a support.

§ 2.—Nor can the earth hang on any thing. A support from above requires a beginning as much as a support from below. We may suspend the earth with a chain from the sky, but what sustains the sky? Another chain from another sky. But what sustains the latter? A commencement must be found, and that can have nothing to sustain it; hence, we find no use in predicating any sustainer and the earth is left without support either from above or below.

§ 3.—The moment a stone is unsupported, it falls. The necessity for a support is precisely what you will discover if you attempt to suspend a stone without a support; but when we apply the same language to the earth, the necessity is merely verbal, like the infinite divisibility of matter, or the race of Achilles and the tortoise, or the fabrication of every thing out of nothing.

§ 4.—*To say that the earth is either supported or unsupported, is equally insignificant.*

That we must finally admit either a first support, which is itself unsupported, or that the earth is without any support, shows that we are employing language insignificantly; that we are wandering in fairy land. Support and unsupported are names of sights and feels: when we apply the words where the sights and feels are undiscoverable, the words lose their significancy: divested of their conventional character, they become again unmeaning sounds.

§ 5.—*The reason which renders the word shape significant when applied to a table, shows that the word is insignificant when applied to the earth as a whole.*

Why must the earth, considered as a single mass, possess a shape? Because all tangible bodies must have a shape. But why? We may thrust back the question as often as we can find new expressions; but when we desire a sensible reply, we must resort to our senses, to whose information alone the necessity refers. Shape is the name of a feel and a sight. If you wish to know why a table must possess a shape, try and manufacture one without a shape, and you will discover the necessity. It will be just what you will experience. But why must the earth possess a shape? Here the necessity is verbal. I cannot refer you to your senses, as in the case of the table, but I must refer you to the table, or some other tangible object; nay, the reason which renders a shape indispensable to a table, is conclusive that it is inapplicable to the earth. Shape is indispensable to a table, because the word names a sight and a feel, which tables exhibit; but it is inapplicable to the earth, (considered as a whole,) because it names a sight and a feel that the earth never exhibits.

§ 6.—*The word shape, when applied to the earth, will signify any thing to which the word refers.*

[To say that the entire earth must have a certain smell or taste, would be deemed puerile; but the assertion is not more puerile than to say the whole earth must have a shape. Why we predicate of the earth a shape I have endeavoured to show; and I may employ a similar process to explain why we do not consider a smell equally essential. Both results are the effects of our experience in the tangible bodies that surround us, and apart from these bodies neither result has any significance.]

To assert that the earth possesses a shape, is significant when we refer to the appearance of the moon under an eclipse, or to the gradual disappearance of a ship in its recession from the shore, or when we refer to any other sensible information; but the moment we desire to make the assertion signify more than sensible references, we desire more than language can accomplish.

§ 7.—*That the shape which we attribute to the earth must be some shape that experience has revealed to us, shows that the predication of any shape is significant of nothing but our experience.*

But if the earth possesses a shape, it must be a plane, a globe, a cone, an oblong, a rhombus, or a square, &c., to the end of our vocabulary of shapes. But why must the shape be one of these? Because no other shape can be found. Why? Try if you can make a shape that is not one of these, and you will discover. Here, again, the language evidently refers to our experience only.

§ 8.—*No verbal necessity is significant of any thing but the sensible information to which it refers.*

But of what shape is the earth? A plane. No; the earth cannot be a plane, for a plane would exhibit some place (of land or water) where we might fall off. Why? Because every plane must possess a termination. But why? You will discover if you attempt to construct a plane that shall be interminable.

§ 9.—If the surface of the earth has no termination, what shape must the earth possess? Round or oval. Why? Because to admit that no termination exists, implies that the shape is round or oval. But whence this implication? Try to make such a surface, and the necessity of a rotundity is just what you will experience. Hence, when I say that a surface which possesses no commencement or termination must be round, the necessity is significant so long as it refers to an apple, or any thing in which the necessity is discoverable; but when the proposition is applied to the earth, the necessity of a roundness is merely verbal. The roundness may refer to the various phenomena which we relate in proof of the earth's sphericity; but if it refers to nothing more, it means no more.

§ 10.—*The forms of language cease from being significant when the phenomena to which the forms refer cease from being discoverable.*

If you take an artificial globe and pierce it with pins, so that their points shall all be directed to the centre, some heads must hang down diametrically opposite to the heads of some of the other pins. Why? Make the experiment, and you will know. But to what do we advert when we say, that in some part of the earth the feet of the inhabitants are diametrically opposite to our feet? That the pins have antipodes is a result of our experience; but the necessity for antipodes to men exists in the forms of language only: forms that cease to be significant where the phenomena to which they refer cease from being discoverable. [Show me a man who exhibits the same appearance in relation to the earth, as the pins exhibit in relation to the artificial globe. You cannot:—hence the nullity of the position.] The moment we attempt to make language significant of more than our senses can experience, we become transported into an enchanted world, where the wonders are more incredible than those which amuse infancy.

§ 11.—*We are correct in calling the earth a sphere, but we are incorrect when we deem the name an authority for attributing to the earth sensible properties which our senses cannot discover.*

But are not the phenomena exhibited by the earth conclusive that it is globular, since you cannot produce similar appearances with any other shape? Granted. The necessity of admitting its sphericalness refers to our operations. It is a sphere by the same necessity that impels a child to admit an automaton is animated. He never saw any thing inanimate which could open and close its eyes, move its feet, hands, and head; hence the automaton must be animate. The child is, however, correct, if he employs the word animate to name what he discovers merely; and we are correct in calling the earth a globe, if we use the word to name what we discover: but the child is wrong when he, by virtue of the name which he has attached to the automaton, imputes to it a power to eat, drink, and sleep; and we are equally wrong when, by virtue of the name that we have given to the earth, we maintain that its inhabitants, of different places, must carry their heads diametrically opposite; that no two lines perpendicular to the earth can be parallel, &c.

§ 12.—*We are correct in saying that the arch of a circle can never coincide with a straight line; but we are incorrect when we deem the assertion capable of either revealing to us physical facts which our senses cannot discover, or of contradicting physical facts which our senses can discover.*

Mathematicians demonstrate that a line may be divided interminably: thus, draw a line AC, and another (BM) perpendicu-

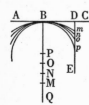

lar to it. The latter line must be interminable in the direction toward Q. Draw also another line (DE) parallel to BM. You may now take any point (P) in the line BQ, and from P, as a centre, describe, at the distance PB, the arch Bp. In the same manner you may take the points O, N, and M, and from each, at the distance of B, describe the arches Bo, Bn, and Bm. Evidently the further the centre is taken from B, the more nearly the arches will approach to D; and the line ED will be divided into parts that will diminish in size at every approach. But the line BM may be interminably extended beyond Q; therefore, the line ED may be interminably divided into parts whose length will continually diminish; because an arch of a circle can never coincide with the straight line BC.

§ 13.—Why can the arch of a circle never coincide with a straight line? Because the terms imply that it cannot. But how came the terms to possess this implication? Try to make an arch coincide with a straight line, and you will discover. The incompatibility alludes to our sensible experience only. After adopting the phrase, we, however, make its authority superiour to that of our senses; for we can form a circle so large that its arch will coincide with a short straight line. Hence the line ED cannot be divided in infinitum except verbally. You will soon produce so large an arch that it will coincide with BD; and then the further division of the line ED will cease from naming any thing sensible, and become division minus division—a sound divested of its signification.

§ 14.—The verbal process which divides ED in infinitum,

will prove that water is not level; for if the earth is round, the surface of a fish-pond is the arch of a circle, and therefore cannot coincide with a straight line.

§ 15.—*That bodies are divisible into parts is a physical fact, which possesses no authority but our experience; hence the fallacy of continuing the division verbally, beyond the authority of our senses, and even against their authority.*

Mr. Reid, in speaking of the divisibility of bodies, says, "nothing seems more evident than that all bodies must consist of parts." Why? Because the word body implies an aggregation. But whence this implication? We may, as heretofore, proceed in a round of questions without arriving at any result. If, however, you undertake to discover a body which cannot be divided, you will learn why all bodies must consist of parts. The necessity of parts possesses no meaning but our experience; hence the absurdity of predicating the necessity, after our senses testify that no parts are discoverable. We may employ the proposition of Mr. Reid to prove that an atom is divisible in infinitum, since every division still leaves a body which is composed of parts; but our language loses its significancy in the process, and the parts which we are dividing become sounds signifying nothing.

§ 16.—*Conclusions respond verbally to premises, as a parrot responds to questions which we may ask it. Whether the answer shall be significant or not, depends on something other than the parrot.*

One moon, multiplied by three, makes three moons. This is as true verbally as that an orange, multiplied by three, makes three oranges. The two cases are, however, radically different. The position is true in relation to oranges, because it refers to a sensible fact; but it is true in relation to the moon, only because the words of the proposition have acquired a relative meaning that enables the premises to imply the conclusion. The conclusion responds to the premises as a parrot may be taught to say three when you ask him any question. Whether the answer shall be sensible and pertinent will depend on the question. He will continue to answer three whether you ask him how much is one apple multiplied by three, or how much is nothing multiplied by three. Like the above is the language which speaks of the divisibility of bodies. The divisibility must continue verbally; but whether the language shall or not signify any thing, depends upon the subject that is to be divided. The division will be sensibly significant when it refers to an orange, but it will be insignificant when it refers to no sensible existence.

[Locke, in his Essays, says, "our idea of space is boundless. Any bounds, even adamantine walls, cannot arrest the mind in its progress through space and extension, for so far as that body reaches, no person can deny extension; and when we arrive at the extremity of body, what can there satisfy the mind that it is at the end of space?"

[Yet, when we reach the walls, why can we not say we are at the end of extension? Endeavour to constitute a wall that shall not possess extension, and you will discover why we cannot say that a wall is the end of extension. But when we arrive at the termination of the wall, why can we not then say, that we are at the end of extension? Attempt to construct a wall that will enable you to make such a declaration, and you will learn why we cannot. The difficulty will be just what you experience. To this experience language refers, and further, words have no signification. We may amuse ourselves with framing propositions such as Locke's, but we mean nothing but what our senses discover.]

§ 17.—*The ultimate cogency of all reasoning refers to our sensible experience.*

"Why," says Locke,[1] "does no person think of infinite white-

---

[1] In Johnson (I) this reads:

But why, says Locke, does no body ever think of infinite sweetness or infinite whiteness, though he can repeat the idea of sweet and white

ness? Because," replies Locke, "if you take the idea of white which was yielded yesterday by a parcel of snow, and join it in your mind with the idea of whiteness that is yielded to-day by another parcel of snow, the two ideas embody into one, and the idea of whiteness is not increased." But why? He answers not. The answer is, however, extremely simple. Why, then, cannot one piece of snow be made whiter by the addition of another piece? Conjoin them, and you will discover. The term "cannot" refers to this experiment, and not to verbal reasons. They possess neither authority nor significance, except as they refer to our sensible experience.

§ 18.—"But," says Locke, "every person who possesses an

as frequently as those of a yard or a day? Because, answers Locke, only those ideas which have parts are capable, by repetition, of producing the idea of infinity. But why? Because, says Locke, with this endless repetition of ideas there is a constant enlargement. But why? Locke does not answer. I will answer for him. The words refer to our operations, and the phenomena with which we are conversant. This stick must be longer if you add to it another stick. Why? Make the experiment and you will discover. The necessity has no other reference: and hence the absurdity of using it where no phenomena are discoverable.

Why does no body think of infinite sweetness, or infinite whiteness, though he can repeat the idea of sweetness and whiteness as frequently as the idea of a stick? Because, says Locke, to the idea of the whitest whiteness, if I add another of a less or equal whiteness, it makes no increase or enlargement of my idea. Why? Because, he remarks, if you take the idea of white, which was yielded yesterday by a parcel of snow, and join it in your mind with the idea of whiteness that is yielded to-day by another parcel of snow, the two ideas embody into one, and the idea of whiteness is not increased. But why? He answers not. The answer is, however, extremely simple, and shows that language has no meaning when it does not refer to sensible phenomena. Why, then, cannot one piece of snow be made whiter by the addition of another piece? Conjoin them and you will discover. This is a simple reason, but no other is so good. The term, "cannot" refers to this experiment, and not to verbal reasons. They have neither authority nor significance, when they are used without a reference to phenomena.

idea of a foot, finds that he can repeat the idea; and joining it to the former, make the idea of two feet, and so on without ever arriving at an end of his increase, whether the idea so enlarged be a foot or a mile, or the diameter of the earth, or the orbis magnus."

§ 19.—I ask, however, what he enlarges? While he speaks of joining one foot to another, he speaks significantly; but when he talks of doubling the diameter of the earth, the process becomes verbal, and the necessity which compels us to admit the enlargement exists in the forms of language only:—forms that owe their significance to sensible existences, and become insignificant the moment they are applied where no corresponding existences are discoverable.

§ 20.—In Gill's Body of Divinity is the following proposition: "Though angels possess no bodies, and so are not in place circumspectively; yet, as they are creatures, they must possess a somewhere in which they are definitively."

Why? If you attempt to dispose of this book so that it shall exist, and still possess no location, you will discover the impracticability. But when the same impracticability is predicated of angels, it exists only in the forms of language; forms which possess no more substantiality, when the sensible phenomena to which they allude are subtracted, than the muster-rolls of an army, when the soldiers are all deserted.

§ 21.—The writer proceeds with his verbal discoveries: "where existed a place for angels before heaven and earth were made? Nowhere." Why? Because we are referring to our sensible experience. The writer, however, thinks he is proving that the heavens or the earth must have been created before angels. Yet even this obvious consequence of his premises is authoritative only because it refers to our operations: thus, you cannot mark with chalk till you have something on which to inscribe the mark. Why? Try, and you will find. Our senses affix to the inability a signification; but when we apply the language to angels, the inability is verbal only.

§ 22.—Locke says, "number applies to men, angels, actions, thoughts, and every thing imaginable." If any proposition is inherently significant, this of Locke must be the one. Yet even this is indebted for its significance to our operations and experience. Why must apples be either one or more? Try to prevent the necessity, and you will discover. The necessity depends not on the structure of language, but on our experience. But why must angels be either one or more? The necessity here is merely verbal. Number may be applicable to angels by virtue of the authority of revelation, but not by virtue of our logick. Number is a name given by us to certain sights and feels, &c.; where these exist not, number is a word divested of its signification. [Suppose we were to apply numbers to darkness, insipidity, or vacuity, we should speak unintelligibly; because these objects exhibit not the sights and feels to which numbers are ordinarily applied. This illustration may assist you to apprehend that where all the phenomena with which we are conversant should be absent, the word numbers would have no signification; hence it may not be applicable to angels. We affix it to them in compliance with the forms of language.]

§ 23.—I have now shown, that when language forces us to admit that apples must be either one or more, the necessity of admitting the conclusion is founded on our experience. I have also shown that when propositions have thus obtained an authoritative character, we apply them where no corresponding experience exists: as that angels must be either one or more. In such applications, the necessity of admitting the conclusion is merely verbal, and therefore fallacious.

§ 24.—*The solicitude which philosophical writers usually evince for the establishment of names and definitions, arises from the verbal deductions which they intend to draw from the names.*

Examples of the foregoing fallacies might be further accumulated without difficulty, but I have probably stated a sufficient number and variety to show that the errour enters deeply into all our learning. We shall now be able to discover a reason for the solicitude evinced often about names and definitions. For instance, if a mathematician wishes to demonstrate that the surface of a fish-pond is not level, the earth must be denominated a sphere, and the sphere be properly defined; after this preliminary, the fish-pond will constitute a part of the circumference of a sphere, and the surface of the pond cannot be a straight line. The further consideration of this solicitude of abstruse writers is important to the view which I wish to present of language, and it constitutes the theme of our next lecture.

Lecture XVII

PHILOSOPHICAL SPECULATIONS ARE OFTEN NOTHING BUT VERBAL DEDUCTIONS FROM NAMES AND DEFINITIONS

§ 1.—*What we have experienced in an orange, we deem predicable of every thing that is called an orange; without reflecting that every word possesses as many meanings as it possesses applications to different objects.*

THEORISTS are solicitous about names and definitions, because speculations are often verbal deductions from such names: for instance, if you wish to prove that the surface of a pond is not level, you can accomplish it verbally by premising that the earth is a sphere, and the pond a part of the circumference.*

§ 2.—Words possess as many significations as they possess applications to different phenomena; consequently, though the assertion is true when applied to an artificial sphere, that no part of its circumference is level; yet the assertion is sophistical when the word sphere is applied to the earth, because sphere possesses then a different signification.

* My illustrations may be defective and otherwise inaccurate; but, if they enable the reader to ascertain the principles which I seek to illustrate, my object will be attained.

§ 3.—*What we infer from given facts is not identical with what we discover by our senses.*

I lately asked a friend what he meant by saying the earth was round. He said it was round like any other round body. I desired an example. He pointed to an artificial globe. "But," said I, "does the earth present the same sight as the globe, or the same feel?" "Neither:—but when a fly walks over the globe, he produces an appearance similar to what a receding ship exhibits to spectators on the shore. Again, when a ship sails in a continued course westwardly, it returns to the country whence it originally departed: as a fly returns when he walks on an artificial globe. Besides, the shadow of an artificial globe resembles the appearance which is exhibited on the moon when eclipsed: an appearance which astronomers say is the shadow of the earth."

§ 4.—The word sphere, therefore, when applied to the earth, is not the name of a sight and feel, (as it is when applied to an artificial globe,) but the name of the above and some other phenomena. To prove by argument that an artificial globe is spherical, would be idle. The word names what we see and feel in the artificial globe. But the earth has been repeatedly subjected to experiments, for the procurement of data from which its shape might be inferred; and the word sphere, when applied to the earth, is a name of these data only.

§ 5.—*Phraseology is not important while we employ it (say the word Cæsar) to designate any thing; but phraseology is very important when we infer from the word Cæsar that an individual must be a Roman emperor.*

Whether the earth be named a sphere or a plane is of little consequence, so long as we use the name to only designate certain data; but the name becomes essential, if we employ it to determine whether the surface of a pond is level, or to determine whether two perpendicular poles that stand before me are parallel. If I use the word sphere, the two poles are not parallel, maugre all that seeing and feeling can testify to the contrary; because you can mathematically demonstrate that no two lines perpendicular to the surface of a sphere can be parallel.

§ 6.—If I admit that my hand touches fire, you may deduce therefrom that my hand will be burnt. The conclusion seems inevitable. But you ought to know first whether I apply the word fire to what you have always found productive of such a result. Perhaps I hold in my hand paper on which the word fire is written. This, however, you would denounce as a quibble. It is a quibble; and the above, together with a vast many philosophical conclusions, are produced by a process similar in character to the quibble, though not so obvious to detection.

[If we employ language simply to refer to phenomena, no serious evil can arise from the terms we adopt; but if we select words to draw from them logical deductions, the slightest change of phraseology may produce in philosophy revolutions which no man can foresee till he has found all the consequences that may be logically deduced from the new names which he introduces. The metaphysician who concludes his book by asserting that nothing exists exterior of his mind, might have concluded it by asserting that every thing is exterior, if he had only named the objects of his knowledge impressions instead of ideas.]

§ 7.—The phenomena exhibited by the heavenly bodies are equally apparent to all men; and we may call them the motion of the heavenly bodies around the earth, or the motion of the earth around its own axis, and around the sun. The choice of phraseology is unimportant, so long as we employ the words to only designate phenomena which our senses discover: but when we employ the words to make discoveries beyond our senses, the phraseology is very important. By adopting the latter phraseology, we make all mankind travel at a giddy velocity of more than a thousand miles a minute in one direction, and about a thousand miles an hour in another direction. By adopting the first phraseology, we escape from disturbing the quiescence of the earth; but we unmercifully cause the sun and stars to travel with a rotation of about twenty-five thousand miles every minute.

§ 8.—Again: if, with Newton, we call the sun a body of fire, the language is harmless, so long as we use it to merely designate the phenomena which the sun exhibits, or to designate any thing; but if we intend to deduce consequences from the word fire, the phraseology is essential: thus, as the planet Saturn is ten times further from the sun than our earth, and as fire dispenses heat and illumination in a degree which distance diminishes in a ratio inverse the square of the distance, we enjoy a hundred times more light and heat than Saturn. This piteous conclusion is accordingly predicated of Saturn. The poor inhabitants of that planet are, however, not permitted to exist with these privations only, but more adventurous speculators urge the deductive process further, and prove that water exists among them in solidity only, and consequently they know not the luxury of fish. Humanity must rejoice that these distressful consequences are avoidable, by the simple contrivance of a late philanthropist, who has extinguished the solar fire, and converted the sun into a radiating fluid, which becomes hot only when it falls on solid bodies: as water evolves heat when thrown on unslacked lime. We need, therefore, no longer wonder why comets are not vitrified. Mercury is made salubrious, and even Herschel a pleasant retreat.

§ 9.—Again: the phenomena exhibited by the barometer and air-pump were formerly designated nature's horrour of a vacuum. Latterly we call them atmospherical pressure. Which of the two expressions we adopt is immaterial, so long as we intend to only designate the phenomena; but the expression becomes important when we design to make discoveries with it beyond the reach of our senses: thus, if a column of water ascends in a vacuum by reason of atmospherical pressure, we can prove that every man sustains a pressure of fourteen tons. This immense burden was first imposed on us about two centuries ago, and it may now be removed if we return to the old phraseology of nature's horrour of a vacuum. However, let us continue the burden, (as we carry it conveniently,) and the new theory accords with more phenomena than the discarded theory.

[I might accumulate deductions which, like the foregoing, depend for their significance on the name by which speculative men designate their premises; but I have probably produced enough to disclose the principle on which such speculations are founded. Every person may find as many further examples as he desires, for he can resort to no science in which they are not prodigally scattered.]

§ 10.—*We should discriminate between theoretical agents and sensible agents. A sensible agent is something which our senses discover; but a theoretical agent is something which is only supposed to exist.*

Theories are beneficial to science;[1] but when we say that water ascends in a vacuum by means of the pressure of the atmosphere, we should discriminate the theoretical pressure

---

[1] In Johnson (I) this reads:

It may be proper to remark that, while I descant so freely on received theories, I do not wish to depreciate their usefulness. My whole object is to illustrate the nature of language. If theories are beneficial to science, it is also beneficial that we should discriminate between theoretical agents and the realities of nature: for example, when we say that water ascends in a vacuum, by means of the pressure of the atmosphere, the word pressure is the theoretical agent by which we account for the ascent of the water. Now, if we would escape from the delusions of language, we must steadily distinguish that this theoretical agent is wholly different from the feel to which the word pressure is ordinarily applied. The feel is a reality of nature, but the pressure, which is attributed to the atmosphere, is merely verbal. It cannot be felt or seen, nor is it palpable to any of our senses. We see the water ascend in the vacuum, but the pressure, which we say causes the ascent, is merely the verbal machinery by which we account for the ascent.

from the feel to which the word pressure is ordinarily applied. Pressure, like every other word, possesses no invariable signification, nor any inherent signification. Its signification is governed by the existence to which we attach it. When it refers to the effort of my hand against this table, it names a feel; and when applied to the ascent of water in a vacuum, it names the ascent. If we suppose it names also some insensible operation of the air on the water, this is merely our theory, which signifies nothing; or rather it signifies all to which we refer in proof of the pressure.

§ 11.—If we keep in view this distinction between theoretical agents and the realities of nature, we shall at once discover the absurdity of continuing the employment of theoretical agents beyond the uses which they subserve to science. If the attribution of a pressure to air enables us to methodise numerous phenomena which are exhibited by the air-pump and barometer, &c., the attribution is valuable; but we should not continue the verbal machinery beyond this utility, and much less should we deduce therefrom that every man sustains a pressure of fourteen tons;—a conclusion which I believe is not subservient to any use, and is therefore only an evidence that the persons who make the deduction are ignorant of the true nature of language.

§ 12.—*Theoretical agents are of man's fabrication, and partake of the mutability of their creator.*

That we may better understand these verbal agents, I will in our next lecture examine the principle which governs us in the selection of them. They are creatures of our own fabrication, as their mutability evinces. At one time we prop up the heavens with the shoulders of Atlas, or support the earth on the back of a tortoise; at another we remove both the props and support, and sustain the earth by attraction and propulsion. The character of these instruments is alike, though they vary in usefulness. The shoulder of Atlas would be preferable to the attraction and propulsion of Newton, if it would apply consistently to a greater number of sensible revelations, or subserve a greater number of useful purposes.

§ 13.—*When we employ language for the purpose of deducing consequences from names, a change of phraseology is productive of a new system of philosophy.*

Dugald Stewart says, "the assertion of Berkeley, that extension and figure possess merely an ideal existence, tends to unhinge the whole frame of the human understanding, by shaking our confidence in those principles of belief which form an essential part of its constitution."

§ 14.—What serious consequences from the use of a new phrase! But, if we consider the language of Berkeley as merely a designation of sensible information, his phraseology will be unimportant. We may call extension and figure either ideal existences, or material existences, and our language will mean— What? Just what you see and feel. If, however, we use language for the purpose of deducing consequences from names, the phraseology is important; but the importance is founded in ignorance of the nature of language.

§ 15.—Again: Mr. Stewart says, "In consequence of the writings of Reid and a few others, the word idea itself is universally regarded as a suspicious and dangerous term; and it has already lost its technical or Cartesian meaning, by being identified as a synonyme with the more popular word notion."

§ 16.—Here philosophy is improved by simply substituting the word notion for the word idea. But why? Because the verbal consequences which we deduce from the word idea cannot be deduced from the word notion. The change of phraseology is an improvement, because we make an improper use of language.

§ 17.—*The choice of phraseology is conventional, and subject to the judgment and caprice of men; but the realities of creation are unaffected by our phraseology.*

In the system of one philosopher, "ideology is stated to be a branch of zoology, and to have for its object an examination of the intellectual faculties of man and of other animals." Mr. Stewart is startled at this phraseology, and says—"the classification is extraordinary, and it is obviously intended to prepare the way for an assumption which levels men with the brutes."

§ 18.—A very serious effect from a cause so trivial! If philosophers can, with a dash of their pen, level men with brutes, we may account as authentick history the enchantments of Circe. But the most which any writer can accomplish is to transform names. Philosophers may apply to brutes, as well as men, the phrase intellectual faculties; but the phenomena exhibited by men and brutes will not become identical from possessing the same name. Philosophers can extend to quadrupeds the term man, but even this will not level men with brutes; it will level the name only. The sensible realities of creation will continue distinct and inconvertible.

Lecture XVIII

OF THE AGENTS WHICH WE EMPLOY IN THE CONSTRUCTION OF THEORIES

[IN MY last Lecture, I showed that theorists deduce consequences from names, without regarding the fact, that names vary in signification with the objects to which they are applied. The word Caesar, which, in one application, is an emperor; becomes, by another application, a quadruped. Even thus varies the signification of round, when applied to the earth, from what the same word signifies when it designates an artificial sphere.

[This error is most effective in the verbal agents with which we construct our theories. The earth's motion around its axis, at the rate of 700 to 1,000 miles an hour; and its motion around the sun, at the rate of 58,000 miles in the same period, are the theoretical agents by which we account for the phenomena exhibited by the heavenly bodies. Few persons estimate this motion as a word which is significant of nothing but the phenomena that it is applied to elucidate, but they estimate it as possessing the same signification as when it is applied to the rotation of a coach wheel; and, in despite of their senses, believe that they are travelling at the above velocity, in the same sense as they travel in a stage coach.

[This example is sufficiently striking to show that there is no limit to the infatuation by which the deductions from names are confounded with sensible phenomena. The deduction of another theory teaches us that the whole globe, if it could be so crushed as to lose all porosity, would occupy a space no larger than a nutmeg; and on the contrary, a cubic inch of our atmosphere, if transported five hundred miles from the earth, would be so released from circumambient pressure that it would dilate sufficiently to fill a sphere of more millions of miles in circumference than I can easily enumerate.

[In the present Lecture I am to examine the nature of the theoretical agents by which we arrive at such monstrous results—results which the ignorant estimate as the necromancy of learning, and which the learned believe from a misapprehension of the significancy of language.

[If we examine our theories, we shall find that the agents employed to effect any object are such as our experience has discovered similarly employed. Every thing falls to the earth by reason of the earth's attraction. But why is attraction the agent? Because we find in magnets that attraction produces similar phenomena. If what is literally named attraction had never been experienced, we should not have attributed it to the earth—we should have employed some other agent.]

§ 1.—*We can employ no theoretical agents, but such as experience has taught us can produce effects similar to those which we seek to account for. In a rude age, theoretical agents are rude; in a refined age they are subtile.*

In a new colony, where more suitable materials are not procurable, I have seen wooden latches, wooden wash-bowls and drinking-cups, wooden candlesticks, and even wooden wicks. Theorists are similarly limited in the agents which they employ. The philosopher of an early era must theorize with the gross agents which surround him. He supports the earth on the back of an elephant, and the elephant on a tortoise. But why not on a butterfly? Because he refers to his experience of the strength of an elephant and the endurance of a tortoise. If he finds the channel of a vanished river, he ascribes the disappearance to a mammoth, which, descending from the hills, drained the river at a draught. His deities war against evil spirits with bows and arrows; and the pleasures of a future world are hunting, where game is exhaustless, and fishing, where tempests are excluded.

§ 2.—We smile at theories in which the agents are so rude; and from the phenomena that industry has accumulated for us, we select instruments more subtile. We support the earth by a projection or push, which the earth received at its creation, and by an attraction or pull that is exerted by the sun. But why must the motion have been produced by a push? Because we refer to our operations. Try if you can protrude a billiard ball without some impulse. But why must the earth feel an attraction or pull? Because a push could move the earth in a straight line only, and not drive it round the sun. Why? Strike a billiard ball, and you will discover. You can find a reason in no way but in that or similar experiments.

§ 3.—Some of the ancient heathen philosophers introduced men into the world by the following process: "Where the country was suitable, wombs grew out of the earth, fixed to it by roots." But why fixed to the ground? Why affixed by roots? and why wombs? The whole process shows, and the instruments show grossly, that we construct theories with the materials which our operations dictate.

§ 4.—In Brown's Philosophy I find the following:—"The addition of a new sense might probably communicate, in a few hours, more knowledge of matter than is ever to repay the physical labours of man; disclosing, at perhaps a glance, the slow revelations of nature, that are singly, and at great intervals, to immortalize future.sages."

§ 5.—Why must the instruction be conveyed by a new sense? Because we know of no other agent that can effect the object. The information, too, is to be acquired at a glance. Why at a glance? Because we know of no means by which any sense can yield instruction but by a glance, a touch, a smell, a taste, or a sound: therefore we must select from these the manner in which the new sense is to operate.

§ 6.—*Every discovery in the arts furnishes us with new theoretical agents.*

Formerly earthquakes were caused by the struggles of giants, whom Jupiter had confined beneath huge mountains. After Jupiter's dethronement, earthquakes were produced by subterraneous fires, which, confined within vast caverns, burst into lightning and rent the caverns. On the invention of gunpowder, theorists new-modelled their machinery. Keith says, "Earthquakes are caused by nitrous and sulphureous vapours enclosed in the earth, and accidentally ignited where there is no vent."

§ 7.—Here, however, is a difficulty: how is this internal and self-elaborated gunpowder ignited? Mr. Keith relates the process: "the vapours may take fire by fermentation, or by the accidental fall and collisions of rocks and stones in hollow places of the earth." But why must fermentation or the collision of rocks be the agent to ignite the vapour? Because the theorists know of none more suitable: a simple but an efficient reason.

§ 8.—Since the potency has been discovered of steam, philosophers have acquired an agent which will supercede every other in the production of earthquakes. The new process is thus related in Gregory's Dictionary of Arts and Sciences:—"The sudden explosion that occurs from volcanoes depends on the accumulation of a quantity of water which enters through some fissure connected with the sea. If the water is sufficient, it will extinguish the volcano; if not, it will be converted into steam, the expansive force of which exceeds the force of gunpowder."

§ 9.—How easily we convey water into the depths of the earth! The sea is an exhaustless reservoir, and a fissure can be made by pronouncing the word. But why must a fissure exist? Because it is the only invention by which you can convey water into the depths of the earth. The process alludes wholly to our operations.

§ 10.—Elasticity was anciently explained by saying that elastick bodies are composed of particles which are coiled up like watch springs. Magnetism furnished philosophers with a new agent. The watch springs were dismissed, and every particle of elastick bodies was surrounded by a repulsive power. To trace how theories have been successively modified as discoveries have furnished new agents, would be instructive. Magnetism and electricity have, however, been more fruitful than other discoveries in the supply of theoretical agents. The alternation of summer and winter, of day and night, of the tides, and of a list of events, from the fall of a sparrow to the projection of a bomb, are effected by magnetick and electrical agents. Magnetism and electricity furnish us with agents, whose subtility answers the exigency of our notions better than any other agents. Even acids, which long produced their pungency by puncturing our tongues with the sharp angles that mechanical philosophers gave to the insensible particles of every acid, now borrow their potency from the phenomena of magnetism.

§ 11.—*All the words and concomitants of a theory refer to our sensible experience for their significance; hence the fallacy of the language when the sensible existences are not discoverable.*

Odours become perceptible by infinitely small corpuscles that are wafted through the air, and strike our olfactory nerves.

Why must the corpuscles be wafted? Because that is a convenient means of bringing them. Can you convey to me yonder feather unless you strike, carry, or blow it? If the odorous corpuscle is either struck or carried, an agent must be provided to strike or carry it; but wafting requires the air only, and this is constantly around us.

§ 12.—"We know," says Mr. Keith, "that the heat of the sun draws vast quantities of vapours from the sea." Why is drawing the agent which the sun employs to raise the vapour? Because we know of no better agent. The dictionary of any language contains all the agents which can be predicated by the persons who speak the language. That the vapour cannot be pulled up we know from our experience. The sun may suck or draw it up, for we can also.

§ 13.—Doctor Halley imagines, that the saltness of the sea proceeds from salts which rivers convey to it from the earth. Other persons maintain that the taste is produced by a great number of salt rocks at the bottom of the sea. Why must salt be the agent? Because you cannot give water a similar taste without the agency of salt. Chymists may discover some other process by which a salt flavour may be communicated, and then we shall be able to afford the sea a different agent: why the salt has not been elaborated already in some recesses of the ocean, out of muriatick acid and soda, is a marvel.

§ 14.—To say that heavy bodies fall to the earth because the sun shines, would not be tolerated. What connexion, we should exclaim, can exist between the two phenomena. For the same reason, we should laugh at a philosopher who might tell us that bodies fall because the earth attracts them, had we not discovered in magnets that attraction produces what resembles the fall of bodies.

§ 15.—If a philosopher were to account for the fall of bodies by saying that matter possesses an inherent love of matter, we might estimate this a rational exposition. We experience that love produces a desire of contaction, to which the fall of bodies is sufficiently congruous. I wrote thus far without recollecting that love has been an agent in theories. Nitrick acid and copper combined, because they had a strong affinity for each other. The acid would leave the copper and unite with iron, because its love for iron is stronger than for copper. A similar principle caused the ancient theory of nature's abhorrence of vacuity.

§ 16.—That the heat of the sun proceeds from combustion, will be the only theory among men who are unacquainted with any other cause of heat; but when we find that chymical combinations, &c., evolve heat, we are possessed of a new agent; and can say, that the warmth experienced from the sun proceeds from a combination of its beams with the body on which they fall: the warmth is the calorick which escapes from the sunbeams, as they pass from a fluid state to a fixed.

§ 17.—*When a theory, in some of its results, conflicts with our experience, the theory is usually abandoned.*

Combustion itself was formerly attributed to the agency of phlogiston, a very subtile and insensible agent. Phlogiston was so light, that some bodies became heavier by losing it. When a theory is driven to conclusions so repugnant to our operations, its dissolution is near;—accordingly, phlogiston had to relinquish its agency in combustion to a more accommodating instrument.

§ 18.—Combustion is now performed by means of oxygen. When combustible bodies arrive at a certain temperature, oxygen loves to unite with them; and as it passes from the form of air to a fixed state, it liberates the calorick which distended it, and for which it no longer possesses any use. The deserted calorick scatters indignantly, and is the heat which we experience.

§ 19.—*Every theory and theoretical agent are significant of the sensible information to which they refer.*

This theory is congruous to a great number of phenomena,[1] yet, like every other theory, it is significant of nothing but the data which are adduced in proof of the theory: as, for instance, combustibles will not burn without oxygen; phosphorus will acquire, by combustion, as much weight as is lost by the air in which the phosphorus is burnt, and the remaining air will be devoid of oxygen, &c.

§ 20.—Why, however, must the heat which ensues in combustion have existed in the oxygen? Because no other source accords so well with our experience. This is a good reason while it lasts, but a similar reason may induce us to-morrow to attribute the heat to another cause. The language is truly significant of the sensible facts only to which it refers; and with this limitation we can never err, adopt what phraseology we please.

§ 21.—Again: why must the oxygen unite with the body which is consumed? Because we can account in no other way so well for the disappearance of the oxygen, &c. The reason is good, and the disappearance of the oxygen will continue to be thus accounted for, till experience may furnish us with a more congruous process.

§ 22.—Beattie, in his Essay on Language, says—"Some of the brute creation alter their voices when the weather is about to change. Their bodies are affected by atmospherical alterations

---

[1] In Johnson (I) this passage reads:

This theory is congruous to a great number of phenomena, and may never be superseded; still, like every other theory, it is significant of nothing but the phenomena which are adduced in proof of the theory. That combustibles will not burn without oxygen, that the residuum &c. of burnt phosphorus will acquire, by combustion, as much weight as is lost by the air in which the phosphorus is burnt, and that the remaining air will be devoid of oxygen, are truths which I do not dispute. Still, that the oxygen unites with the phosphorus, and that the heat which ensues is the discarded caloric of the oxygen, are the mere verbal machinery by which we reconcile to our own operations the phenomena which we discover.

which we cannot perceive; and they are expressing pleasant or painful sensations, even as an infant when it smiles or cries."

§ 23.—But why make the alterations of the weather a theoretical agent to affect the sensations of brutes? Because we experience such results in ourselves:—the weather affects our corns, old wounds, fractures, &c.

§ 24.—*Theories enable us to connect with pleasing illusions what would be otherwise disconnected facts.*

Theories are useful. We are acquainted with no mode of creating a science, but by embodying facts in some theory. Besides, when certain conclusions are deducible from a theory, we resort to experiments for their realization, and thus many new facts are occasionally developed. [The experiments made on the mountains Chimborazo and Schiehallion, were to discover the attractive power which was deduced from the theory of Newton.

[Again: as the attraction of cohesion was affirmed of every body, many efforts to consolidate air have been made with all the faith which could be inspired by an ignorance of the nature of language, and with all the zeal of enlisted opinion. But such experiments are valuable, even when, like the above, they are unsuccessful. To know that air cannot be compressed into solidity, is ascertainable by experiment alone; and the knowledge of what is impracticable is, in utility, only one grade below the knowledge of what is practicable.]

§ 25.—Theories enable us also to associate our knowledge with pleasing illusions. If astronomers had not applied the terms mountains, chasms, lakes, seas, and volcanoes, to the appearances of the moon, they would not have gazed so intently at that luminary. Newton would probably not have so ardently devoted his great faculties to astronomy had he supposed that he was establishing nothing but an ingenious fiction, significant of the phenomena only that he could discern. He estimated these as the most unimportant part of his knowledge;—the mere loop-

holes by which he was enabled to pry behind the curtain of nature;—a curtain erected to resist the gaze of vulgar eyes, but
pervious to his acute conjectures.*

§ 26.—*Theories are human contrivances by which we artificially associate sensible realities, and by familiar processes,
account for their production.*

But if theories are merely human contrivances, by which we
artificially associate sensible realities, and artificially account
by familiar processes for their production, what can we know
more than the information which our senses and internal experience reveal? This question is important. It seems also to be
misunderstood by every description of persons. The wise and
the simple, the learned and the ignorant, propound questions
without knowing what will constitute a solution; and investigate
nature without knowing when to be satisfied. I shall undertake
to elucidate these points, and I have entered on no topick more
practically important.

---

* We are accustomed to say that Newton discovered the laws which regulate
the motions of the heavenly bodies. We should speak more appropriately were
we to say that he discovered laws which coincide with the motions, &c., of the
heavenly bodies.

PART FOURTH

OF LANGUAGE WITH REFERENCE TO SOME OF THE
USES TO WHICH WE APPLY IT

Lecture XIX

[MUCH OF my life was passed with persons who employed
nearly ceaseless interrogatories. Questions, at length, became
to me a species of persecution; and I can now scarcely hear
one propounded without an impulse towards irritation.]

§ 1.—*Questions have interrogated every thing but themselves.*
No subject is less understood than questions. They constitute
a field which is not ungleaned merely, but unreaped. Every
thing pertaining to them is unmarked by the feet of curiosity,
and untrained by the hand of cultivation. As the eye sees every
thing but itself, so questions have interrogated every thing but
themselves. To supply this deficiency is the object of the present
discourse.

[In a late gazette a person is introduced who had perforated
the earth to discover a salt spring. At a given depth he found
water, and observed the continued ascent of inflammable air.
He solicits philosophers to tell him whether the gas exists naturally at the bottom of his perforation, or is caused by the decomposition of water.

[The above inquiry coincides with the opinion which is generally entertained of philosophy. A philosopher is deemed a
species of necromancer. He is thought capable of making discoveries without the agency of his senses. He is required to
know sights which he never saw, feels which he never felt, &c.;
or possibly he is required to announce what is not discoverable
by any person; not only what eye hath not seen, but what no eye
can see. Notions, in relation to philosophy even so vague, are
found, not with the illiterate only, but with the learned; and
hence the absurdities which are frequently dignified with the
title of philosophy. The whole proceeds from an ignorance of
the nature of questions; from not knowing what to inquire after,
and what answer to be satisfied with.]

§ 2.—*All questions which relate to the external universe must be directed to our senses.*

What is the shape of a taste, or the colour of a sound?[1] The questions are insignificant. They inquire after no information of our senses. Every interrogation which possesses a similar defect, is equally trifling, provided the question relates to the external universe:—our senses being the only means which we possess of knowing the external universe.

§ 3.—*A question which the senses cannot answer is insignificant.*

Should a spark of fire fall amid a room full of gunpowder, what effect will occur? Should a spark of fire fall amid the

---

[1] In Johnson (I) this passage reads:

I hope you recollect that in the progress of our Lectures I taught that language can effect no more than to refer us to phenomena. This position will enable us to see that every question is insignificant when it does not inquire after some sensible existence. If I should ask what is the shape of a taste, or the colour of a sound? every person would exclaim against the inanity of the questions; but the only cause of their insignificance is that they inquire after no sensible phenomenon. Every interrogation which possesses a similar defect is equally trifling.

Children employ such questions more frequently than men, and more grossly. In children the practice is deemed an exercise of laudable curiosity by persons who know as little on the subject as children. Such questions are ably ridiculed by Sterne. "By the right use and application of the auxiliary verbs, in which," says he, "a child's memory should be exercised, there is no idea can enter his brain, how barren soever, but a magazine of conceptions and conclusions may be drawn from it, thus: Did you ever see a white bear? Have I ever seen one? Might I ever have seen one? Am I ever to see one? Ought I ever to have seen one? Can I ever see one? If I should see a white bear, what should I say? If I should never see one, what then? Is there no sin in a white bear? Is it better than a black one?"

Sterne proceeds much further than I have copied; and we may find questions equally insignificant in grave speculations. In a work professedly philosophical (Theory of Agreeable Sensations), I find the following: "Actors, when they either laugh or weep, affect spectators with

satellites of Jupiter, what effect will occur? These questions are grammatically alike, yet the last is insignificant, while the first is significant. The significant question inquires after information which my senses can furnish, while the insignificant queston inquires after no information which the senses can furnish. What if the sun should wander from the zodiac? This question was propounded once in ridicule by Sterne. Every person knows it to be insignificant, though perhaps few persons can tell what constitutes the insignificance.[1]

---

the sensations which the drama expresses. But by what mechanism do the vibrations of the fibres of the actor's brain transmit themselves to that of other persons?"

You may think the author is speaking figuratively, and that his literal intention is to direct us to the interesting phenomena which we experience at scenic representations; but nothing is further from the fact. He is soberly asking a question, to which he has duly subjoined an answer that affords proof (if further proof were necessary) that the question was not intended to refer to any sensible phenomenon; hence it differs not from the above questions propounded by Sterne, or from another of Sterne's questions which I omitted: namely, what if the sun should wander from the zodiac?

[1] In Johnson (I) the passage reads:

A writer, whose name I do not recollect, says, "it is not the ignorant who should ask questions, but the wise." The ignorant can, however, ask questions, but they hazard words which may be insignificant: thus, I may ask what the effect will be if a spark of fire should fall amid gunpowder? The question is significant, not from the collocation of words, but because they refer to a sensible phenomenon. The same question will become insignificant the moment I refer to no phenomenon. Suppose I ask what the effect will be, if a spark of fire should fall amid the satellites of Jupiter?

When insignificant questions are propounded, it is well to ask the querist what he is inquiring after. In this way I have disconcerted many profound interrogatories. The moment a person knows not what he is inquiring after, his question is assuredly insignificant to himself.

[Seeing a shadow on a wall, a person asked me if there was any thing on the wall when he was not looking at it? Certainly: I can see the shadow as distinctly when your eyes are shut as when they are open. But what will become of the shadow when no man has his eyes on it? Precisely what you have named. Will the shadow be on the wall? If you enable me to know what phenomenon you are inquiring after, I can answer your question; but if your question relates to no discoverable existence, it means nothing.]

§ 4.—*Our senses alone can answer questions. Words can only refer us to what our senses reveal.*

[The nature of questions will be better understood by investigating the nature of answers. You will recollect that words can effect no more than to refer us to phenomena; hence no answer can effect more than to refer us to phenomena.]

When the Lord answered from the flaming bush the inquiry of Moses, by saying "I am that I am," the answer was wonderfully expressive of the nature of language, which can in no instance accomplish more than it effected in that. We may say to life, What art thou? and to death, What art thou? and we may address a like inquiry to the sun, the earth, the sea, the revolution of the seasons, the alternations of day and night, the fluctuation of the tides, the attraction of magnetism, and the gravitation of stones; but language can furnish them with no better answer than, I am that I am. Would we learn more in relation to them, we must seek it from our senses. Every sight, sound, taste, feel, and smell, which an object exhibits spontaneously, or which it can by any art be made to exhibit, is an answer to our question; but we may as well attempt to enlarge our family by multiplying the names of our children, as increase our knowledge of an external existence by multiplying words upon it. What our senses discover we may relate, and in such language as we deem most appropriate; but the moment we attempt to make our answers more comprehensive, we are employing language for purposes that are beyond its capacity. We may fabricate theories and definitions, but we cannot enlarge our knowledge of the external universe by an arrangement of words, any more than a conjurer can look into futurity by arranging the figures of a pack of cards.

§ 5.—*When we attempt to use language for some other purpose than to refer to our sensible experience, we are like a blind man speaking of colours.*

How does a magnet attract iron? Exhibit the magnet and the iron, and let the querist see the operation; he can receive no reply which will be so authoritative. But he sees the fact only, and not the cause. Let him examine further, and see every thing that is visible; touch every thing that is tangible, and employ similarly all his senses; if he wants to find what his senses cannot discover, his search is not only fruitless, but it is unmeaning. When he would speak of the object of such a search, language itself fails him. His sentences may be grammatical, but they will possess no sensible signification. When a blind man talks of colours, the word is sensibly insignificant to him; and every word is equally insignificant to us when it refers to the external universe, and attempts to speak of what our senses cannot discover.

§ 6.—*As colours can depict sights only, so words can converse of nothing external which is not sight, sound, taste, feel, or smell.*

Nero threatened to decapitate a painter unless he should produce three pictures on subjects that should be given to him. The first was the emperor's favourite horse. The painter finished the likeness, and it was satisfactory. He was then required to paint the emperor, and in this he also succeeded; but the last requirement was that he should paint the sound of the emperor's flute. The requirement was not within the power of colours, and the painter was beheaded.

§ 7.—That colours are unable to depict sounds, tastes, and

smells, we are aware; but we know not that words are unable to discourse of any thing external which is not a sight, sound, taste, feel, or smell. The inability in both cases possesses the same foundation in nature. Colours are sights; hence, no combination of them can represent what is not visible. In the same way, words, which relate to the external universe, are in effect sights, sounds, tastes, feels, and smells; hence, no combination of them can discourse of what is not sight, sound, taste, feel, or smell.

[The boundary which separates the phenomena that may be represented by colours, from those to which colours are inadequate, is, therefore, sufficiently defined; but no writer has imagined that there is a limit beyond which words also cannot discourse. Nor is the latter position easily conceived, for we can no more exemplify with words that there is a limit to their applicability, than a painter can demonstrate with colours, that there are phenomena which colours cannot delineate.]

§ 8.—*An external thing that is not sensible, is as incongruous a thing as an insensible elephant.*

Even to speak of any thing external which my senses cannot discover, is a contradiction; because the word thing, when it refers to the external universe, signifies some revelation of my senses. Endeavour to teach a Frenchman the meaning of the word thing. If you cannot speak French, nor he English, no ingenuity of yours, and no aptness of his, can enable you to convey to him a meaning of the word thing, unless you make him understand that it signifies some sight, sound, taste, feel, or smell, which you may present to his senses. An external thing which none of our senses can discover, is a word divested of signification. We may as well talk of an insensible horse, as an insensible external thing:—both words admit equally the existence of a sensible revelation.

§ 9.—The same difficulty occurs, employ what word you will in the place of thing. You cannot more readily teach the Frenchman a meaning of the word existence, than of the word thing. You must appeal to his senses for the meaning of existence, precisely as you must for the meaning of the word horse or elephant; hence, an insensible external existence is a contradiction; for the word external existence admits the cognizance of your senses, as much as the word white or horse.

§ 10.—*Every question which relates to the external universe implies (as essential to its signification) that it seeks some sensible information.*

What is lightning? The phrase is elliptical. It means what thing is lightning; and we have already shown that the word thing signifies a sensible existence; hence, the question truly inquires after the information of the senses, and can be answered by their information only. The same result follows if you supply the ellipsis with the word existence, or with whatever other word you may substitute as the substantive of the pronoun what.

§ 11.—*When we attempt to forsake sensible information, it is still present with us.*

We are situated in relation to the senses, like St. Paul in relation to evil. He says, "when I attempt to do good, evil is present with me";—so, when we attempt to forsake sensible information, it is still present with us. Apple is the name of something which can be seen, felt, and tasted. The word admits these qualities; hence, to speak of an insensible apple is to contradict what must be admitted, to make the word significant. A like difficulty occurs with every word. External existence names some thing that can be seen, felt, tasted, heard, or smelled; hence, to speak of an insensible external existence is to contradict the admission which gives signification to the phrase. We may, with no greater impropriety, speak of an invisible brilliancy, an inaudible noise, or any other contradiction. Boys in the country wear, attached to their shirts, a false collar, which is called a dickey. This is usually much starched, and sometimes surrounds the boy's neck, so as to bury his chin and mouth. A boy who was thus annoyed, was seen by his schoolmaster to jump repeatedly; and on being asked why he jumped, said he was attempting to spit over his dickey. The boy's attempts are analogous to ours when we endeavour to exalt our meaning beyond our senses. The sensible meaning of words cannot be detached in our flights, any more than the boy could jump without carrying his dickey upwards with him.

§ 12.—*Diminution is one of the means by which we attempt to conceal the absurdity of employing the names of sensible existences, where the existences are not discoverable.*

The original of all matter is, we are told, atoms, which are so small that millions of them must be aggregated before the mass becomes sensible. Still, these little insensible primitives are atoms. Were we told that they are gwho, we should scorn the unmeaning affirmation. Atoms seems intelligible, though we forget that it is applied where our senses can discover none of the sensible information which gives the word its signification; hence, that the word, when thus used, possesses no more sensible signification than the word gwho.

§ 13.—*Subtilization is another means by which we attempt to conceal the fallacy of employing the names of sensible existences, where the existences are not discoverable by our senses.*

Attraction is attenuated as we discover it in magnetick and electrick experiments; but when we wish to predicate attraction where our senses cannot discover it, we are forced to subtiliate it verbally, till it becomes too subtile for our senses. In this condition, it is the most potent agent that is employed in verbal philosophy. It not only holds together the insensible atoms which constitute a diamond, but it upholds the earth, sun, and planets. The only difficulty is, that when we subtract from the word attraction its sensible qualities, we leave an empty sound:—as empty as the word apple when we abstract from that word its sensible references.

§ 14.—*Insensibleness is as much a negation of external exist-ence, as death is a negation of life, or absence a negation of presence.*

Insensible evaporation, insensible perspiration, insensible heat, &c., are agents by which also we attempt to penetrate be-yond the sensible realities of the universe. By affixing to them the adjunct insensible, we endeavour to account for our in-ability to discover them by our senses; but insensibility is as much a negation of all which gives signification to the words, as death is a negation of life. We read in the Arabian Nights of a facetious rich man, who tendered a sumptuous entertainment to a hungry mendicant:—"Eat, brother, of this ragout, and spare not this stewed lamb and pistachio nuts." To the poor man's senses, the table was unfurnished with viands of any kind; and though his complaisance induced him for a period to accompany his host in the evolutions of eating, his stomach gave him practical admonitions of the nature of insensible ragouts.

Evaporation, perspiration, attraction, &c., are so subtile in their sensible form, that we see not the inanity of depriving them entirely of sensible properties; but the same principle which nullifies an insensible ragout, nullifies an insensible vapour, &c.

§15.—*All that Providence has placed within our power, in relation to the external universe, is to note what our senses discover.*

Finally, all that Providence has placed within our power in relation to the external universe, is to note and record what our senses discover. To this end, we may compound elements and analyze compounds. We may examine causes and trace effects. While our language is confined to what our senses disclose, every word is significant. Within this circle, we may propose significant questions and receive significant answers; but the moment we step beyond the circle, we can neither propound a significant question nor frame a significant answer. We are worse than blind men when they attempt to talk about colours; for though their language is sensibly insignificant to themselves, it is significant to others; but when we attempt to discourse about external realities which no person's senses can discover, language itself fails us, and becomes insignificant. Our language may retain a verbal meaning, but it will lose its sensible meaning; it may be significant of theories, definitions, mathematical calculations, and other verbal processes; but it will not be significant of the realities of the external universe.

§ 16.—If we examine the speculations of philosophers, we shall find that no truth is so little known as the above. As the stars appear at sunset to supply the light of the absent sun, so philosophy commences its revelations where our senses terminate their revelations. But here the parallel ceases. The stars possess a little light that is inherent and independent of the sun; but words possess no inherent meaning in any case, and no external meaning independent of the senses.

§ 17.—*Language cannot enable us to penetrate beyond the range of our senses.*

To deem ourselves shut up in the universe with no capacity to know or even speak any thing of it but what our senses reveal, seems a narrower range than we are accustomed to attribute to our knowledge. Still, such is our situation. Language cannot enable us to pass the barrier of our senses. We may as well attempt to construct a dwelling house which shall be undiscoverable by the senses, as construct a proposition which shall signify something of the external universe that cannot be discovered by the senses. The same difficulty obstructs both attempts. We possess for the house no materials but such as are sensible; and we possess no words for the proposition but such as refer for their signification to sensible information.

§ 18.—I have now, I trust, shown that every question which relates to the external universe is insignificant if it cannot be answered by our senses. It is insignificant because we can frame no question that will not, in its terms, relate to sensible information; and secondly, because we possess no means of knowing any thing of the external universe but what our senses reveal.

Lecture XX

EVERY QUESTION WHICH RELATES TO WHAT IS INTERNAL OF MAN, IS INSIGNIFICANT IF IT CANNOT BE ANSWERED BY OUR CONSCIOUSNESS

§ 1.—HAVING shown in my last discourse that every question which relates to the external universe is insignificant if it cannot be answered by our senses, I must add that every question which relates to the universe within ourselves, is insignificant if it cannot be answered by our consciousness.

§ 2.—*We cannot readily designate by words the phenomena which constitute our internal consciousness.*

When a flash of lightning crosses the horizon, it appears as vividly to persons around you as to you; hence, when you attach a name to it, every person knows what the name signifies. But when you become conscious of some phenomenon within yourself, and wish to speak of it, much difficulty occurs in making other persons know the phenomenon to which you allude. This difficulty embarrasses all discourse which relates to what we experience internally.

§ 3.—*Every man recognises the items of his own consciousness, how unable soever he may be to designate them by words to other men.*

If you ask me to tell you how I felt at beholding the decapitation of a felon, I may be unable to give you any verbal definition of my feeling, or any verbal description of it; still, I know precisely what I experienced on the occasion.* The feeling may say to me, I am that I am. You cannot transmute me into words. You may reflect on me, and note in relation to me

---

* Or I knew while I was experiencing the feeling.

all that you experience. You may refer to me in any words that you deem appropriate, but your words are not me. I am myself alone. Your words cannot alter me, or enlarge or abridge me. They are the breath of your own body. So far as they refer to me, you must look to me alone as the only true expositor of myself.

§ 4.—*Every question which relates to our internal consciousness is best answered by the mute revelations of consciousness itself.*

What constitutes personal identity? What enables you to know that you are the individual who, thirty years ago, arrived in this city? The usual answer to this question would be words, but the true answer is independent of all words. It is simply what you discover it to be. A dumb mute possesses on this subject all the knowledge which you possess, and usually in much greater clearness and purity than you possess it; for with you, the answer is probably so confounded with words that the phenomena of nature (which constitute the real answer) are but little regarded.

§ 5.—What are thoughts? What is memory? What is an idea? What are conscience and consciousness? They may severally answer, I am what I am. No answer is so good as this, because none is so little likely to mislead the inquirer. Would we know further what they are, we must resort to our experience, and in its mute revelations alone can we receive the answer. What is lightning? Should the clouds exhibit to me a flash, it would constitute the best answer that the question is susceptible of. Precisely thus, when I ask what is memory. Should the recollection occur to me of a flash of lightning, the recollection would constitute the best answer which the question about memory is susceptible of.

§ 6.—*In relation to the realities of nature which are not external of us, language possesses no signification but as it refers to our internal experience.*

To experience the recollection of a flash of lightning will tell you only what the word memory names. You may say that you wish to know how memory is caused, and what constitutes its nature. Recur, then, again, to your consciousness. Experience all which you can in relation to memory, and receive the experience as the only answer which the questions admit. If experience will not answer the questions, language cannot; for language possesses no signification in the premises, except what it derives from its reference to your experience.

§ 7.—*Questions are insignificant when they seek what consciousness cannot answer.*

We can answer every question which inquires after any thing that we can experience, either by our senses or our consciousness; but a question which inquires after none of these is an inquiry after nothing. How would memory look if we could see it? How would it feel, taste, smell, or sound? Does it die, or continue to live in the soul after the death of the body? If it is a property of the soul, why does it decay in old men? If it is a property of matter, is it confined to a particular piece? Does it possess gender and number? We may form as many such questions as we can form syntactical sentences; but the questions are like a numerical sum whose figures refer to nothing. The figures may be multiplied, divided, added, and subtracted, according to the rules which figures obey; but if the figures possess no ulterior reference, their product will possess no ulterior signification. Our questions also may be subjected to all the rules of logick that are applicable to the words; but so long as the words possess no ulterior reference, the answers which may be elaborated from them will possess no ulterior signification.

Lecture XXI

INQUIRIES AFTER A THEORY WE MISTAKE FOR AN INVESTIGATION OF NATURE

§ 1.—*The words cause and effect are, like all other words, insignificant when they refer to nothing; and are never sensibly significant of any thing but the sensible particulars to which they refer.*

WHEN WE disengage from our grasp a stone, and see it fall to the earth, we inquire into the cause of its descent. The inquiry is proper, but we can know nothing of the external universe except what our senses disclose; hence we must seek a sensible cause. This, however, is not our practice. We invent a verbal cause which we confound with the sensible realities of the external universe. The verbal cause is created by attributing to the stone and its descent some agent that we know to possess (were it present) the power to produce the descent. We discover in magnets a power to attract iron; hence, by attributing attraction to the earth, we make the descent of the stone congruous to our notions of causation. Nearly every movement of our body, and every volition of our mind, causes a sensible effect. We are conceived, born, and we die, by a sensible process of cause and effect. All our business, cares, and pleasures, are a combination of causes and effects. We need not wonder, therefore, that men are usually unconscious that cause and effect are only certain discoverable relations; and that where the relations are undiscoverable, the words cause and effect can be applied with no more propriety than we can apply the word elephant where no quadruped is discoverable.

§ 2.—*To invent a verbal cause that will make a unique operation of nature, congruous to operations with which we are familiar, is mistaken for a physical discovery.*

"The little bodies which compose water are," says Locke, "so loose from one another, that the least force separates them.

Nay, if we consider their perpetual motion, they possess no cohesion. But let a sharp cold come, and they will unite and not be separated without great force. He that could make known the cement that makes them adhere so closely, would discover a great secret."

§ 3.—Nothing is easier than to discover the cement if it refers to any sensible information. We may examine water, and note all the information which it can yield our senses in its transformation into ice. But this was not what Locke was seeking. He wanted a theory that would make the transformation of water into ice, analogous to some of our accustomed operations. This, however, was not seeking for any thing that exists in the external universe, but for a process of words.

§ 4.—*Verbal causes may be predicated in infinitum; hence, they are characteristically distinguished from the realities of nature.*

Admit that a philosopher shall say he has discovered the cement which holds frozen water in solidity. "Then," continues Locke, "this discovery aids us very little without he can discover the bonds which hold together the cement." Grant that the philosopher shall discover these also. "This will not avail," says Locke, "unless he can discover the cement which holds together the particles of the bonds"; and thus he must proceed without end: for every cement must be composed of parts which, equally with the first, will require to be cemented. If any person chooses to divert himself by constructing such speculations, I entertain no objection; but let us not confound them with the sensible realities of the external universe. When we seek causes, we must seek a sensible existence; and where none is discoverable, we must be content to note the deficiency as part of our sensible knowledge.

§ 5.—*The verbal causes which a theorist adopts are usually selected with a reference to his own occupations.*

When the fabled inhabitants of a besieged city consulted as

to the best means of defence, the masons recommended ramparts of stone, a carpenter recommended that they should be made of wood, and the tanners thought leather preferable. So, if you examine the various theories of philosophers, you will generally be able to divine the science with whose phenomena the philosopher is familiar. If the formation of rocks is to be accounted for by a chemist, they are caused by a chemical precipitation among the waters of a flood, by crystallizations, and by chemical combinations. If a physician becomes geologist, the interiour of the earth suffers convulsions; volcanoes vomit up rocks, and the ocean fractures them into smaller stones. If such speculations can subserve any useful purpose, I would not reject the benefit in contempt of the machinery; but that such speculations should be mistaken for the realities of nature is as curious an errour as human weakness ever exhibited.

§ 6.—*We must discriminate between inquiries after a theory, and inquiries after the realities of creation.*

To inquire sensibly into the structure of the earth is to record all which our senses can discover. To inquire verbally is to select from our experience, and apply to the earth, such agents as we have found competent, in other cases, to produce and arrange rocks, or something analogous to rocks.

§ 7.—*Natural operations which are peculiar, we find difficult to subject to a theory.*

We are perplexed when we attempt to account verbally for the generation of animal life, or for any other operation to which our sensible experience furnishes no analogous operation. If the embryo animal can be deemed the production of either an egg or a seed, we are satisfied. These are accordingly one theory. Animalculæ are said to be discoverable in certain seminal fluids; and as we are familiar with the growth of animals from small to large, we can easily account for the large if we can assume the small; hence, animalculæ are another theory of generation.

§ 8.—But out of what was the first material object created? This is the most perplexing question that theory undertakes to answer. All the creative operations which we experience proceed from some material. An animal requires an egg; a tree requires a seed; but the first matter could proceed from neither egg nor seed; hence, we must either admit that matter is without a beginning, or we must produce the first matter without egg, seed, or other material. We adopt the latter alternative. Matter was produced, we say, by the fiat of Deity. We know not how;—or, in other words, we know of no analogous process, and hence can make no theory.*

§ 9.—We are satisfied with the vivification of eggs, provided we can discover in the animal which produces them any thing

---

* Inductive philosophy consists in inventing verbal causes for sensible operations. Newton's laws for philosophising are properly rules for the construction of theories:—that is, rules for the finding of verbal causes. We think a cause must exist, hence we see not the absurdity of attributing verbal causes. Cause and effect are, however, mere words. Nothing gives them significancy but our experience. Why, then, should not our experience be permitted to teach us that causes are not universal? An uneducated Ethiopian believes fluidity to be inseparable from water; but experience teaches us that the Ethiopian is mistaken. We gain nothing but delusion when we will not limit our knowledge by the revelations of nature. The relation of cause and effect is like the relation of fluidity and water. Both relations exist where we discover them to exist, and they exist not where we discover that they exist not. Air is, I believe, the only substance which presents to us tangibility without visibility. Had we not this example, we should deem visibility inseparable from tangibility. We should be correct, also, in such a belief; for the universality of the position would signify our experience only. But can any thing exist without a cause? The question is insignificant except as it refers to our experience, and no answer is sensibly significant beyond what we experience. To reject a negative instance is as fallacious as to reject an affirmative instance. Our knowledge of the realities of the universe cannot be extended beyond our sensible experience.

ED. NOTE.—Newton's laws for philosophizing given in his *Principia*, Bk. III:

1) We are to admit no more causes of natural things than such as are both true and sufficient to explain their appearances.

2) Therefore to the same natural effects we must, as far as possible, assign the same causes.

3) The qualities of bodies, which admit neither intensification nor remission of degrees, and which are found to belong to all bodies within the reach of our experiments, are to be esteemed the universal qualities of all bodies whatsoever.

4) In experimental philosophy we are to look upon propositions inferred by general induction from phenomena as accurately or very nearly true, notwithstanding any contrary hypotheses that may be imagined, till such time as other phenomena occur, by which they may either be made more accurate, or liable to exceptions.

analogous to sexual organs and sexual intercourse; but some oviparous animals present the singularity of no sexual organs. Some animals, also, (oysters,) possess no power of locomotion, and therefore can possess no sexual intercourse. These cases are perplexing to our modes of theorizing; but we avoid the difficulty by attributing verbally to each animal a double sex, and thus its increase is reconciled to the exigency of our experience in other cases.

§ 10.—We discover that some plants blossom without producing fruit, and that others of the same species blossom and also produce fruit. We discover, also, that blossoms which bear fruit, will not fructify when they are secluded from the blossoms that bear no fruit. These facts we reconcile to our experience in other matters, by a theory which attributes sex to plants. The fructiferous blossoms are female, the barren are the male; while a certain farina acts as a seminal agent. This is transported to the female organs by insects, or currents of air; and the gross machinery is completed, and fructification rendered satisfactorily intelligible to us.

§ 11.—*A sensible cause is a sensible existence, and produces a sensible effect; but in a theoretical cause, nothing is sensible but the effect.*

If we exhaust the air out of a tube, (an ordinary pump,) water will ascend thirty-four feet in the pump. Quicksilver will not rise higher in the pump than thirty inches. These facts are as interesting without a theory as with. Still we desire some theory that shall make the ascent analogous to operations with which we are familiar; hence, we say that the atmosphere presses the fluid, and pushes it up the tube. If the push existed, it would perform the office which we assign to it; therefore, we assume its existence; but after we accumulate all the phenomena to which the theory is applicable, (and they are many,) the push is but the verbal agent, by which we make the phenomena conform to other processes with which we are familiar.

A sensible pressure is something in itself. It is a feel; (sometimes a sight and a feel;) but the pressure which the atmosphere exerts on water and quicksilver can be neither seen nor felt. All we see is the ascent of the water and quicksilver.

§ 12.—*While we employ verbal causes to account for a sensible effect, the process harmonizes with our experience; but when we employ a verbal cause to produce verbal effects, the process leads us to manifest absurdities. The further we proceed in a catenation of such causes and effects, the more evidently we recede from the realities of nature.*

That water will ascend in a vacuum thirty-four feet is attributed theoretically to the weight of the atmosphere. The assumed weight is the verbal cause, and it makes the ascent of the water congruous to our own manual operations, and hence is satisfactory to us. But we proceed further:—assuming that the verbal weight of the atmosphere is a reality of the external universe, we deduce from it that a man of ordinary dimensions sustains on his body a pressure of fourteen tons weight of atmosphere. Every instance in which we thus react on verbal causes produces a monster as astounding as the above. The result alone ought to teach us that the process is fallacious; especially as the absurdities which the process creates become more glaring, if possible, the further we proceed with it; hence, by a tacit agreement, philosophers usually refrain from deducing any verbal effects from the ability of man to sustain a weight of fourteen tons.

§ 13.—*Inquisition concerning the realities of the external universe is limited to the discoveries of our senses; but verbal inquisition is boundless.*

I have probably adduced examples enough to show that before we answer any question, we must determine whether the answer is to be verbal or sensible. If the answer is to be restricted to the realities of the external universe, the answer will be limited by what our senses can discover, and we must announce their information in any words which we deem most likely to designate the sights, sounds, feels, tastes, and smells, to which we refer. But if the answer is to be a theory, we may descend into the centre of the earth, or ascend to the centre of the empyrean; we may talk of what happened before the flood, and what shall occur after the universal conflagration; we may with Newton crush the earth into a size which shall be less than a nutmeg; or, with Descartes, dilate a wine glass full of air till it shall fill all space. But let no man confound such answers with the realities of the external universe. Ingenious they may be, and they may refer to certain sensible experiments; but beyond the sensible existences to which they refer, they are words; and besides words, they are nothing.

§ 14.—*In questions, also, which relate to our internal consciousness, we must discriminate whether the answer is to be a theory, or the revelation of consciousness.*

All the remarks which I have made on questions that refer to the external universe, apply equally to questions that relate to the universe within ourselves. In this branch of the subject, an answer may either be theoretical or experimental; and before we answer a question, we must ascertain the kind of answer which is required of us: for instance,

"Our soul possesses the power," says Locke, "of exciting motion by thought; but if we inquire how the soul produces such an effect, we are entirely in the dark."

[The difficulty arises from a misconception of the nature of inquiries. If to inquire is to observe phenomena, we act as absurdly in saying we cannot inquire, as a man would who should insist that he cannot walk. When we say to him, you are now walking, he may reply, this is not what I call walking. But what does he call walking? He cannot tell. He knows only that he is unable to walk. He determines that nothing which he can do shall be called walking; hence nothing will make him admit that he can walk. To inquire, means only to seek all the phenomena which a subject exhibits. We create obstacles by claiming for the process an unknown and occult signification: a signification which we cannot elucidate by any phenomenon. We divest the word inquire of every sensible signification, and then puzzle ourselves with the assertion, that we cannot inquire.]

Motion is produced by thought precisely as I experience when I raise my hand to my head. I may find a difficulty in designating by words what I experience; but my knowledge on the subject is complete, for I know the process itself. Locke, however, wanted some theory that should make the process analogous to some external sensible operation, and hence the difficulty.

§ 15.—*Theories are usually derived from our familiar physical operations; hence, we cannot invent satisfactory theories for mental operations;—the two departments of creation not being sufficiently analogous.**

When the ascent of water succeeds a vacuum, we reconcile the ascent to our familiar manual operations, by attributing a pressure to the surrounding atmosphere; but we possess no external operation that is analogous to the succession of volition and motion; hence, the difficulty of answering the question of Locke:—we possess not the means of inventing a satisfactory theory. Locke evidently attributes the difficulty to a mystery of nature, while it is nothing but the inapplicability to mental phenomena of the verbal process by which we construct theories:—theories are all constructed from our physical experience, but physical experience is not congruous to mental operations.

§ 16.—How does memory perform its operations? Before we answer the question, we should ascertain whether the answer must be a theory or a revelation of nature. If the answer is to be a revelation of nature, the mute developments of our experience yield the only correct answer. Words can refer us

* See ante, § § 2, 3, and 7.

to these developments; but the moment they attempt more than such a reference, we are theorizing:—that is, we are probably attempting to make the operations of memory analogous verbally to our manual operations. Locke somewhere speaks of the operations of memory under the half allegory and half theory of a schoolboy with a slate, writing down certain events, and which writing eventually becomes obliterated. Again he speaks of memory as an agent that runs about the brain in search of faded impressions; like a lackey in search of a mislaid umbrella. The analogies are so gross, that they are asserted more as an illustration of memory than as a theory; but they evince the usual unacquaintance with the distinction which exists between an inquiry after a theory, and inquiry after the realities of nature.

§ 17.—How are remote objects visible? Just as we discover. This would be deemed a very foolish answer; still, it is the best that can be given, for it refers us to the revelations of experience, which alone can yield us a correct answer. But the answer is peculiarly dissatisfactory because the question seeks a theory. When we are satisfied of this fact, the above answer is indeed improper. Lord Monboddo answers the question by saying that the soul leaves the body, and emanates to the distant object. The contact which is thus verbally produced makes vision analogous to our accustomed manual operations, and hence supplies what we require. The reflection of light, and the camera obscura which is produced by a dissected eye, furnish us with a theory that is more congruous to our accustomed operations than even Lord Monboddo's; hence, vision is now performed by the light which rebounds to our eye from visible objects, and produces on the retina a small miniature of the external object. When we get a distant object thus into the eye, we find but little difficulty in understanding how (according to our own operations) an external and distant object becomes cognizable to our minds.

§ 18.—Want of contact with external objects is, you perceive, the difficulty which must be obviated before seeing can be made congruous to our physical operations. A like difficulty pertains to hearing and smelling, and we vanquish it, as in the case of seeing, by a theory which supplies the contact. The air constitutes a medium through which are floated theoretical atoms of odour, and theoretical appulses of sound, from the objects heard and smelt, to the olfactory and auditory nerves.

§ 19.—*The silent revelations of experience can alone teach us the realities of our mental nature.*

"Actors, when they either laugh or weep, affect spectators with the sensations which the drama expresses. But by what mechanism do the vibrations of the actor's brain transmit themselves to that of other persons?"

§ 20.—Is the answer to be a theory, or a revelation of nature? We must ascertain before we undertake to answer. To know how in reality an actor affects us, we must resort to our experience. The answer will not be words, but the phenomenon itself. If, however, we desire a theory, we must invent some verbal machinery that will make the operation congruous to our manual operations.

§ 21.—Though we deem any mental phenomenon inexplicable unless we can show it to be analogous to physical operations, we deem the operations of Deity well explained when we can show them to be analogous to mental operations. "The Lord said, let there be light, and there was light." But how could light be produced by such a declaration? Very easily: creation follows the volition of Deity, just as our limbs obey the volition of our minds. This theory makes the whole satisfactory; hence, we may see that nothing is essential to the construction of a theory, but the predication verbally of some means which we have experienced to be capable of producing a result like that which we are striving to explain. But however this may be, I hope you now perceive that we mistake inquiries after a theory for investigations of nature. The two inquiries are wholly different, and are dependent on different principles. By confounding the inquiries we shall gain nothing but delusion. By separating them, we shall at least discriminate between the verbal ingenuity of man, and the realities of creation.

Lecture XXII

INQUIRIES AFTER THE DEFINITION OF WORDS WE MISTAKE FOR AN INVESTIGATION OF NATURE

§ 1.—*We should discriminate between the verbal significa-tion of a word and its sensible signification, if we would cor-rectly appreciate either language or the sensible universe.*

As WE inquire after a theory and mistake the inquiry for an investigation of nature, so we inquire after the verbal significa-tion of words, and mistake the inquiry for an investigation of nature. What is a point? A name which we have given to a certain sight or feel: as, for instance, what I see when I look at the end of a needle;—or, what I feel when I touch the end of the needle. But these, say mathematicians, are not a point. A real point cannot be seen or felt. It possesses no length, breadth, nor thickness. The difference, however, between me and mathe-maticians is, that they are speaking of the verbal meaning of the word point, whilst I am speaking of the sensible meaning. The two meanings are distinct, and we must discriminate to which we refer if we would correctly appreciate either language or the sensible universe.

§ 2.—*Nothing is more common than to confound the verbal meaning of a word with the sensible.*

What is a line? Something which possesses length without breadth or thickness. You cannot exhibit such a line, nor can you feel one. Every line that you either see or feel will possess breadth as well as length. The line which possesses neither breadth nor thickness is verbal, and your words constitute its verbal meaning. Let no man, when he investigates the verbal line, suppose that he is investigating the realities of the external universe, though nothing is more common than such mistakes.

§ 3.—*Before we can tell what an atom is, we must know whether the question refers to the verbal meaning of the word, or the sensible.*

A sensible atom is discoverable by my senses. The word is properly applied to a sight and a feel, as an atom of sand; but we may apply it to an odour or a sound, or any other sensible information to which we may deem the word appropriate. But a verbal atom is a quantity of words; for instance, the following:—"Atoms are the primitive material particles of which all bodies are composed. An atom is not so small as a mathematical point, because an atom must possess length, breadth, and thickness, or no aggregation of atoms could produce sensible bodies:—things without length, breadth, and thickness, cannot acquire length, &c., by aggregation. Atoms are, however, so small, that a greater number of them than the sands on the sea shore are emitted every instant from a lighted candle. Those which, in the form of light, are radiated from the sun, fall millions of miles, and with inconceivable rapidity, yet hurt not the eye on which they strike, though an organ of sensation the most tender of any with which we are acquainted." A verbal atom differing thus from a sensible atom, you will perceive in all inquisition which relates to atoms, the necessity of understanding whether the questions refer to the verbal meaning of atoms, or to the sensible meaning.

§ 4.—You find that atoms must possess length, breadth, and thickness, or they will be unsuited to the duty of constituting the material universe. But now occurs a difficulty:—If atoms possess length, they are divisible in infinitum; for we can no more annihilate length by division, than we can create length by an aggregation of bodies which possess no length. If, therefore, every atom is divisible in infinitum, we can never arrive at the primitive atoms out of which bodies are formed. This difficulty has not been found insurmountable: we are told that the primitive atoms are indivisible from no lack of parts, but from a hardness which renders them indivisible.

§ 5.—*Every word which possesses a sensible meaning possesses also a verbal meaning.*

Let us now examine the division to which the atoms ought to have been subjected interminably, if Deity had not specially interposed an impassable hardness. What is division? The sensible meaning is a sight or a feel, and usually both a sight and a feel. The word may signify also the information of the other senses; hence, we may speak of dividing a taste or a sound. In these cases, as in all other sensible significations of the word, it will mean the sensible information to which it refers.

§ 6.—But this division will not answer when we undertake to divide interminably. We must employ a division which is composed of words: for instance, "to cut in two,—to make two of what was previously one." With this division we can accomplish wonders. The moment we apply it to an invisible atom, the atom becomes two, and we may continue the process interminably.* The two divisions being thus radically different, (the sensible division being a sensible operation, while a verbal division is a process of words,) nothing is more important, when we are required to answer any question which relates to division, than that we should know whether the question refers to the verbal meaning of the word or the sensible meaning.

§ 7.—*The external sensible universe is very different from the verbal universe of philosophers.*

"One grain of pure gold can be hammered so as to cover a surface of fifty square inches. But after the leaf is hammered to the extent of our ability, it still possesses an upper surface and an under surface, and hence possesses parts which are divisible,

---

* See Lecture XVI, § 16.

though we possess not the skill to divide them. If the leaf could be divided, it would again possess an under surface and an upper, and therefore could be again divided, and thus in infinitum, till the surface would equal not only that of the whole earth, but be infinitely larger."

§ 8.—The above process is copied from Rees's Cyclopedia, but we can plainly perceive that the division spoken of possesses only a verbal signification. If the writer, when he thus spoke of dividing the leaf in infinitum, had asked himself whether he was referring to the sensible meaning of the word division, or the verbal meaning, he could not have failed from discovering the true character of his speculation. It is verbal, and the external universe is not concluded by it or concerned in it.

§ 9.—*The question How? refers usually to a theory,—the question What? to a definition: we mistake both for physical inquiries.*

"That the principle which thinks and is within us, should in vain ask itself what constitutes thought, is a contradiction," says D'Alembert, "which, even in the pride of our reasoning, cannot fail to confound us."

§ 10.—D'Alembert[1] was inquiring after the verbal signification of the word thought, and he could devise no satisfactory definition. If he wished to know what thoughts are, independently of language, nothing can be more easy than to discover.

---

[1] In Johnson (I) this passage is developed as follows:

But what kind of answer is required? Verbal. And here lies the difficulty. Independently of words, nothing can be more easy than to know what thoughts are: they are precisely what we experience. Language can in no way effect more than to refer us to the phenomena. We are ignorant of this simple truth, and therefore perplex ourselves with verbal elucidations.

When we attempt to explain phenomena by the aid of words, we act as unwisely as if we were to teach a child the signification of whiteness, not by directing his eyes to the sight, but by telling him that whiteness is the reflection on his retina of all the coloured rays of light. Language

They are what we experience. What is whiteness? The name of a certain sight; for instance, the colour which you discover in snow. Much perplexity is, however, experienced when you seek the verbal meaning of whiteness. We may parody the words of D'Alembert, and say of whiteness, "that the principle which sees whiteness and is within us, should in vain ask itself what constitutes whiteness, is a contradiction which in the pride of our reasoning cannot fail to confound us." But what do we wish to effect? We wish to employ some words that shall not merely designate the phenomena to which the word whiteness refers, but we wish to convert whiteness into words. We may as well be surprised when we cannot transmute sunbeams into gold, as when we cannot transmute whiteness into words. Whiteness is a sight, and words possess no affinity to it:—words are sounds, and they cannot be converted into whiteness.

§ 11.—*Every existence is its own best interpreter, and its only physical revealer.*

This asking what is whiteness, what is thought, &c., proceeds on the supposition that whiteness, &c., is not itself, but something else. Now, in all cases, whiteness or thought, &c., is itself. Words can refer us to the existences which we name whiteness, but words can effect no more:—they cannot become whiteness.

---

is indebted for its signification to the phenomena to which it refers, but we reverse the principle. We act as if the nature of a phenomenon was governed by the language that we apply to it.

This gross perversion is almost universal. If I should discover a strange substance, the first question with every beholder would be, What is it? It is what you see. This answer would be thought very absurd. No person would be satisfied till some bystander affixed a name to the new discovery, when the crowd would immediately disperse, and imagine themselves possessed of every requisite information. They would not appear to know that the name is merely a human invention, and that all which gives it significancy is the appearance, feel, and other sensible phenomena which the substance before them exhibits, and which they disregard.

§ 12.—*The verbal meaning of a word is usually founded on some theory.*

What is magnetism, aurora borealis, attraction, gravity, &c.? To answer these questions sensibly is to refer us to what our senses reveal; but such answers are rarely given and rarely expected. The querist seeks usually the verbal meaning of magnetism, attraction, &c., and without the slightest suspicion that his investigations are verbal. The verbal answer is a definition founded on some theory. I object not to it, and it may be useful; but I wish to discriminate between the verbal answer and the sensible, that men may not seem to disagree, where perhaps they merely misunderstand each other:—that they may not waste their efforts on verbal disquisitions, when they wish to obtain knowledge of the external universe.

§ 13.—*The process which deems words the ultimate objects of inquiry, may, like all other verbal processes, be continued without end.*

What is conscience, hope, faith, courage? The natural meaning is what we can discover by our consciousness, while the verbal meaning is such a definition as approved authority shall have imposed: for instance, "conscience is the monitor within us,—the internal man,—the principle which regulates our moral conduct, &c." Like every other verbal process, this, also, may be continued in infinitum: thus, What is conscience? The moral sense. What is the moral sense? A. And what is A? B. What is B? The process admits of no end, for the last answer is as questionable as the first.

Lecture XXIII

IN ALL INQUIRIES WHICH RELATE TO THE SENSIBLE UNIVERSE, WE MUST DISCRIMINATE THE SENSE TO WHOSE INFORMATION THE INQUIRY REFERS

§ 1.—*Distance names a sight and a feel; hence the duplicity of asking whether seeing can inform us of distance.*

CAN seeing inform us of distance? Do you mean the sight

distance, or the feel? The moment we thus discriminate the information to which we refer, the question about distance loses its interest. Seeing cannot inform us of the feel distance, any more than feeling can inform us of the sight distance. We are playing a game of bo-peep when we discourse of distance, without discriminating the sense to which we refer.

§ 2.—*When we know that the word external is restricted to the information of feeling, we shall not wonder that hearing, tasting, smelling, and seeing, cannot reveal what we mean by the word external.*

A French philosopher attempted to elucidate human knowledge by a statue which is successively endued with the five senses. When it possesses no sense but smelling, its consciousness consists in the perception of odours, without any knowledge that the odours proceed from an external existence. The statue acquires hearing next, but still it obtains no consciousness that any thing external of itself exists. It acquires tasting and vision:—the tastes seem to be nothing but such as we occasionally experience when we complain of having a bitter taste in our mouths. They are accompanied with no extrinsick connexions. Vision also presented nothing but a succession of sights which passed internally before the mind, like images painted on it. Finally, the statue obtained the sense of feeling. Then, for the first time, it learnt the existence of external objects. It found that its pedestal was external, the floor was external, &c.

§ 3.—The mystery vanishes when we discriminate the sense to whose phenomena the philosopher refers for a signification of the word external. External names feels, hence the statue possessed no acquaintance with external till he acquired the sense of feeling. The statue possessed no acquaintance with heat also, and pain, till it acquired the sense of feeling; but this intelligence is not enumerated among the mysteries of the case, because heat and pain are known to name feels only. External seems different. The word names usually sights as well as feels. The French philosopher restricted its signification to the phenomena of feeling. When we know this, we need no statues to teach us that if we possess no sense of feeling, we shall be acquainted with none of its information.

§ 4.—*Above and below name sights; hence, hearing cannot inform us in relation to either above or below.*

Another philosopher tells us that though we believe hearing can designate the place from which a sound proceeds, yet the ear is indebted for this intelligence to experience, without which hearing cannot tell whether a sound proceeds from above us or below, &c.

§ 5.—I agree with this philosopher, but his doctrine is but little mysterious if you discriminate the senses to whose phenomena we refer by the words above us and below. Above is the name of a sight and a feel. Below is also a sight and a feel; hence, hearing cannot inform us of either above or below. Hearing cannot perform the office of seeing or feeling.

§ 6.—*Before we can answer whether colour is connected with external objects, we must know the sense to which the word connected is intended to refer.*

Professor Stewart says, "a few moments' reflection must satisfy any one that the sensation of colour can reside in the mind only; yet our constant bias is to connect colour with external objects."

§ 7.—Before we altercate, we must discriminate the sense to whose information we refer for the meaning of the word connected. If we mean the feel connected, (the feel produced by the links of a chain,) nothing is more puerile than to assert that colour is not connected with external objects. Colour is a sight; hence, it cannot produce the feel to which we refer by the word connected. Colour exhibits the sight connected, which is the only connexion that is applicable to colours.

§ 8.—*Colour is not spread over the surface of bodies when*

we refer to feeling for the signification of the phrase; but colour is spread over the surface of bodies when we refer to seeing for the signification of the phrase.

"But," continues Mr. Stewart, "our natural bias is to conceive white, blue, and yellow, which exist in the mind only, as something spread over the surface of bodies."[1]

Let Mr. Stewart tell us to what sense he refers. He will admit that oil and paint can be spread over the surface of bodies, and this elucidates the whole matter. He is referring to the feel

---

[1] In Johnson (I) this passage reads:

"But," continues Mr. Stewart, "our natural bias is to conceive white, blue, and yellow, which exist in the mind only, as something spread over the surface of bodies."

A painter might startle if he should be informed that white, blue, and yellow are not spread over the surface of bodies. Has he suffered a delusion which you are about to dispel? No; you are using the phrase, "spread over the surface," as no man ever used it, when applied to colours. You insist that the phrase has but one signification, and because that signification is undiscoverable in colours, you conclude that mankind are suffering an egregious error. The error is, however, in language, which has not a peculiar term to express every phenomenon, but employs the same term to name several phenomena. You transfer a defect which exists in language, to our senses, where it exists not.

What is the spreading over the surface to which Mr. Stewart refers? He will admit that baize can be spread over the surface of a table—this affords an elucidation of his error. The spreading referred to by Mr. Stewart is the feel spreading. It is where we can feel the body that is covered, and the body that covers. All, then, which Mr. Stewart means is, that colour cannot be felt;—a sight cannot be felt. The word spread, when thus restricted, is so far from what we naturally believe of colour, that no man ever entertained so unnatural an opinion. We may as well insist that a man who calls his dog Pompey mistakes him for the dictator of Rome.

Mr. Stewart will admit that the oil and lead which compose colour can be spread over the surface of bodies. It is the sight colour which produces the difficulty. The sight never can be spread over the surface of a body so long as we confine the signification of the phrase to the phenomena of feeling.

"spread over the surface." But when we say colour is spread over the surface of bodies, we allude to the sight spread and the sight bodies. To say colour is not spread over bodies, (meaning thereby the information of feeling,) is to quibble:—though such a use of language was not intended by Professor Stewart. He was misled by not knowing the chameleon character of words.

[Again: Mr. Stewart deems it erroneous to say, that "light strikes the eye." Why? Because strike is the name of a feel; therefore it cannot be predicated of light, which is a sight. Mr. Stewart supposes that strike possesses but one meaning. It possesses, however, as many meanings as it has applications to different phenomena. Sometimes it is the name of a sound, as when we say a sound strikes our ear. It has no inherent applicability to one phenomenon more than another; and when it refers to no phenomenon it becomes insignificant.

[The correct meaning of a word is the sight, feel, taste, or other phenomenon to which the word is appropriated by approved custom. So long, however, as a word designates any phenomenon, it has a signification. To say a sound looks like another sound, is to use licentiously the word looks, which is the name of a sight; still, if the speaker refers to the similarity of two sounds, the word has every requisite to render it significant. A philosopher who should contend that sounds cannot look alike (meaning thereby a sight) would be more in error than a man who should maintain that they resemble: for the assertion of the philosopher would involve a quibble, whilst that of his opponent would only be an impropriety of phraseology.]

§ 9.—*Before we can tell whether greenness is in grass, we must know the sense to which the word is intended to refer.*

When I look at grass, is greenness in the grass? No, says Professor Stewart. But to what sense does he refer for the signification of the word in? The answer to this question settles the controversy. He refers to the information of feeling, as when I say my hand is in my pocket. But the feel in is not applicable to colour. Greenness is in grass when we refer to the sight in and the sight grass, and these alone are pertinent to colour.

§ 10.—*Before we can answer the question that inquires where colour is situated, we must decide on the sense to which the word where shall refer for signification.*

But where in truth is colour situated? Before the question can be answered, you must decide on the sense to which where shall refer. If you mean the feel where, colour is nowhere; but if you mean the sight where, you will find no difficulty in designating where colour exists.

§ 11.—When I place my hand on grass, I may say colour is not here. Nothing is here but a certain texture of parts. But I refer to the sense of feeling. Feeling is not pertinent to colour. Feeling possesses no cognizance over it. The here which relates to colour is a sight. You may therefore place your hand on grass, and say colour is here; provided you refer to seeing for the meaning of the expression.

§ 12.—*Before we can answer whether sweetness is in sugar, we must ascertain the sense to which the word in is intended to refer.*

"Nothing is in sugar," says Locke, "but a certain texture of parts, which are so formed as to produce on our organs of taste the sensation of sweetness. Sweetness itself is not in sugar." But to what sense does Locke refer for the signification of in? If he refers to feeling, sweetness of course is not in sugar. No man believes that he can feel sweetness in sugar. Sweetness is in sugar when we refer to the sense of tasting for the signification of the word in, and no other sense possesses any cognizance over the subject.

§ 13.—*The senses alone can answer questions which relate to the external universe, and we must designate the sense to whose authority we are appealing.*

When I smell a rose, is the fragrance in the rose or in my

mind, &c.? Suppose we ask the senses. They alone can answer the question. What says feeling? He can feel all that is in the rose, but he will aver that he cannot feel fragrance. He can feel nothing in the rose but texture, substance, figure, &c. What says seeing? It can see every thing that is truly in the rose, but it cannot see any thing like fragrance. We may with no better result ask tasting and hearing. They will severally affirm that they can taste and hear all that is in the rose, but they can find no fragrance. When, however, we ask smelling, it can discover fragrance in the rose. The in must refer to the information of this sense. To ask whether fragrance is in the rose, meaning the feel in, the sight in, &c., is to talk absurdly.

Lecture XXIV

WE INTERPRET THE INFORMATION OF OUR SENSES BY WORDS, INSTEAD OF INTERPRETING WORDS BY THE INFORMATION OF OUR SENSES

§ 1.—*The sensible signification of a word is as various as the objects to which the word is applied.*

CREATION is immense; still, the names of created objects form the one use to which language is appropriated. Every feeling, every desire, every action, can be recorded by language. No event is so eccentrick, no imagination so wild, no situation so peculiar, but language can publish it. To effect these innumerable appliances we possess but a few thousand words:—hence, every word must possess a multitude of meanings.

Nothing is more definite than colours; still, in the application of language to them, we shall find that every word is employed diversely. White is applied to snow, to paper, to the glass of our windows, to our skin, to the floor of this room, to the walls, to light, air, water, and to silver.

§ 2.—*Instead of interpreting words by sensible information, we interpret sensible information by words.*

The versatility of language produces no embarrassment in the ordinary concerns of life. When a man tells us that the floor of our room is white, we look at the floor and interpret the word white by what we discover in the floor; but in speculation we reverse the mode of interpretation:—instead of examining the floor to ascertain the meaning of the word white, we investigate the word white to ascertain the colour of the floor.

§ 3.—*We mistake verbal criticism for an investigation of nature.*

My hand is in my glove, the moon is in the sky, hardness is in iron, heat is in the fire, sweetness is in sugar, colour is in grass. The word *in* is employed differently in each of the above cases. When I say my hand is in my glove, the in names a feel; when I say the moon is in the sky, the in names a sight; and when I say heat is in the fire, the in names a feel which is different from the feel to which I refer when I say my hand is in my glove. A perfect language should perhaps not use one word to express so many different sensible revelations. It should possess a separate word for each. Such, however, is not the nature of our language. We apply a word to numerous cases which we deem homogeneous or analogous. Practically, no evil arises, for we interpret the word by the sensible revelation to which it is applied,—deeming Cæsar at one moment a dog, and at another moment a Roman emperor. In speculation, however, we interpret the natural existence by its name. If I say heat is in fire, you will estimate the meaning of the word in by perhaps what you allude to when you say your hand is in your glove; hence, you will deny that heat is in the fire. You are thus investigating the meaning of the word in, to determine the relation which heat bears to fire; instead of examining heat and fire to ascertain the meaning of the word in.

§ 4.—"A few moments' reflection," says Professor Stewart, "must satisfy any one that the sensation of colour resides in the mind only; yet our constant bias is to connect colour with external objects."[1] Suppose, then, a man should assert that the colour of baize is connected with the baize, must I interpret his assertion by what I discover in the baize and colour? No, says speculation. What you discover in them must be subjected to the meaning of the word connected; and when you find that the colour and the baize exhibit phenomena that are different from what the word connected is applied to in some other cases, (the links of a chain, for instance,) you must say that the colour and the baize are not connected. We thus interpret the information of our senses by words, instead of interpreting words by the information of our senses.

§ 5.—Again, we say iron is hard, and the hardness is in the iron. Must I interpret these assertions by what I discover when

---

[1] In Johnson (I) the passage reads:

"A few moments' reflection," says Professor Stewart, "must satisfy any one that the sensation of colour can reside in the mind only; yet our constant bias is to connect colour with external objects."

But wherein am I mistaken, when I assert that the colour of this baize is connected with the baize? The error lies in the restriction which Mr. Stewart places on the word connexion. The word is generally appropriated to a sight and a feel: to the feel which is produced when I endeavour to separate two links of a chain, and to the sight which is experienced when I look at the links. To suppose, however, that the word has the same signification when I assert that colour is connected with the baize, is to suppose that I am asserting a nullity: for how can colour, which is a sight, be thus connected with baize, which is a feel? It cannot be by the feel connexion, because that involves the absurdity that colour can be felt; nor can it be by the sight connexion, because that involves the equal absurdity that baize (*i.e.* the feel) can be seen. The only way then in which the word connexion can be significant when applied to the sight colour and the feel baize, is as a name of the peculiar phenomenon to which the word then refers. To insist that connexion shall not be thus construed, but that it shall always mean the phenomena which are exhibited by two links of a chain, is as absurd as to insist that no two men shall have the same name, under the penalty of being deemed either one person, or of one of them being considered a nonentity.

I touch iron? No, says speculation; you must estimate what you discover when you touch iron by the meaning of the word in; and when you find that the iron and hardness produce feelings that are different from what the word in is applied to in some other cases, (as when you say your hand is in your glove,) you must say that hardness is not in iron.

§ 6.—Again, when we apply a spark to a mass of gunpowder which explodes, we say that the explosion is caused by the spark. The spark is the cause, and the explosion is the effect. We say, also, that a connexion exists between the cause and the effect. But must I interpret the meaning of the word connexion by what I thus discover in the spark and explosion? No, says speculation; what you discover in the spark and explosion you must subordinate to the meaning of the word connexion; and when you find that the spark and the explosion exhibit appearances that are different from what the word connexion is applied to in some other cases, (the links of a chain, for instance,) you must say that the spark and the explosion are not connected:— "they are only associated together," says Hume. "One succeeds the other, but they are not connected."

[Hume says, "our senses inform us of the colour, weight, and consistence of bread; but neither sense nor reason can inform us the qualities which fit it for the nourishment and support of the human body."

[So long, however, as the proposition of Hume has any signification, it is untrue. Our senses can discover every phenomenon which is exhibited by bread, therefore they can discover the qualities that fit it for nourishment. To use the word quality insensibly makes the discovery difficult indeed; for we prosecute it under this disadvantage, that nothing which we discover can be the object sought. The very circumstance that our senses discover it being conclusive against it; for the conditions of our search are "that neither sense nor reason can inform us."

[A man may insist that he does not know what causes the

sweetness of sugar. Do you want to see what causes the sweetness, then the information which you desire is some sight. Perhaps you want to hear what causes sweetness; the information which you wish is some sound. If you desire these, or to smell, feel or taste what causes the phenomenon in question, I can conduct you where you can employ all your senses in analytically or synthetically examining sugar, and the operations which are connected with its production and refinement. If you desire none of these your question must be insignificant. Language can effect no more than to refer us to phenomena. If you choose to frame a proposition which has no such reference, the words may seem to be significant, but they are divested of signification, and are vacated sounds.

[It is laudable to seek the causes of phenomena, but we ought to know when we have succeeded in our search. Practically causes are known by every person, but speculatively by no one. To speak, to move, to sit, to stand, we can all perform unhesitatingly; but if we speculatively inquire into the cause of any of these operations, we confound ourselves with subtleties.

[If, however, we seek correctly, there is no more difficulty in discovering speculatively the cause of any phenomenon, than there is in exerting the cause practically. The speculative cause and the practical one must be identical. To assign a cause that refers to no phenomenon, divests the word of signification. It becomes a vacated sound, a cause minus cause.

[What, then, causes the motion of my hand, when I raise it to my head? The effort which I am conscious of making when I raise my hand. Whether this effort has a name or not does not affect the inquiry. We all know how to produce the action, and that which we perform when we produce it, is the cause.

[But some person may wish to investigate further. He may ask, what is the cause of this effort which I speak of? But here the investigation becomes verbal only, and may be pursued in infinitum. If we assign any thing, say A, as the cause of the effort, he may immediately repeat his question, what is the cause of A? It is B. And what is the cause of B? and so without end. But there must be an end, if we wish our language to retain any significance: The series must end, when there is no phenomenon to which the word cause can apply.

[We may now see more plainly the futility of the question which asked, by what mechanism the vibrations of an actor's brain, are transmitted to the brains of the audience? The cause sought was not intended to be any phenomenon, and the answer agreed with the intention. The writer says, when the motions of the body, the colour of the face, and the directions of the eye, depict the state of our soul, there is in unison a chain which extends to the spectator, and communicates the vibrations of one brain to that of another.

[The writer shows extensively how the above can be performed; but I will not quote further from so idle a speculation. It differs, however, in no essential particular from any effort which essays to employ language for other purposes, than to refer to sensible existences.

[Burke inquires similarly, "why visible objects of great dimensions are sublime?" That he was not seeking any sensible phenomenon, we may learn from the answer.—He says, "though all the light reflected from a large body should strike the eye in one instant, yet the large body is formed of a vast number of distinct points, and a ray from each makes an impression on the retina. So, though the image of one point should cause but a small tension of this membrane, yet another stroke, and another, and another, must, in their progress, cause a very great one; till the tension arrives at the highest degree, and the whole capacity of the eye, vibrating in all its parts, must approach to the nature of pain, and produce an idea of sublimity."

[Evidently the actors in the above explanation are all verbal personages. The tension of the retina, the reiterated strokes which it experiences, the images which strike, and the vibrations of its parts, are words divested of their sensible signification, and therefore nullified.

[Finally, we must steadily remember, that all which Providence has placed in our power, is to record the phenomena that our senses discover. While we keep within this circle, every word is significant. We may investigate causes, and trace effects; propose questions, and receive answers; compound elements, and analyze compounds; but the moment we step beyond this circle, the charm dissolves: the magician and the magic sink together; the universe vanishes, and even language loses all its significance.]

§ 7.—*To interpret nature by language causes frequently much amazement.*

A thread passes through the eye of a needle; a bullet passes through a board; light and colours pass through solid crystal; sound passes through a block of stone; electricity passes through a bar of iron; a thought passes through the mind; a pain passes through our head; a bird passes through the air; and perspiration passes through the pores of your hand. These expressions refer to diverse existences, though they possess a sufficient analogy or homogeneity to make the phrase "pass through" applicable to them all. Practically, we interpret each application by the phenomenon to which it refers. This interpretation leaves nature as boundlessly diverse as our senses declare it to be. Speculation, however, interprets each phenomenon by the phrase "pass through"; for instance, let the passage of a thread through the eye of a needle be selected as the only correct "pass through"; we may then be much amazed that light should pass through solid crystal. The exhibition of nature we have been familiar with without exciting any surprise; but when we interpret it by the phrase "pass through," we are amazed.

[An ignorance of the principle which we are now considering, occasions also much admiration; thus Professor Stewart, in his Philosophy, says, "an expert accountant can enumerate, almost at a glance, a long column, though he may be unable to recollect any of the figures which compose the sum."

[Thus far the statement of Mr. Stewart creates no perplexity; but when he adds, "nobody doubts but each of these figures has passed through the accountant's mind," the case seems altered. The accountant begins to wonder that he does not recollect the several figures. Passing through the mind, he supposes to mean something different from what he experiences in addition. He does not know that words mean, in every case, the phenomena to which they refer. He supposes rather that the passage of the figures through the mind signifies the same as the passage of an army through the gate of a city.]

§ 8.—*Nature is no party to our phraseology.*

Water is fluid, air is fluid, quicksilver, light, blood, electricity, lightning, ether, magnetism, fused iron, are all fluid. The word is correctly applied, for they possess the homogeneity which justifies the application to them of the word fluid; but we err greatly when in our speculations we interpret by the word fluid these various revelations of nature. Nature is no party to our names. We are told that God brought every thing to Adam that he might name them. The same process continues. We may apply the word fluid whenever we discover that the name is appropriate; but we must not afterwards interpret the object by the name which we thus attach to it. The name must, in every case, be interpreted by the object to which it is attached.

§ 9.—*Much of what is esteemed as profound philosophy is nothing but a disputatious criticism on the meaning of words.*

A thought strikes my mind, a project strikes my imagination, a sound strikes my ear, a light strikes my eye, an odour strikes my olfactory nerves, a stone strikes my hand, the wind strikes my face, lightning strikes a house, a hat strikes my fancy, a pain strikes my shoulder. These are only a few uses of the word strike. We discover in the objects referred to a sufficient conformity to make the word strike appropriate to them all; but they exist precisely as we discover. Each is peculiar, and might have been designated by a separate word, if so much nicety of discrimination had been deemed desirable. In speculation, however, the sameness of their name, and the difference in their nature, produce difficulties. We select one of the cases, and deem it a peculiarly correct exposition of the meaning of strike, and then decide by it that light does not properly strike the eye, a thought does not strictly strike my mind, &c. I object not to this verbal criticism, but I wish to show that it is verbal. It affects the meaning of the word strike, but it affects not the phenomena to which I refer when I say light strikes my eye, and a thought strikes my mind. These exist precisely as I discover; and whether I apply to them or not the word strike may concern the propriety of my phraseology, but not the character of natural revelations.

§ 10.—*We resort to language to explain the information of our senses, instead of resorting to our senses to explain the meaning of words.*

"Some of the ablest philosophers in Europe are now satisfied," says Professor Stewart, "not only that no evidence exists of motion's being produced by the contact of two bodies, but that proof may be given of the impossibility of such a process:—hence they conclude that the effects which are commonly imputed to impulse, arise from a power of repulsion, extending to a small and imperceptible distance around every element of matter."

§ 11.—If John says that two billiard balls weigh a pound, and Thomas insists that they weigh only ten ounces, the balls can be placed in counterpoise with a pound weight, and the controversy be decided. But we cannot contrast thus the motion of the balls with the word impulse, because the word impulse possesses no fixed sensible signification, but conforms to the sensible object to which it is applied.

§ 12.—Professor Stewart, however, employs the words impulse and repulsion as John employs the pound weight. John asks the pound weight to tell him the specifick gravity of the two balls; and Mr. Stewart asks the words impulse and repulsion to explain what he is beholding in the movement of the balls.

Lecture XXV*

WE OFTEN MISTAKE THE INAPPLICABILITY OF A WORD FOR AN ANOMALY OF NATURE

§ 1.—*The word demonstrate may be restricted in its signification so as to be inapplicable to colours.*

[I MAY offer to demonstrate that the wall of our room is as white as the paper which I hold in my hand. The demonstration will be accomplished, if I place the paper against the wall, and enable you to see that the colours correspond. The word demonstrate you will not object to, because you will understand the process to which it alludes.

[In speculation, however, the case is different.] Locke says, "We cannot demonstrate the equality of two degrees of whiteness, because we have no standard to measure them by. The only help we have are our senses, which in this point fail us."

§ 2.—The difficulty is not imputed to the inapplicability of the word demonstrate, but to our senses, which fail in affording us the requisite help by which to measure the degrees of whiteness. What kind of demonstration does Locke allude to? To counting, as when we measure the equi-numerance of two bags of dollars; or to weighing, as when we ascertain the equiponderance of two bars of lead; or to measuring, as when we determine the extension of two lines. But the word demonstrate, when thus restricted in its signification, is not applicable to colours. We may as well say that we cannot taste the difference between two degrees of whiteness. Taste is not applicable to whiteness. The difficulty is not in our senses, but in the inappli-

---

* This and succeeding lectures were described in Johnson (II) as fragments.

cability of the language. Our senses do not, as Locke alleges, fail us in our attempt to demonstrate the equality of two degrees of whiteness; but the word demonstrate (as Locke restricted its meaning) is inapplicable to whiteness.

[With such a restriction on the word demonstrate, Locke may as well have asserted the most puerile proposition as the above. His was precisely such a mistake as was committed by an African king, who executed a sailor for imposition, because the sailor declared that he had crossed the ocean in the Elephant: a name which the African thought applicable to an animal only.]

§ 3.—*The word connexion may be restricted in its signification so as to be inapplicable to the relation which is discoverable between a cause and its effect.*

Hume insisted that no visible connexion exists between any cause and its effect. We apply a spark to gunpowder, and an explosion ensues; "but," says Hume, "we see not that an explosion is necessarily connected with a spark." Cause and effect seem, therefore, either to possess some anomaly, which prevents us from seeing that cause and effect are connected, or they are not connected. But what connexion does Hume allude to as not visible in cause and effect? He alludes to the connexion which is exhibited by the links of a chain. Such a connexion is inapplicable to the nature of cause and effect. Cause and effect exist successively. One only can be present; the other must be either future or past. To talk, therefore, of seeing a cause and its effect connected, as we see the connexion of two links, is to talk of seeing at the same time either a present sight and a past, or a present and a future. The phrase of Hume, when thus limited, (and thus Hume evidently limited it,) is inapplicable to cause and effect.

§ 4.—The inapplicability is still more glaring when we refer to phenomena which are invisible: for instance, when we say that we can see no visible connexion between sugar and sweetness. Here, in addition to the former difficulties, we are required by Hume to see sweetness—to see a taste. The taste is one link of the chain, and sugar the other link. To see them connected we must see them both:—see a taste!

§ 5.—*The word connexion may be so restricted in its signification, as to be inapplicable to the relation which exists between colour and the body which is coloured.*

Professor Stewart says, "a few moments' reflection must satisfy any one that the sensation of colour can reside in the mind only; yet our constant bias is to connect colour with external objects."

§ 6.—The green which seems in connexion with this baize, is therefore not connected with it. The difficulty is not imputed to the word connexion, but to some delusion of our senses. What connexion does Mr. Stewart allude to? The connexion which exists between the links of a chain. It is a feel. But the word connexion, when restricted to a feel, cannot be applicable to colours, for we cannot feel a sight. Our constant bias is to connect green with the baize, not by the feel connexion, but by the sight. To limit the connexion to a feel is to make the word connexion inapplicable to colour; hence the difficulty of Mr. Stewart is not in our senses nor in nature, but in the inapplicability of the word connexion.

§ 7.—*The word know may be so restricted in its signification as to become inapplicable to a large portion of our knowledge.*

"Though we suppose generally that external objects cause in other persons similar sights, tastes, feels, sounds, and smells, to those which they produce in us, yet," say metaphysicians, "no man can know this with certainty."

§ 8.—Apparently a mysterious contradiction exists in the above position; for while we wonder at the alleged want of knowledge, we are confident of a practical possession of it.[1]

---

[1] In Johnson (I) the passage reads:

Apparently there is a mysterious contradiction in the above meta-

The difficulty proceeds from the restriction which metaphysicians place on the phrase "to know." The controversy relates not to nature, but to language. What we experience will not be affected by the phrases which we apply to it. If the phrase "to know" shall be restricted to the information of my own feeling, I cannot know how fire affects your hand; for I cannot feel with your hand. When, however, I assert that I know how fire affects your hand, the assertion does not include that I can feel the operation of fire on you. The assertion refers simply to my experience, conjoined with various facts and expressions that I derive from you.

§ 9.—*Whether we can be certain that we shall die, depends on the meaning of the word certain. The question relates to language and not to nature.*

I once heard a divine contend in his sermon, that "except on the authority of revelation, no individual can be certain that he shall die." The zest of the proposition consists in the restriction which the preacher places on the word certain. Whether we shall or not employ the word certain will not affect our sensible knowledge. A deaf mute knows in relation to death all that we

---

physical assertion; for while we wonder at the alleged impossibility, we are confident of its practical inefficiency. But the difficulty proceeds from not knowing that the word similar has several meanings, and that it is used diversely in the above positions. When I say, that the heat which I am feeling is similar to what I felt yesterday, the word similar refers to the antecedent feel and the present. So long as I restrict thus its meaning I cannot know that fire produces in you a similar feeling to what it produces in me. I cannot feel with your organs.

But we intend a different meaning, when we affirm that the feel which you experience is similar to mine. The word similar means now that you display, under the operation of heat, appearances like those which I exhibit; or that you describe your feelings in the same language, &c. In short, I cannot know that the feel which fire produces in you is similar to what it produces in me, and I can know. The assertions refer to different phenomena.

know, provided his intercourse with men has yielded him the experience which we possess. To apply to our knowledge the word certain, or to withhold the application, relates to the propriety of our phraseology, and not to nature. We are so accustomed to subordinate nature to language, that probably not one of the preacher's auditors discovered that the sermon was nothing but a disquisition on the meaning of the word certain. The decision of the controversy, however, (either against the certainty of death or in favour,) would practically change neither their feelings nor conduct; for how perplexed soever we may become by verbal speculations, the realities of nature control our conduct. The preacher restricted the use of the word certain to events which were already consummated; hence the future death of an individual is not a certainty.

Lecture XXVI

WE MISTAKE THE UNINTELLIGIBILITY OF A WORD OR PROPOSITION FOR A MYSTERY OF NATURE

§ 1.—*Language permits us to frame propositions which possess a very ambiguous meaning, and sometimes no meaning.*

"OF THE substance and essence of either mind or matter we know nothing, and can know nothing."

Here, then, are two words, which are assumed to name something, but we know not what. If, however, we neither know what they name, nor can know, we neither know nor can know that they name any thing. Our knowledge of their significance cannot exceed our knowledge of what they signify. But because language permits us to thus frame propositions which are unintelligible, we attribute the defect to a mystery of nature, though it is truly nothing but a misuse of language.

§ 2.—*The meaning of a word cannot exceed what man can know in relation to it.*

"We are conscious of various internal movements and energies to which we give the names of faculties, sensations, ideas, passions, emotions, &c.; but of the nature and qualities of that by which these movements and energies are produced, and in which they inhere, we neither know any thing, nor can know."

§ 3.—The above quotation assumes, as a part, I suppose, of some theory, that something exists by which certain of our movements and energies are produced, and in which they inhere; but what this something is we neither know nor can know. This word, then, this something, possesses confessedly but little meaning, if any. It is a sound of our own creating, the mere breath of our own body, and dependent for its signification on the discoverable revelations to which it refers. Its meaning, therefore, cannot exceed what we know, and our knowledge of it, we admit, is nothing; still, its unintelligibility and insignificance are not imputed to the word as a defect, but to nature as a mystery.

§ 4.—*We impute to nature the ambiguities and unintelligibility which are produced by a misuse of language.*

"By the mediation of our corporal organs," says the same writer, "we receive an almost infinite number and variety of impressions from material objects; but of the nature and qualities of the material objects from which these impressions proceed, and what the objects are, independently of these impressions, we neither know any thing nor can know any thing."

§ 5.—The above quotation contains the same errour as the former. If we know not what the nature and qualities are, we know not that our language is significant. Its significance cannot exceed our knowledge, for it is the creature of our invention, possessing originally no more signification than the wind which whistles over the strings of an Æolian harp. We, however, impute the unintelligibility of the proposition to nature, instead of knowing that it proceeds from the use of words in an ambiguous sense, and even without any definite sense.

§ 6.—"The most gigantic intellect," says the same author, "when it attempts to grasp a subject which lies beyond the boundaries of human knowledge, (in the region not of the un-known merely, but of the unknowable,) is as impotent as the most ordinary mind."

§ 7.—The proposition premises of the word subject, that its meaning shall not be unknown merely, but unknowable; and the complaint is not that language permits us to make so un-meaning a proposition, but that nature prevents us from under-standing it. The word subject is a mere sound, indebted for all its signification to the natural revelations to which it may refer; yet, after admitting that it refers to nothing, and hence admit-ting its insignificance, we allege that nature is very mysterious in not enabling us to comprehend the meaning of the word.

Lecture XXVII

LANGUAGE CANNOT BE MADE SIGNIFICANT BEYOND OUR KNOWLEDGE

§ 1.—*The limitation of meaning which pertains to words, we mistake for a limitation of our faculties.*

IN CERTAIN essays on human knowledge, published some years since, the author asserts, that "he will endeavour to ex-plain the extent to which mind and matter are knowable."

§ 2.—The phrase "mind and matter" is not deemed to be limited in its signification by our knowledge; but our knowl-edge is deemed capable of teaching us a certain portion only of the signification of the phrase:—a defect in our senses and understanding precluding us from knowing more than a portion of its meaning. What a curious inversion of the truth! What a strange exaltation of language above nature! Instead of teach-ing us "the extent to which mind and matter are knowable,"—the writer can teach us nothing but the extent to which the phrase "mind and matter" is significant language. Our knowledge gives to the phrase all the signification which it possesses; and when we arrive at the extent of our knowledge, the phrase is at the extent of its signification. Beyond the extent of our knowledge, the phrase is as insignificant as the wind which whistles through our window.

§ 3.—*We mistake the unintelligibility and insignificance of certain propositions for mysteries of nature.*

The same writer continues:—"As through consciousness we become acquainted with certain intellectual energies only, without possessing any consciousness of the substance in which they inhere, or of the ties by which they are connected, all speculations concerning such substances and ties must be within the regions of the unknowable, and necessarily abortive."

§ 4.—The writer tests not his proposition by the revelations of nature to discover the signification of the "substances and ties" of which he speaks; but he tests nature by those words; and discovering nothing which answers to the exigency of their requirement, he concludes that nature is mysteriously evading his shrewd examinations.

§ 5.—*Such propositions are formed by the employment of words divested of their sensible signification.*

The words "substance, inhere, and ties," are names of sights, sounds, tastes, feels, and smells, or at least of some revelation of nature. A substance, &c., that cannot be discovered by our senses, is as insignificant as an elephant that cannot be discovered by our senses; both words are equally vacated sounds, when separated from the sensible revelations which give them significancy.

§ 6.—Language can be made as capacious as our experience, but not more capacious. I may insist that nature is so exceedingly subtile, that I cannot taste the flavour of moonshine, nor smell its odour; nor can I feel the texture of the particles of which it is composed. If I catch a handful of them, they elude my grasp before I can convey them into a dark room for closer inspection. This is exceedingly wonderful to a person who sees not that the whole is created by divesting of signification the

words flavour, odour, texture, particles, &c., and uniting the
nullified words into syntactical propositions. Language permits
us to frame unmeaning and unintelligible propositions, but we
impute their unintelligibility and insignificance not to a misuse
of language, but to a mysteriousness of nature, and an inefficiency of our intellect.

Lecture XXVIII

WE MISTAKE THE INAPPLICABILITY OF A PROCESS OF LANGUAGE FOR A DEFECT OR MYSTERY OF NATURE

§ 1.—*Whether we can or not prove the existence of an external universe, or our own existence, depends on the applicability
to it of the verbal processes of logick, and not on nature.*

PERHAPS nothing which philosophy has debated is so mysterious as the assertion that we cannot prove the existence of an
external universe;—nay, that we cannot prove the existence of
ourselves. Descartes supposed that he had accomplished the
proof of his own existence at least. He says, "I think, therefore
I am." "But," replies Doctor Reid, "how do you prove that
you think? If you assume this without proof, you may as well
assume your own existence without proof." Doctor Reid admits
that to prove these facts is impossible, but that we are bound
to believe them, for they constitute a part of our consciousness.
"But," says a subsequent writer, "how do you prove the existence of the consciousness of which you speak?"

§ 2.—You perceive the difficulty lies in our inability to prove
the facts adverted to. That the facts exist, all men are practically satisfied; but that the facts are incapable of proof, is the
marvel and the fallacy. We can prove that the three angles of a
triangle are equal to two right angles; but we cannot prove that
a triangle actually exists in the external universe, or that we
exist who employ the process of mathematicks. What a marvel!

§ 3.—But what is the proof about which we are thus solicitous, and the absence of which is deemed so portentous and

mysterious? It is a process of language;—an artificial process
of human ingenuity. I have heretofore stated* that argumentation and logick consist in showing certain verbal conclusions
to be admitted by certain verbal premises. All demonstration
and proof proceed on the same principle. You must admit certain verbal axioms and definitions; and when the proposition is
shown to be embraced verbally by these admissions, the proposition is demonstrated. The process is verbal. It belongs to
language, and apart from language the process possesses neither
signification nor application. To say, therefore, that we cannot
demonstrate our own existence, without first assuming it, is
merely to state the nature of the process. The sensible realities
of creation are not implicated or affected by our ability or
inability to apply to them our verbal processes of demonstration
and proof, any more than the air is implicated in our ability or
inability to represent it with colours on canvass. Instead, however, of knowing that our inability to prove verbally our own
existence, (without first assuming it,) is a property of language,
we suppose it to be a curiosity of nature, or a portentous mystery. I am acquainted with no errour which shows so mon-
strously as the above, the superiority that language has acquired
over the realities of the universe; and the curious inversion by
which we estimate nature by language, instead of estimating
language by nature.

Lecture XXIX

WE MISTAKE WORDS FOR THE ULTIMATE OBJECTS OF KNOWLEDGE, WHILE
THE REVELATIONS OF NATURE ARE PROPERLY THE ULTIMATE OBJECTS

§ 1.—*The phenomena of life are ultimate to the verbal question which inquires whether I live, though we mistakenly suppose the question to be ultimate to the phenomena.*

"I THINK," said Descartes, "therefore I exist." He invented
this enthymeme for the purpose of proving his own existence;

---

* Lecture XIII.

for we must assume nothing. "Every thing must be proved," he said. The phenomena of life, of which he was momentarily conscious, and the phenomena of thinking, were not deemed the ultimate objects of human knowledge. He sought for something beyond; and by his reposing when he arrived at the above enthymeme, we can discover what he deemed the ultimate objects of human knowledge:—some process of words.

§ 2.—*The revelations of nature are ultimate to the verbal question which inquires after the existence of an external universe; though we mistakenly suppose the question to be ultimate to the revelations.*

Some philosophers have affirmed the non-existence of an external universe; "for," say they, "we know nothing of external existences but what our senses inform us of, and possibly nothing exists but the sensations. Whether the senses are actually excited by extrinsic objects or not, will," say these philosophers, "affect not our knowledge, so long as we experience the sensations." The revelations of nature are, you perceive, not satisfactory to these philosophers. They are seeking for some ulterior knowledge, for some knowledge more authoritative and explanatory. In truth they are inverting the order of nature. They are seeking words as the ultimate objects of human knowledge, while the revelations of nature are deemed secondary and debatable.

§ 3.—How mysterious is death! What can it be? Our senses in vain yield us their information; we are not accustomed to deem the revelations of nature as the ultimate objects of our knowledge. We are accustomed to deem language the ultimate object, and thus most perversely subordinate creation to an artificial contrivance of our own. As Descartes was not satisfied with the reality of his own existence, till language had echoed it in an enthymeme, so we are not satisfied with the revelations of nature in relation to death, till language vents on it some sentences.

§ 4.—*Deaf mutes are exempt from the fallacy of estimating words as the ultimate objects of knowledge.*

Deaf mutes are exempt from the errour of seeking some information ulterior to the revelations of nature; while we, from infancy to the termination of life, are led by the forms of language and by the unsuspected labours of speculative philosophy, to deem words the ultimate objects of knowledge. What is death? what is an earthquake? what is the sun? A man would be laughed at, who should answer these questions by referring us to nature's revelations in relation to them. We desire something ulterior; some theory, or a process of language in some other form.

§ 5.—What supports this candle? The candlestick. And what supports the candlestick? The table. And what supports the table? The floor. And what supports the house? The earth. And what supports the earth? We are arrived at the end of our sensible knowledge, but this prevents us not from pursuing the process verbally, for we know not that the revelations of nature are the ultimate objects of our knowledge. A verbal termination of the inquiry is far more congenial to our habits of philosophising than the termination which is produced by nature.

§ 6.—*We constantly mistake some verbal proposition for the ultimate object of our knowledge.*

We are told by some philosophers, that consciousness proves that we exist. The proposition is deemed ultimate to the consciousness, while, in truth, the proposition possesses no signification but the consciousness. To feel pain, proves that I am a sentient being. The feeling seems to be secondary to the proposition, though it constitutes its ultimate meaning. To taste sugar proves it to be sweet. The taste seems to prove not itself, but something ultimate, which we announce by the word sweet. You perceive that we constantly deem some verbal proposition to be the ultimate object of our knowledge. All our controversies in relation to the existence of an external universe are founded on this errour. No disagreement exists about the revelations of nature, but we deem them not the ultimate objects of our knowledge; hence we dispute whether or not these revelations prove an external universe. The proposition is deemed the most consequential part of our knowledge, while it is the mere mode in which we speak of the revelations of nature.

§ 7.—"I cannot help believing," says Doctor Reid, "that those things really happened, which I remember to have happened." The verbal proposition, "I cannot help believing," &c., seems to be something ultimate from the natural revelation which constitutes the remembrance; but all that is consequential, and belongs to the realities of nature, is the revelation. We may speak of it as we please. We may say with Doctor Reid, that we cannot help believing, &c.; or we may say that we can help believing; but so far as the realities of nature are implicated, the revelation of nature is our ultimate knowledge on the subject, though we perversely mistake the phrase as the ultimate knowledge, and exhaust ourselves in verbal controversy.

§ 8.—The sun is now believed to be a body of fire. At one time it was called a heated stone. Some say it is inhabited, and others that it is uninhabitable. The controversy involved at no time any disagreement as to the discoverable revelations of nature. Were these deemed the ultimate objects of our knowledge, we should readily discover the unimportance of such controversies; but when we deem our verbal propositions the ultimate objects of our knowledge, the errour yields a sufficient reason for controversy.

§ 9.—Does the earth revolve on its axis from the west to the east, or do the heavens revolve on their axis from the east to the west? Does either event occur, or is the motion a mere contrivance of our own to reconcile the discoverable phenomena to our notions of causation? We may estimate these questions as very important, and they may be important so far as they affect our theories; but nature is not necessarily connected with them. All that truly belongs to nature are her discoverable revelations; and if these are alike to all men, we should not mistake our verbal controversies for a disagreement about the realities of nature. We, however, are not accustomed to thus subordinate language to nature. We deem language the ultimate boundaries of our knowledge; hence the undue importance which we attach to our verbal disagreements.

§ 10.—What is the colour of sunshine? Nearly every person will perceive that our ultimate knowledge in this matter is what we discover in nature, and that the name by which we designate the colour is subordinate to the natural revelation. Some persons, however, may, even in this case, not discover the errour which I am striving to illustrate. They may dispute whether the colour is white or orient, &c., and deem the decision the ultimate object of our knowledge.

§ 11.—Some of the ablest philosophers of Europe are now satisfied, that motion proceeds in no case from any impulse produced by the contact of two bodies; such a contact is impossible, owing to the repulsive nature of material bodies. The motion is produced by repulsion, which makes bodies rebound from each other before they arrive at an actual contact. The philosophers who make this discovery receive from nature the same revelation as is received by other philosophers who admit the actual contact of bodies. No disagreement exists as to the sensible revelations of nature, but the revelations are not deemed the ultimate objects of knowledge; hence the controversy in relation to the language that is to be employed.

§ 12.—*When we deem words the ultimate objects of our knowledge, we invert the order of nature.*

I may not have succeeded in becoming intelligible in the above remarks; but to me no speculative position is more important, and no truth more evident, than that we mistakenly invert the order of nature, and deem words the ultimate objects of our knowledge, while we ought to deem the revelations of nature our ultimate knowledge. Are all things material, or are some spiritual? How virulently would this proposition be debated! If the controversy involves any question of fact as to what the Scriptures have declared on the subject, or as to any phenomenon internal or external which we experience, the controversy may be important; but if the disputants are acquainted with the same revelations of nature, and the same revelations of Scripture, their controversy relates not to the ultimate objects of human knowledge, but to the employment of words. To a deaf mute the controversy would be as unmeaning as the chattering of magpies is unmeaning to us. Nature evolves before us her phenomena. These are important, whether we note them or not, or discuss them or not; and we are acted on and act in this evolution of realities without the slightest deference to our speculations, though in our discussions we seem to suppose that the evolutions of nature are controlled by our verbal decisions. Our errour is analogous to the hallucinations of the philosopher referred to in Johnson's Rasselas, who believed that the winds and rains were controlled by his diagrams and volitions; and that a mistake in his calculations would either deluge the earth, or involve it in tempests. Doctor Franklin has left us the soliloquies of an ephemera. It notices the gradual declination of the sun, and asserts that philosophers are generally agreed that a period will arrive, when the sun will entirely disappear at the western extremity of the horizon, and that the whole race of the ephemera will be destroyed with even the mighty leaf on which so many nations exist, &c. Our speculations are like these. So far as our speculations refer to the revelations of creation, they are significant of the realities of creation; but we must estimate these revelations as the ultimate objects of our knowledge of creation. Every animal may possibly possess a language and a train of verbal speculations; but nature moves forward and flows onward with no more natural connection or affinity to the language of one animal than to the language of another. The bird that carols in a forest, and the philosopher who speculates in a closet, are alike employed in the formation and combination of sounds with which the realities of the universe possess no affinity or connexion but such as is produced by an artificial reference of the sounds to the realities referred to.

Conclusion

§ 1.—INSTEAD OF contemplating creation through the medium of words, men should contemplate creation itself. They should estimate what their senses disclose, and the phenomena which they experience internally, as a dumb mute estimates them. Language was designed for a communication between man and man, and not for a communication between nature and man. In passing through a forest, I may see something which I never saw before. I can communicate the sight to you in no way but by words; while the sight itself is the only correct revelation to myself. We are not in the practice of thus contemplating sleep, death, magnetism, light, fire, men, women, thoughts, sun, moon, anger, hope, and all the other phenomena which our senses disclose, or our internal consciousness reveals. We talk to ourselves about them, and thus contemplate them through the defective medium of language which was designed as a mere substitute for our senses, &c., in our intercourse with one another.

§ 2.—By the above errour we interpret creation by words, and, as a consequence thereof, we fail from seeing that words should be interpreted by the revelations of creation. When you utter a number of sentences to tell me what death is, I know not that your sentences must be interpreted by the revelations of my senses, &c.; and that, apart from these revelations, the words are sensibly insignificant.

§ 3.—To illustrate the foregoing positions is the design of all that I have stated. Theoretically, the positions may be admitted by every person, and may be deemed already known; but practically they are violated by all men, and understood by none. That language will eventually receive the interpretation for which I contend, I cannot doubt; but that I possess the ability to make existing errours perceived even, I much question.

§ 4.—I might have inserted an indefinite number of further illustrations of the great principles which I desire to inculcate; but if what I have already presented shall be understood in the manner in which I understand them, enough has been said to excite towards the subject the efforts of men to whom Providence has awarded more leisure and more talents than I possess; while, if I shall not be understood, I have expended already too much effort on a fruitless undertaking.

§ 5.—Our misapprehension of the nature of language has occasioned a greater waste of time, and effort, and genius, than all the other mistakes and delusions with which humanity has been afflicted. It has retarded immeasurably our physical knowledge of every kind, and vitiated what it could not retard. The misapprehension exists still in unmitigated virulence; and though metaphysicks, a rank branch of the errour, is fallen into disrepute, it is abandoned like a mine which will not repay the expense of working, rather than like a process of mining which we have discovered to be constitutionally incapable of producing gold.

§ 6.—Finally, while I dismiss this book, I entreat for it a close investigation at least. It is the painful production of much labour; and though I am aware of the delusion of self-love, I cannot believe that the principles which I have endeavoured to display are wholly undeserving of publick attention.[1]

---

[1] The concluding paragraphs of Johnson (I) are as follows:

I have now completed the first division of what I proposed to say on the Philosophy of Human Knowledge. I have shown, that many phenomena of different senses are so frequently associated, that they are designated in all languages by a single word; and hence we consider phenomena as identical, while the identity exists in language only. These phenomena constitute a large class of existences, and a misunderstanding of this simple ambiguity of language has filled the world with metaphysical disquisitions. As an example of these existences, I would adduce distance, which, though a unity in language, is two distinct phenomena: a sight and a feel. The like may be said of extension, roundness, prominence, &c.

Secondly, I have shown that words are merely sounds, which are indebted for signification to the phenomena only that we, by custom or instruction, apply them to. This seems a very obvious characteristic of words, still we frequently employ them when confessedly there are no phenomena to which they can refer. As a gross instance of this latent sophistry of language, I will say that the air which we are inhaling, and which we deem pure and transparent, is full of scorpions. This sentence is grammatical, and possesses an apparent significance, but the word scorpions, referring to no phenomenon, is nullified. All our learning is corrupted with this error, though, when exhibited in so gross an example as the above, we discover immediately the fallacy.

Thirdly, I have shown that as words have no inherent signification, every word possesses as many significations as it possesses a reference to different phenomena. We all know that when the name George refers to Washington it is dignified and venerated; when it refers to a vagabond reeling through our streets, it has an entirely different signification. The position when thus applied seems too obvious to need a comment; still, when differently used, it constitutes a sophistry which occupies a large space in speculation.

Fourthly, I have shown that language can effect no more than to refer us to phenomena. To judge from the contents of any library, no truth is so little known. We should rather infer that language can effect every thing but to refer us to phenomena. Why cannot the most elaborate disquisition, the whole vocabulary of the most copious language, teach some sagacious blind person the meaning of the word scarlet? We know the attempt was once made; and when the philosopher thought he had succeeded, the blind person said that scarlet must be like the blast of a trumpet. By why is language inefficient in this particular? Is there any peculiarity in colours? No: the difficulty is in language, which can, in no case, effect more than to refer us to some known phenomenon. Every person knows this truth when it relates to teaching the blind sights, and the deaf sounds; but no person seems to understand it, when he hears a discourse to reveal what exists in the centre of the earth, or what is transacting in the republics of the moon.

Fifthly, I have shown that the only use of argumentation is to convince us that what is sought to be established is included in the premises. Or, in other words, we assent to the verbal proposition that a half is less than a whole, when we understand that the word whole implies that it is more than a half. This plain principle also is grossly overlooked; and the oversight is continually inducing men to waste their strength in vain efforts. They disregard the acquisition of mere premises, (an acquisition which alone increases knowledge,) and strive to deduce new conclusions, though that is only varying the language in which their knowledge is clothed. By this perversion of effort we increase our knowledge no faster than a merchant would his wealth, who should close his shop, and employ himself in inventing new phrases to express the money which is lying in his till.

I have shown, next, that it is the phenomena to which words refer, that give one word the power of implying another, and that give premises power to command our assent to certain conclusions. For instance, twice two apples make four; a half of an apple is less than the whole apple—are propositions which we assent to, because our knowledge of the phenomena to which the propositions refer compel our assent. An ignorance of the source of this compulsion, has filled the world with the most fantastic conclusions. Men suppose that their assent to such propositions has no relation to phenomena: hence they say, if a half of an apple is less than a whole, the half of an insensible atom must be less than a whole. They pursue this process, and keep halving the halves as long as fancy suggests; and they suppose that each conclusion is significant and irresistible.

This constitutes one of the most subtle errors which language has betrayed us into, and I have investigated it at an unusual length. I have shown that it governs us in the construction of theories, and that it is the principal reason of the great solicitude expressed by theorists to define the names by which they denote the objects of their speculations. If they call one of the fixed stars a sun, it decides immediately that it is the centre of some group of worlds, whose invisibility adds only to the sublimity of the speculation.

Lastly, I have shown that all which Providence has placed within our grasp, is the sights, tastes, feels, sounds, and smells that our senses reveal to us; that we cannot even ask a significant question unless it refers to these, and every answer is insignificant that has not a similar reference.

What I have to say further concerning the Philosophy of Human Knowledge, may with propriety constitute a separate division: but before I adventure on it, I would fain know whether I can excite interest or convey information. I am too well aware of the insidiousness of self-love, to be satisfied with my own suggestions, and too painfully conscious of the depression of timidity, to retract without an effort. What I have advanced is not the fugitive offspring of a sudden intention, but the slow and painful product of contemplative years. If I have wholly mistaken my abilities, it is time I was undeceived. To the public, then, I confide the question; and though I have no reason to expect a favourable decision, a failure will at least save me from perseverance in a fruitless undertaking.

ABBREVIATIONS USED

In the identification of passages quoted or referred to by Johnson, the following abbreviations are used:

Bacon	Francis Bacon, *Novum Organum*
Bayley	Richard Bayley, *Essay on the Yellow Fever*
Beattie (1)	James Beattie, *Dissertations, Moral and Critical*
Beattie (2)	———, *Essay on the Nature and Immutability of Truth*
Berkeley	George Berkeley, *Essay towards a New Theory of Vision*
Blair	Hugh Blair, *Lectures on Rhetoric and Belles Lettres*
Blake	John Lauris Blake, *Conversations on Natural Philosophy*
Brown	Thomas Brown, *Lectures on the Philosophy of the Human Mind*
Campbell	George Campbell, *Philosophy of Rhetoric*
Condillac	The Abbé de Condillac, *Treatise on the Sensations* (trans. Geraldine Carr)
Cullen	William Cullen, *Synopsis Nosologicae Methodicae* (probably)
Darwin	Erasmus Darwin, *Zoonomia*
Descartes	René Descartes, *Discourse on Method*
Edin. Encyc.	*Edinburgh Encyclopedia*
Ellis	William Ellis, *Polynesian Researches*
Francis	John W. Francis, *Febrile Contagion*
Gill	John Gill, *A Body of Doctrinal Divinity . . .*
Halley	Edmund Halley, *An Account of the Circulation of the Watery Vapours of the Sea, and of the Cause of Springs* (referred to in the article, "Saltness," in *Rees's Cyclopaedia*)
Hauksbee	Francis Hauksbee, *Physico-Mechanical Experiments*
Hume (1)	David Hume, *Enquiry concerning Human Understanding*
Hume (2)	———, *Natural History of Religion*
Hume (3)	———, *Treatise on Human Nature*
Keith	Thomas Keith, *New Treatise on the Use of the Globes* (4th ed.)
Locke	John Locke, *Essay concerning Human Understanding*
Malebranche	Nicolas Malebranche, *Treatise concerning the Search after Truth* (trans. Thomas Taylor)
Newton (1)	Isaac Newton, *Optics* (4th ed.)
Newton (2)	———, *Principia*
Ogilvie	James Ogilvie, *Philosophical Essays*
Paley	William Paley, *Natural Theology*
Parry (1)	Caleb H. Parry, *Elements of Pathology*
Parry (2)	Sir William E. Parry, *Narrative of the Attempt to Reach the North Pole* (probably)
Paul	Paul the Apostle, Epistle to the Romans
Plato	Plato, *Timaeus*
Pouilly	Louis-Jean Lévesque de Pouilly, *Theory of Agreeable Sensations*
Rees	*Rees's Cyclopaedia*, London, 1819
Reid (1)	Thomas Reid, *Essays on the Intellectual Powers of Man*

Reid (2)	———, *Inquiry into the Human Mind on the Principles of Common Sense*
Saint-Pierre (1)	Jacques Bernardin de Saint-Pierre, *Le Café de Surate*
Saint-Pierre (2)	———, *Studies of Nature* (trans. Henry Hunter)
Shakespeare (1)	William Shakespeare, *Julius Caesar*
Shakespeare (2)	———, *Merchant of Venice*
Sterne	Laurence Sterne, *Tristram Shandy*
Stewart (1)	Dugald Stewart, *Account of the Life and Writings of Thomas Reid, D.D.*
Stewart (2)	———, *Elements of the Philosophy of the Human Mind*
Stewart (3)	———, *Philosophical Essays*
Wollaston	William Wollaston, *Religion of Nature Delineated*

IDENTIFICATION OF
PASSAGES QUOTED OR REFERRED TO
BY JOHNSON

PAGE	PAR.	PASSAGE
35	2	Shakespeare (1), Act. II, sc. 1, ll. 25–27
41	fn.	Blair, Lect. XVIII, par. 5 from end
57	3	Berkeley
58	1	Saint-Pierre (2)
60	2	Reid (2), ch. vi, sec. III, par. 7
60	5	Reid (2), ch. vi, sec. III, par. 6
61	fn.	Reid (2), *ibid.*
61	fn.	Hume (1), Sec. XII, pt. I, par. 9
63	5	Hume (1), *ibid.*
64	2–4	*Edin. Encyc.*, art. "Metaphysics"
65	3	Not in Reid (2)
66	5	Locke, Bk. II, ch. 8, sec. 19
69	2	Locke, Bk. II, ch. 8, sec. 16, paraphrased
69	4	Reid (2), possibly a rough paraphrase of ch. v, sec. v, par. 8, or ch. v, sec. II, par. 5; also Reid (1), Essay II, ch. xvii, sec. 5
77	2	Brown, Lect. XII, par. 5
91	2	Parry (2)
92	5	Stewart (2), Vol. I, ch. ii, par. 13 from end
93	6	Blair, Lect. I, par. 9, paraphrased
102	2	Hume (1), Sec. XII, pt. II, par. 2
105	6	Stewart (2), Vol. I, ch. i, sec. II, last paragraph
106	2 ff.	Locke, Bk. II, ch. 8, sec. 13
109	4	Darwin
116	2 ff.	Paley, cf. ch. xxi, sec. 4
119	2–3	Blake, Conversation XVI
120	4	Brown, Lect. XIV, par. 12
121	2–3	Brown (not located)
122	3	Brown, Lect. VII, par. 1
123	1	Brown, Lect. V, par. 20
123	fn.	Brown, Lect. V, par. 17
124	3	Brown, Lect. VII, par. 8
130	3	Parry (1)
130	7	Cullen
132	3	Francis
132	3	Bayley
134	3	Stewart (2), Vol. I, ch. iv, sec. v, par. 4
135	1	Plato, 56–57
135	4–6	Saint-Pierre, Study XIII, of Paris, par. 7 from end
135	7 ff.	Malebranche, Bk. II, ch. v, quoted in Stewart (2), Vol. 1, notes and illustrations, note (S)

PAGE	PAR.	PASSAGE
242	fn.	Pouilly, ch. ix
247	5	Paul, Rom. 7:21
254	4	Locke, Bk. II, ch. 23, sec. 26
255	4	Locke, *ibid.*
260	4	Locke, Bk. II, ch. 23, sec. 28
263	3	Pouilly, ch. ix
267	4	D'Alembert, quoted in Brown, Lect. XI, par. 4
270	3	Condillac
271	6 ff.	Stewart (2), Vol. I, ch. i, sec. 2, par. 4
273	2	Stewart (2), Vol. I, ch. i, sec. 2, par. 14
274	6	Locke, Bk. II, ch. 8, sec. 18, paraphrased
276	4	Stewart (2), Vol. I, ch. i, sec. 2, par. 4
278	2	Brown, Lect. VI. Brown discusses Hume's views in connection with these examples. Johnson apparently turns the reference into a quotation
278	3	Hume (1), Sec. IV, pt. ii, par. 3
281	5	Stewart (2), ch. ii, par. 19
283	3	Stewart (2), ch. i, sec. ii, last paragraph
284	4	Locke, Bk. IV, ch. 2, sec. 13
285	4	Brown, Lect. VI; see item for page 278, par. 2, above
286	3	Stewart (2), Vol. I, ch. i, sec. ii, par. 4
288	3 ff.	Ogilvie, p. 52
290	4 ff.	Ogilvie, p. 55
292	3 ff.	Descartes, Pt. IV, par. 1
292	3	Reid (1), Essay VI, ch. vii, par. 20, paraphrased
296	2	Reid (1), Essay VI, ch. v, sec. 3, paraphrased

INDEX